Genius

FOR
RAYMOND KLIBANSKY
DEMOCRITVS SENIOR

Genius

The History of an Idea

Edited by
Penelope Murray

Basil Blackwell

Copyright © 1989 Basil Blackwell. Chapter 2 copyright © Martin Kemp 1989

First published 1989

Basil Blackwell Ltd
108 Cowley Road, Oxford, OX4 1JF, UK

Basil Blackwell Inc.
432 Park Avenue South, Suite 1503
New York, NY 10016, USA

British Library Cataloguing in Publication Data
A CIP catalogue record for this book is available from the British Library.

Library of Congress Cataloging in Publication Data
Genius : the history of an idea.
  Bibliography: p.
  Includes index.
  1. Genius—History. 2. Creation (Literary,
artistic, etc.)—History. 3. Europe—Intellectual
life. I. Murray, Penelope.
BF412.G44 1989 153.9′8 88–35122
ISBN 0–631–15785–9

Typeset in 10 on 12 pt Baskerville
by Hope Services, Abingdon
Printed in Great Britain by T.J. Press Ltd, Padstow

Contents

Acknowledgements

I should like to thank the European Humanities Research Centre at the University of Warwick for giving me the opportunity to organize a conference on the theme of genius in April 1987 at which some of the contributors to this book delivered papers, which formed the basis of their chapters as they now appear. I am grateful to the British Academy and to Barclay's Bank for their generous financial support of this conference.

Notes on Contributors

Penelope Murray is lecturer in Classics at the University of Warwick.

Martin Kemp is Professor of Fine Arts at the University of St Andrews. His books include *Leonardo da Vinci: The Marvellous Works of Nature and Man* (London, 1981) and *Leonardo da Vinci* (New Haven and London, 1989).

Glenn Most is Professor of Classics at the University of Innsbruck. He is the author of *The Measures of Praise: Structure and Function in Pindar's Second Pythian and Seventh Nemean Odes* (Gottingen, 1985).

Jonathan Bate is a Fellow of Trinity Hall, Cambridge. His books include *Shakespeare and the English Romantic Imagination* (Oxford, 1986).

Michael Beddow is Professor of German at the University of Leeds. He is the author of *The Fiction of Humanity: Studies in the Bildungsroman from Wieland to Thomas Mann* (Cambridge, 1982).

Drummond Bone is lecturer in English at the University of Glasgow. He writes on Byron and English Romanticism.

Michael Tanner is a Fellow of Corpus Christi and lecturer in Philosophy at the University of Cambridge. He is compiling a complete discography of Richard Wagner.

Christopher Norris is Professor of English at the University of Wales, Cardiff. His books include *The Deconstructive Turn* (London, 1983) and *Paul de Man* (London, 1988).

Wilfrid Mellers is Emeritus Professor of Music at the University of York. His books include *Beethoven and the Voice of God* (London, 1983) and *The Masks of Orpheus* (Manchester, 1987).

Clive Kilmister is Emeritus Professor of Mathematics at the University of London. His books include *General Theory of Relativity* (Oxford, 1973) and *Schrödinger: Centenary Celebration of a Polymath* (Cambridge, 1987).

Neil Kessel is Professor of Psychiatry at the University of Manchester. He is the author of *Alcoholism* (Harmondsworth, 1965).

Anthony Storr is an Emeritus Fellow of Green College, Oxford. His books include *The Dynamics of Creation* (London, 1972) and *The School of Genius* (London, 1988).

Introduction

The archetypal image of genius for the twentieth century is probably that of Albert Einstein, a man whose radical creative insight into the nature of space and time profoundly altered our perceptions of the world. In calling him a genius we acknowledge his extraordinary creative powers, powers which distinguish him from men and women of talent, and which are certainly beyond the reach of ordinary mortals like the rest of us. Scientists and mathematicians can explain what it is about Einstein's work which compels us to speak of him as a genius, and psychoanalysts may seek the sources of such creativity in the personality and upbringing of Einstein the man, but there remains something fundamentally inexplicable about the nature of such prodigious powers. We attribute the extraordinary quality of, for example, Shakespeare's poetry, Mozart's music and Leonardo's paintings to the genius of their creators because we recognize that such works are not simply the product of learning, technique, or sheer hard work. Of course we can trace sources and influences, and we can analyse the effects of a work of art in terms of its formal qualities, just as we can assess the virtues of a mathematical insight or a scientific discovery, but no amount of analysis has yet been able to explain the capacities of those rare and gifted individuals who can produce creative work of lasting quality and value. If we ask how Mozart was able to compose music of such purity and perfection (significantly Einstein himself is said to have remarked that Mozart's music was so pure that 'it seemed to have been ever-present in the universe, waiting to be discovered by the master'[1]), we can only answer, 'because he was a genius', which is tantamount to saying that we do not know. For in each age and in each art, genius is that which defies analysis.

Although it is tempting to follow the example of Johann Caspar Lavater, who never defined genius, on the grounds that he who has genius knows it not, he who does not have genius cannot know what it is,[2] some definition is obviously necessary in order to clarify the general scope of this book. I begin with the definition of genius given in the *Oxford English Dictionary* (head 5):

Native intellectual power of an exalted type, such as is attributed to those who are esteemed greatest in any department of art, speculation, or practice; instinctive and extraordinary capacity for imaginative creation, original thought, invention, or discovery. Often contrasted with talent.

This notion of genius is essentially an eighteenth-century development, part of that radical shift in aesthetic theory so brilliantly explored by M. H. Abrams in *The Mirror and the Lamp*.[3] A corollary of this view is that the person endowed with such extraordinary capacities becomes a privileged individual representing, in Herbert Dieckmann's words, 'the acme of mental and creative endowment'.[4] By the end of the eighteenth century the genius, and in particular the artistic genius, comes to be thought of as the highest human type, replacing such earlier ideal types as the hero, the saint, the *uomo universale* and so on.

In exploring the origins of this idea we should first of all look at certain developments in the history of the word genius. In modern usage the term is intimately connected with creativity and originality, an association which goes back to the eighteenth century, when the word first acquired its familiar modern meaning, defined above. This was also the period when the word was used for the first time to denote a person endowed with such superior powers, as in the phrase 'Newton was a genius.' But before the eighteenth century genius had a variety of different meanings, none of which correspond to our modern use of the term. Of the various earlier meanings of genius defined in the *OED* three are of particular importance for our purposes: (1) genius as attendant spirit; (2) genius as characteristic disposition or natural inclination; (3) genius as natural ability or innate endowment.

The first sense derives directly from the Latin *genius*. In Roman religion the *genius* was originally the spirit of the *gens* (the family), whose cult, like that of the *Lares* and *Penates*, was associated with the household. Precise details of its early significance are disputed and obscure, but by the time of our first literary references in Plautus (around the turn of the third and second centuries BC) the *genius* appears to be a kind of tutelary spirit embodied in each man, not quite identical with him, but intimately connected with his personality. Like the Greek *daimon*, the Roman *genius* was born with each man and accompanied him throughout his life, as we can see from Horace's classic definition in *Epistles* 2.2 (lines 187ff.). Why two brothers should have completely different personalities and lifestyles, Horace says, only *genius* knows, 'the companion which rules the star of our birth, the god of human nature, mortal for each individual, varying in countenance, white and black' (*natale comes qui temperat astrum, / naturae deus humanae, mortalis in unum / quodque caput, vultu mutabilis, albus et ater*).[5] This spirit or deity was worshipped by every man on his birthday, the modern birthday cake being a vestige of the offerings a Roman would have made to his *genius* on the anniversary of his birth. *Genius* in this sense of guardian spirit was attributed not only to individuals but also, by extension, to groups of people (the *genius populi Romani*, for example) and to places, the celebrated *genius loci*: cities, towns, houses, marketplaces and street corners all have their own presiding deity. The notion of *genius* as an attendant spirit allotted to every man at his birth was central throughout the Latin Middle Ages, and remained one of the dominant meanings of the English word 'genius' (as of the French '*génie*' and Italian '*genio*') until the eighteenth century. But during the course of that century a striking and fundamental change occurs in the meaning of the word: up till this time, genius as a personal, protective spirit had been something every man possessed, now genius as an extraordinary creative power becomes the prerogative of a highly selected and privileged few.

Part of the complexity involved in defining the various meanings of our English word stems from the fact that, unlike the first sense of 'genius' as attendant spirit, the second and third senses, listed above, derive from the Latin *ingenium*, meaning both 'natural disposition' and 'innate ability', rather than from the Latin *genius*. And in fact, as Edgar Zilsel showed,[6] we can learn as much about the origins of the modern concept of genius from the history of the word *ingenium*, translated variously into modern languages as '*ingegno*' (Italian), '*esprit*' (French) and 'wit' or 'genius' in English, as we can from the history of the Latin word *genius*. For *ingenium* in the sense of 'natural ability' is a quality which cannot be acquired by learning, nor is it a quality which everyone possesses. Already in Sir Philip Sidney's *Defense of Poesie* (1583), where 'genius' is clearly the equivalent of *ingenium*, there is the suggestion that some people are born with certain capabilities which others lack: 'A poet no industry can make, if his own genius be not carried unto it; and therefore is an old proverb *Orator fit, poeta nascitur*'. Increasingly in the following centuries we find 'genius' used in the sense of an inexplicable quality as, for example, in the following quotation from Dryden's *A Parallel of Poetry and Painting* (1695):

A happy genius is the gift of nature: it depends on the influence of the stars, say the astrologers, on the organs of the body, say the naturalists; 'tis the particular gift of heaven, say the divines, both Christians and heathens. How to improve it, many books can teach us; how to obtain it, none: that nothing can be done without it all agree.

or in Pope's justly famous lines:

> In poets as true genius is but rare,
> True taste as seldom is the critic's share.
> Both must alike from Heaven derive their light
> Those born to judge, as well as those to write.
> (*An Essay on Criticism* (1711) lines 11–14)

Although it looks as though we are approaching the modern meaning of genius in these last two quotations, one crucial factor is missing: there is as yet no distinction between genius and talent.

Interesting as it may be to investigate the complex development of the various meanings of the word 'genius', the history of the idea of genius is not the history of a word. For although the modern connotations of the word were nonexistent before the eighteenth century, the idea that certain individuals possess inexplicable creative powers has its roots in the literature and thought of an earlier age. The mysterious nature of man's creative capacities had already been recognized by the Greeks, at any rate in relation to poetry, and from earliest times poets had claimed to be divinely inspired. Plato's doctrine of poetic inspiration as a kind of frenzy or enthusiasm formulated, for the first time in Western culture, a belief in the irrationality of the poetic process, which remained standard for centuries to come and which, in certain important ways, anticipated some of the notions which were later associated with the idea of genius.

In the Renaissance, with the heightened confidence in the manifold capabilities of man which characterizes Italian humanism, we see the emergence of a new conception, that of the poet as creator: as God creates the world out of nothing, so the poet like another god (*'velut alter deus'* in Scaliger's influential description[7]) invents his material, making images of things that do not exist. Applied first to poets, this comparison was also used of the painter's creative power, as for example by Leonardo:

If the painter wishes to see beauties that charm him it lies in his power to create them, and if he wishes to see monstrosities that are frightful, buffoonish, or ridiculous, or pitiable, he can be lord and God thereof [. . .] In fact, whatever exists in the universe, in essence, in appearance, in the imagination, the painter has first in his mind and then in his hands.[8]

The belief in the divine capabilities of the artist is also reflected in the epithet *'divino'*, which came to be used increasingly of artists during the sixteenth century, most memorably in connection with Michelangelo, whom Aretino addresses in a famous pun as: '*Michael più che mortal / Angel divino*' (Michael more than mortal / Angel divine).[9] Michelangelo is not called a genius, but the Renaissance image of the '*divino artista*' clearly prefigures the genius of later ages.

Indeed geniuses obviously existed long before the invention of the concept, as the great eighteenth century exemplars, Homer, Shakespeare and Newton testify. A less commonplace illustration of this point is provided by Plutarch's description of Archimedes as a man who 'possessed so lofty a spirit, so profound a soul, and such a wealth of scientific inquiry that [. . .] he had acquired through his inventions a name and reputation for divine rather than human intelligence.' Of Archimedes' exceptional ability in geometry Plutarch says:

Some attribute this to the natural endowments of the man, others think it was the result of exceeding labour that everything done by him appeared to have been done without labour and with ease. For although by his own efforts no one could discover the proof, yet as soon as he learns it, he takes credit that he could have discovered it [. . .] For these reasons there is no need to disbelieve the stories told about him – how, continually bewitched by some familiar siren dwelling with him, he forgot his food and neglected the care of his body; and how, when he was dragged by force, as often happened, to the place for bathing and anointing, he would draw geometrical figures in the hearths, and draw lines with his finger in the oil with which his body was anointed, being overcome by great pleasure and in truth inspired of the Muses.[10]

Here is a classic description of genius at work. The fact that Plutarch's contemporaries attributed Archimedes' mental powers to natural endowment or hard work rather than to genius merely indicates that it is our perceptions of human creativity and inventiveness rather than the phenomenon itself which changes. Man's capacity to use his imagination to create, invent and discover has always existed, and the problem of human creativity, so far from being simply a modern preoccupation, is one which has concerned many different stages of Western culture whose aesthetic, moral and psychological presuppositons have been very different from our own. The question of why the idea of genius should have arisen at the particular period when it did, and the underlying reasons for the various transformations which the idea has undergone, from its first formulation in the rationalist aesthetics of the eighteenth century, through the excesses of the *Sturm und Drang* and the era of Romanticism, to its ambiguous status in the twentieth century, will be explored in the following chapters of this book.

Today 'genius' is part and parcel of our everyday vocabulary, a word which however devalued, continues to express a belief in human capabilities which is central to our culture: genius is essential, as Richard

Poirier puts it, 'for the very reason that it is vague, and can stand for a dream of human power and mastery that is a challenge to other Gods'.[11] Amongst critics and academics in general, however, the notion of genius tends to be regarded as irrelevant, a mere Romantic fiction, which is primarily invoked in order to avoid the rigorous analysis of texts which is the proper business of criticism. The reasons for this scepticism are not difficult to see, for the idea of genius is, indeed, problematical. How do we define genius, and how do we differentiate between genius and talent? If creativity is an essential ingredient of genius how creative does a person have to be in order to be a genius, and for that matter what exactly is a creative person?[12] We can all, apparently, be creative to a greater or lesser degree, but what is it that makes a genius? If the hallmark of a work of genius is that it stands the test of time, is it only possible to apply the idea retrospectively? For many, the difficulty of answering questions such as these, the very indefinability of genius, makes it a meaningless concept. Furthermore genius is perforce elitist, not only in that it privileges certain individuals, but also because it elevates certain kinds of activity above others: genius forces us to make value judgments, a task which may not be too difficult in relation to scientific discoveries or mathematical proofs, but one which makes us distinctly uncomfortable when it comes to the creative arts.

Again the notion of genius raises questions about the role of the creative individual and his place in society: Nietzsche, as Michael Tanner reminds us, insisted on the 'preposterousness of expecting the exceptional (which alone is valuable) to proceed from someone who leads a model bourgeois existence'. Does the possession of genius, then, allow the individual complete licence to disregard all the rules of the society in which he lives, to be judged by standards quite different from those which are applied to his fellows? It is certainly not difficult to think of instances of geniuses who have produced outstanding and life-enhancing work, but who have been despicable as human beings. And undoubtedly a belief in the alienation and otherness of the creative individual was an essential aspect of the Romantic cult of genius, in which suffering was the inevitable price the genius had to pay, not only for his superhuman powers, but also for the total freedom which it was his duty and privilege to exploit.[13] This complex of ideas is also expressed in the Faustus legend, which, from Marlowe to Thomas Mann, provides the earliest and most continuous example of the Mephistophelean view of genius, epitomized in the cry of Busoni's Faust: 'Give me genius with all its pains.'

This brings us to what is perhaps the most recalcitrant problem of all those associated with the idea of genius, the question of the relationship between the artist and his work. For the study of genius is ultimately the study of human creativity, and its primary interest is in the creative human being rather than in the work he creates (which is no doubt, the reason why psychology and psychiatry are the only intellectual disciplines in which the analysis of genius still flourishes), but it is the work which prompts our interest in the creative individual. This problem is less acute in the case of mathematical insights or scientific discovery where, however intuitive the mental processes involved in such creative activities may be, the end result bears some relationship to verifiable facts or observable truths. But in the creative arts the imagined world which the artist creates inevitably reflects, albeit in a highly tenuous and complex way, the mind of a particular individual. Whereas it is possible to imagine that if Einstein had not formulated the general theory of relativity someone else would have done, it is inconceivable that Beethoven's music or Shakespeare's poetry would have been composed if those particular individuals had not existed. This is not to say that Einstein was any less a genius than Beethoven or Shakespeare, but merely to make the obvious point that there are differences between the nature of genius in the arts and in the sciences.[14] What is essential to the conception of genius in any field is that the work itself should be of lasting quality and value, and this is clearly the reason why the notion of genius has never been applied in any meaningful way to the performing arts. The central problem which genius poses in relation to the creative arts was highlighted very clearly in the discussion which followed the talk given by Raymond Klibansky at the conference on genius out of which this book has grown. When the question was raised as to why there is no tradition of happy genius in Western culture, Professor Klibansky replied, with characteristic directness: 'Could a happy man have written Hamlet?'

The central theme of this book is the development of the idea of genius from its origins in classical antiquity to its current deconstruction in postmodernist criticism. Within a broadly chronological framework, experts in different fields explore the idea from a variety of different viewpoints, reflecting the controversial nature of a subject which demands an interdisciplinary approach. Rather than providing a continuous narrative, or attempting to be comprehensive, the book focuses on certain points in the history of the idea of genius, or on certain themes, which are particularly interesting or significant. Separate chapters are devoted to music and to mathematics, since these are the two areas in which the idea of genius is still applied with some of its traditional force, at least by the population at large, if not by practitioners of these subjects. The greatest contribution to the study of genius which the twentieth century has made, however, is in the field of psychiatry, and it therefore seemed fitting to end the book with a chapter on genius and psychoanalysis. What future the

idea of genius has in the increasingly utilitarian culture which we now
inhabit remains an open question.

Notes

1 See B. Hoffman, *Einstein* (London, 1975), p. 252.
2 Johann Caspar Lavater, *Physiognomische Fragmente*, (Leipzig, 1778) vol. 4; and
   see H. M. Jones, *Revolution and Romanticism* (Cambridge, Mass., 1974), p. 283.
3 M. H. Abrams, *The Mirror and the Lamp* (New York, 1953).
4 H. Dieckmann, 'Diderot's Conception of Genius', *Journal of the History of Ideas*, 2
   (1941), p. 151.
5 For a detailed discussion of these lines and the complex of ideas that lie behind
   them see C. O. Brink, *Horace on Poetry: Epistles Book Two* (Cambridge, 1982),
   pp. 385–6, 441–4. For the importance of the Horatian lines for the medieval
   conception of genius see J. C. Nitzsche, *The Genius Figure in Antiquity and the
   Middle Ages* (New York, 1975).
6 E. Zilsel, *Die Entstehung des Geniebegriffes. Ein Beitrag zur Ideengeschichte der Antike
   und des Frühkapitalismus* (Tübingen, 1926), pp. 293ff. On the history of the
   English word see also Logan Pearsall Smith, *Words and Idioms* (London, 1925),
   pp. 95–114; M. L. Wiley, 'Genius: a problem in definition', *Studies in English*, 16
   (1936), 77–83.
7 See Abrams, *The Mirror and the Lamp*, pp. 272–85; E. N. Tigerstedt, 'The Poet
   as Creator: Origins of a Metaphor', *Comparative Literature Studies*, 5 (1968), 455–
   88. In general on the concept of creativity in the arts see M. C. Nahm, *The
   Artist as Creator* (Baltimore, 1956); R. Williams, *The Long Revolution* (Harmondsworth, 1965), pp. 19–56; W. Tatarkiewicz, *A History of Six Ideas* (Warsaw and
   the Hague, 1980), pp. 244–65; P. O. Kristeller, ' "Creativity" and "Tradition" ',
   Journal of the History of Ideas, 44 (1983), 105–13.
8 Quoted from J. P. Richter (ed.), *The Literary Works of Leonardo da Vinci*, 3rd edn
   (2 vols, London, 1970), vol. 1, p. 54. Cf. M. Kemp (ed.), *Leonardo on Painting*,
   (New Haven and London, 1989) p. 32.
9 See Martin Kemp's discussion in chapter 2 of this book.
10 Plutarch, *Marcellus* xvii 4–6. I have quoted the translation in I. Thomas (ed.),
    Selections Illustrating the History of Greek Mathematics, (London, 1941) vol. 2, pp.
    31–2. I am grateful to David Fowler for drawing my attention to this passage.
11 Richard Poirier, 'The Question of Genius', *Raritan*, 5, 4 (Spring 1986), 102–3.
12 See, for example, R. J. Sternberg (ed.), *The Nature of Creativity* (Cambridge,
    1988).
13 See in particular R. Currie, *Genius, an Ideology in Literature* (London, 1974).
14 See for instance, S. Chandrasekhar, *Truth and Beauty: Aesthetics and Motivations in
    Science* (Chicago, 1987), especially chapter 3.

1
Poetic Genius and its Classical Origins

Penelope Murray

> The creative aspect of life which finds its clearest expression in art baffles all attempts at rational formulation. Any reaction to stimulus may be causally explained; but the creative act, which is the absolute antithesis of mere reaction, will for ever elude the human understanding.
>
> C. G. Jung, *Modern Man in Search of a Soul*

Interest in the nature of creativity began with the Greeks, to whom we owe the central image of the Muses, symbol of the poet's inspiration for more than two thousand years in the history of European culture. The Greeks did not have a word for genius, or indeed for creativity; nevertheless it is clear that from the earliest beginnings, long before the invention of aesthetics, they recognized that there was something inexplicable in the creative act. In their attempts to fathom this mystery they formulated ideas which were of fundamental importance in the subsequent history of aesthetics.

In this chapter I shall explore the classical origins of the concept of genius. My discussion will focus in general on the portrayal of the poet, and in particular on two ideas about the nature of poetic creativity which played a vital part in the development of the notion of genius in later ages. One is divine inspiration, that is the belief which attributes the apparently inexplicable element in poetic creation to the temporary influence of an external force; the other is the notion that the poet himself has innate talent or natural ability which is in some sense 'given', and cannot be acquired through learning. These ideas, first formulated by the Greeks, have existed in one form or another ever since, for some kind of 'given' factor in poetic composition has rarely been denied, even in periods when the emphasis of critical theory has been on rules and technique, and the dominant image, that of the poet as craftsman.

In considering the origins and development of these ideas I shall base my analysis on a series of passages from ancient authors, all of which are of interest and importance in their own right. But some have acquired a significance out of all proportion to their original status because of the way in which they have been subsequently read and interpreted. For it is characteristic of the influence exerted by the classical tradition that particular texts or authors which may have been marginal or untypical in their own day have often assumed a central role in the literature and thought of later ages. For example, as Klibansky, Panofsky and Saxl show in their classic study *Saturn and Melancholy*,[1] the Renaissance conception of creative melancholy derives ultimately from a passage in the pseudo-Aristotelean *Problems*, a text quite outside the mainstream of classical literature. Indeed, as the authors of *Saturn and Melancholy* point out, 'ancient writers record its main thesis, that all great men are melancholics, with either a certain remote astonishment or else with frank irony.'[2] Similarly, Longinus' treatise *On the Sublime* was of only marginal interest until Boileau's translation, published in 1674, sparked off the whole eighteenth-century discussion of 'the Sublime', making Longinus compulsory reading for every educated man.[3] My purpose in what follows, therefore, is to explore the origins of two highly influential ideas about the nature of poetic creativity, and to set in context various passages from ancient authors which have played a significant part in shaping the history of the idea of genius since the Renaissance.

The two concepts of inspiration and natural talent which are at the centre of my investigation are usually traced back to antiquity, to Plato and Pindar respectively; but I believe that already in Homer it is possible to distinguish between two distinct attitudes to poetic creativity which foreshadow the later concepts.[4] In early Greek literature, poets attribute their power to the Muses, who inspire their protégés in two main ways, which are distinguishable, even if they are not in fact distinguished by the poets themselves. They give inspiration in a temporary sense, as we can see, for example, from the description of the bard Demodocus at *Odyssey* 8.73: 'The Muse moved the bard to sing of the glorious deeds of men,' or from the invocations to the Muses, such as we find in the opening line of the *Iliad*: 'Sing, goddess, the anger of Peleus' son Achilleus.' But they also give permanent poetic ability. In the *Odyssey* the blind Demodocus is described as 'a goodly bard, whom the Muse especially loved. She gave him both good and evil, for she took away his eyes and gave him sweet song' (*Od.* 8.62–4). These words clearly imply that the gift of song is as permanent as the blindness which accompanies it, and which is frequently associated with bards:[5] in return for his ordinary mortal sight, Demodocus is blessed with the poet's divine insight which the Muses confer. His poetic gift is further defined by Alcinous at *Od*. 8.43–5: 'Call here the divine bard, Demodocus; for to him above all others has the god given the gift of song, to give pleasure in whatever way his spirit moves him to sing.' Once again the gift which the god bestows is a permanent one which the bard may use as he likes, rather than a temporary access of inspiration. It is this idea of *permanent* endowment which, I believe, foreshadows subsequent notions of the genius as a person with special gifts.

Apart from bestowing the gift of poetry, the Muses are also commonly said to teach poets: Odysseus, for example, praises Demodocus, saying that either a Muse or Apollo must have taught him (*Od*. 8.487–8); Hesiod claims that the Muses taught him fair song (*Theogony* 22), and Solon refers to one who has learnt the gifts of the Muses (*frag*. 13.51). The precise meaning of such statements is not clear, as Aelius Aristides, sophist of the second century AD, somewhat disparagingly remarked: 'How then do the Muses teach? By opening a school like elementary teachers?' (*In Defence of Oratory* 91). But in general the teaching metaphor emphasizes the craft aspects of the poet's vocation, whilst at the same time underlining its divine origin: poetic ability is a skill, but one which comes from the gods. What is perhaps surprising is the absence of any references in early Greek literature to the possibility of one poet teaching another, and this in spite of the emphasis placed on the skilled nature of the poet's craft. In an oral culture the novice must in fact have learnt the rudiments of his craft by listening to those more experienced than himself, yet teaching is presented as the prerogative of the gods. Aristides' comments are again apposite: when Odysseus prefaces his praise of Demodocus with the general statement that bards deserve honour because the Muse has taught them and loves them (*Od*. 8.479–81) it is, he says, 'as if Homer were afraid on his own behalf that someone might say that he learned from another, and not from the Muses themselves' (*In Defence of Oratory* 90).

Poetic ability is not the only human endowment which was thought to originate from the gods, but one of several, including physical beauty, strength, wisdom, eloquence, skill in handiwork and prophecy. On the whole the gods do not bestow more than one gift on a person, a belief which persists in early Greek thought even when outstanding ability is attributed to nature rather than to divine causation. Men cannot choose their skills, but must simply accept what the gods have given them and live their lives accordingly. What is significant about the gift and teaching metaphors is that they are used primarily to describe outstanding abilities and distinguishing features; indeed this is why it is gods who teach them, not men. We have the converse situation in a fragment from the *Margites* (*fr*. 2), where someone is described as having no skills at all because the gods have not taught him anything. Poetic ability and others like it are conventionally described as gifts of the gods, because, as John Stuart Mill observed of the maxim '*nascitur poeta*', there is 'a common tendency among mankind to consider all power which is not visibly the effect of practice, all skill which is not capable of being reduced to mechanical rules, as the result of a peculiar gift'.[6]

Once a person has received a gift of this sort, he continues to be a favourite of the gods. So, for example, craftsmen are under the protection of Athena and Hephaestus, Apollo protects prophets, and poets are sacred to the Muses. What distinguishes poets from other groups in early Greek literature is the frequency of references to the poet's special status and the emphasis placed on his links with the divine. Of course this is partly, no doubt largely, due to the fact that poets are our primary source of information during this period: when considering the status of the poet in early Greek literature, what we are actually doing is looking at the poet's conception of himself. But even when due allowance is made for any discrepancy between what the poet says of himself and his actual social status, it is clear that poets did enjoy considerable prestige in early Greek society;[7] and it is significant that the lofty conception of their role which they projected persisted into later periods. Why else would Plato have tried so hard to undermine the role of the poet?

Homer and the early Greek poets do not speculate about the reasons or circumstances surrounding the bestowal of gifts and skills on men, but the gift and teaching idioms presuppose an actual meeting between gods and men. This underlying implication is first made explicit in Hesiod's account of the momentous occasion on which the Muses appeared to him on Mount Helicon and summoned him to be a poet:

Once they taught Hesiod fair song, when he was tending his sheep at the foot of sacred Helicon. These were the words which the goddesses first spoke to me, the Olympian Muses, daughters of Zeus the aegis-bearer: 'Shepherds dwelling in the fields, shameful wretches, nothing but bellies, we know how to speak many false things as though they were true; but we know, when we wish, how to utter true things'. So spoke the daughters of great Zeus, ready of speech. And they plucked a branch of flourishing laurel and gave it to me as a staff, a wonderful thing, and they breathed into me a divine voice so that I might celebrate the events of the future and the past. They bade me sing of the race of the blessed, eternal gods, but always to sing of themselves first and last.

(*Theogony* 22–34)

That Hesiod is the first self-conscious European poet, fully aware of his own special nature, has often been pointed out, and the question of the status of the description – whether it reflects a genuine religious experience, or whether it is merely conventional – has been much debated.[8] But what I wish to consider here are the implications which this passage has for Hesiod's conception of his art: clearly he ascribes his poetic ability not to any innate talent or qualities which he has, but to the grace of the Muses, who have singled him out and bestowed on him their gifts. His vocation as a poet began when the goddesses first set him on the path of song, as he later recalls (*Works and Days* 659). Interestingly enough, Maximus of Tyre (*Dialexis* 38), writing in the very different cultural milieu of the second century AD, regarded Hesiod's description, and other similar tales of untaught sages receiving divine inspiration, as allegories to explain innate talent, but Hesiod himself does not see it that way.

In fact the early Greek poets appear to have no conception of poetic, or for that matter any other, ability being innate. We can perhaps see the beginnings of this idea in Phemius' claim (*Od.* 22.347–8) that the god implanted (*enephusen*) in him the pathways of song, the first instance of the *phusis* word group in connection with poetry, although it is not altogether clear whether this implanting took place at birth. Some commentators translate *enephusen* as 'made to grow' so that the whole phrase would mean 'the god has made the pathways of song grow in me'; but parallels suggest that the word *emphuō* is normally used of physical entities or spiritual qualities that are rooted or stuck fast in a person or thing. Possibly, therefore, Phemius' claim anticipates the later idea that poetic ability is innate and cannot be acquired.

There is no indication, however, that poetic talent was thought to be inherited or passed down from generation to generation, which is perhaps surprising in view of the importance attached to lineage and descent in the Homeric poems. Certainly the gift of divination was regarded as hereditary, at least in the case of Theoclymenus (*Od.* 15.225), whose lineage is traced back through a succession of seers to the legendary Melampus.[9] A similar, though less elaborate, genealogy is given to the craftsman Phereclus in the *Iliad* (5.59–60), which certainly indicates that his skill had been handed down from earlier generations, and might imply that skills such as his were thought to be hereditary. No such genealogies are given for poets in the early period, though it has been suggested[10] that when Hesiod says in the *Theogony* (94) that singers are 'from the Muses' (*ek Mouseōn*) the expression could refer to lineal descent in the literal sense. But this is to interpret the phrase in the light of the later vogue for tracing the ancestry of famous poets such as Homer and Hesiod back through the legendary figures of Orpheus, Musaeus or Linus to the Muses; and even in these genealogies the emphasis is on the divine nature of poets and poetry rather than on inheritance.

The idea that divine gifts could be bestowed at birth is implied in Achilles' grimly pessimistic words to Priam on the miseries of mortal existence (*Iliad* 24.525–42): life without pain is impossible, he says, for men's fortunes are allotted to them by Zeus from twin urns of blessings and evils. For some life is wholly wretched, but others have a mixture of good and bad fortune, like his own father Peleus, who had many sorrows even though he had been given glorious gifts by the gods from the time of his birth (*ek genetēs*). That same phrase occurs in connection with musical ability in the Homeric *Hymn to Apollo* (dated to not later than the seventh century BC) when the god, amazed at the sound of the newly invented lyre, asks Hermes: 'Have these marvellous deeds accompanied you from birth, or did some god or man give you the glorious gift and teach you heavenly song?' (440–2). A more significant example of the gift at birth motif occurs in Hesiod's *Theogony*, where the Muses bestow their gifts at birth, although on this occasion the gift is eloquence in prose rather than poetic ability, for the recipient is a king rather than a poet: 'Whomsoever of the kings who are fostered by Zeus the daughters of great Zeus honour, on him they look when he is born, and they pour sweet dew on his tongue and honey-sweet words flow from his mouth' (*Theogony* 81–4).[11] The difference between this description of the bestowal of the Muses' gifts on kings and Hesiod's account of his own meeting with the goddesses highlights the special nature of the poet's gifts: whereas the king has his powers of arbitration and peace-making from birth, Hesiod is singled out to receive his gift of poetry on a momentous occasion during his life. Quite clearly he regards himself as a special being, and implicit in his account of the revelation granted to him by the Muses is the belief that he is in some sense set apart from other men by his experience.

The notion that men are born with certain qualities, both good and bad, begins to emerge during the course of the sixth century, notably in the poetry of Theognis, who asserts the superiority of the aristocracy on the basis of noble birth. Wealth may have corrupted the social order, making the poor man rich and the rich man poor, declares this gloomy and embittered spokesman for the decaying ideals of the past, but you can never teach virtue or make a bad man good. It is birth alone which determines these qualities. The idea implicit in the work of Theognis, that excellence depends on innate qualities, receives its fullest and most powerful expression in Pindar, who proclaims again and again that no achievement is possible without inborn ability. 'Everything that is natural is best' (*to de phua kratiston hapan*), he asserts at *Olympian* 9.100, where the word *phua* is used to denote the qualities and aptitudes with which a man is born, and which make up his essential nature. The superiority of natural or inborn qualities over learning is a frequent motif in his poetry as, for example, at *Nemean* 3.40–2 where he contrasts the power of the man whose excellence is inborn with the impotence of one who has merely learnt, 'a man without light, blowing now this way, now that, nor does he enter the contest with sure foot, but tastes countless virtues with ineffectual mind'.

Pindar reinterprets the Homeric idea that men excel in different ways according to the gifts that the gods have given them in terms of the concept of *phua*. Thus at *Nemean* 1.25–6 he says: 'Different men have different skills. But a man should walk along straight paths and strive according to his nature.' Here and elsewhere Pindar ascribes to nature what Homer and others ascribe to the gods; but it would be a mistake to regard innate ability and divine gifts as mutually exclusive alternatives, for nature is itself god-given, a connection which is made explicit at *Pythian* 1.41–2: 'All means of mortal excellence come from the gods; for it is they who make men naturally wise and strong and eloquent.' This fact, though generally recognized, has led to a certain confusion amongst classical scholars; for it is sometimes assumed that Pindar replaces the idea of temporary inspiration, which we find in earlier poets, with the concept of inborn talent or natural ability.[12] But Pindar's frequent invocations to the Muses to help him in his song indicate that this idea of inspiration is present in his poetry just as it is in Homer's. What the concept of *phua* does replace, or rather redefine, is the earlier idea that the Muses grant permanent poetic ability. Whereas Homer and Hesiod regard poetic ability as a gift bestowed on a man on some momentous occasion during his life, Pindar regards it as a gift of nature, divinely bestowed, but innate.

More self-consciously than any other Greek poet, Pindar presents himself as a chosen individual, the prophet and herald of the Muses, who rides in their chariot. It is symptomatic of his conception of himself as an elevated and superior being that he avoids using the traditional terminology for poets and poetry, preferring instead to use the terms *sophos* and *sophia*. Pindar was not the first to use these terms in the context of poetry, but he invests them with a new significance: as Bruno Snell has shown,[13] these words were originally used in early Greek poetry to denote practical ability and knowledge rather than wisdom, and were applied to a wide variety of activities including carpentry, seamanship, generalship, the art of the seer, musical skill, and poetry. The emergence of *soph-* words to mean wisdom in a more intellectual sense was a gradual process, and one in which Pindar played an important part. In his poetry the *sophos*, whether he be poet, patron or victor, is a man of superior intellect, set apart from his fellows both by his inborn nature and by his communion with the gods. The essence of this view is expressed at *Olympian* 2.83–8: 'There are many swift arrows in the quiver beneath my arm, which speak to those who understand; but for the majority they need interpreters. Wise is he who knows many things by nature (*sophos ho polla eidōs phua*). Let those who have merely learnt chatter in vain, like garrulous crows, against the holy bird of Zeus.'

In later ages, Pindar was to become a symbol of overwhelming natural force too great to be constrained by the conventional rules of art, a paradigm of wild and untutored genius.[14] This view was fostered in large measure by Horace's celebrated description of him in *Odes* 4.2, which so influenced the conception of the Pindaric ideal from the seventeenth century onwards:

> *monte decurrens velut amnis, imbres*
> *quem super notas aluere ripas,*
> *fervet immensusque ruit profundo*
>   *Pindarus ore,*
>
> *laurea donandus Apollinari,*
> *seu per audacis nova dithyrambos*
> *verba devolvit numerisque fertur*
>   *lege solutis,*
>
> *seu deos regesque canit*

(As a river which rains have swollen beyond its banks rushes down from a mountain, so deep-voiced Pindar seethes in a torrent of song, worthy of Apollo's laurel whether he rolls new words in bold dithyrambs, carried away in rhythms freed from rules, or sings of gods and kings)

But Pindar's own insistence on the superiority of nature over learning appeared to corroborate this image. So Addison classed Pindar together with Homer, the Old Testament prophets and Shakespeare as one of those natural geniuses who 'by the meer Strength of natural Parts, and without any assistance of Art or Learning, have produced Works that were the Delight of their own Times, and the Wonder of Posterity';[15] and Edward Young singles him out from ancient writers with an explicit reference to *Olympian* 2: 'A Star of the first magnitude among the Moderns was *Shakespeare*; among the Ancients, *Pindar*, who (as Vossius tells us) boasted of his No-learning, calling himself the Eagle for his Flight above it.'[16]

The contrast which Pindar draws between natural ability and learning is rightly regarded by commentators as an early contribution to the general debate in the fifth century on the relative merits of *phusis* (nature) and *technē* (art), a debate which continued for centuries, particularly in relation to poetry and oratory. The question as to which of the two, art or nature, was the more important became a commonplace of ancient literary criticism. In almost every case it would be anachronistic to regard nature (*phusis* in Greek, *ingenium* or *natura* in Latin) as anything more than natural talent or aptitude. The one exception is the treatise *On the Sublime* attributed to Longinus. According to this work, sublimity (*to hupsos*), defined as a kind of eminence or excellence of discourse, is the hallmark of the greatest poets and prose writers, who can overwhelm us, sometimes in a single phrase, with the lightning force of their emotions, transporting us in spite of ourselves into the realms of inspired imagination. Although Longinus specifically rejects the idea that this effect can be achieved by nature alone without the aid of art, nevertheless the most important source of sublimity is natural greatness (*to megalophuēs*) which confers both the ability to conceive great thoughts and the power to generate strong and inspired emotion (ch. 8). The way in which he describes the 'natural greatness' necessary for sublimity is certainly quite different from the traditional acknowledgement of natural talent as a prerequisite of the orator or poet; for Longinus treats sublimity as a product not of technique but of character: those whom nature has endowed must develop their minds in the direction of greatness, cultivating noble thoughts, for 'sublimity is the echo of a noble mind' (ch. 9). This concentration on the personality of the writer combined with his frequent use of the language of enthusiasm and inspiration raise Longinus' *megalophuēs* (natural greatness) to an altogether different level from the mundane *phusis* of other critics. It is indeed difficult to avoid using the term 'genius' when translating Longinus, particularly in the famous comparison (chs. 33–36) between the flawless products of mediocrity and the inspired but erratic sublimity achieved by *hai hupermegetheis phuseis* ('exceedingly great natures'). D. A. Russell's translation captures exactly the spirit of the original:

So when we come to great geniuses in literature (*tōn en logois megalophuōn*) [. . .] we have to conclude that such men, for all their faults, tower far above mortal stature. Other literary qualities prove their users to be human; sublimity raises us towards the spiritual greatness of god.[17]

The language of inspiration which Longinus uses in his treatise to describe both the effects of sublimity and the emotion necessary to produce it owes much to Plato, whose concept of '*furor poeticus*', the notion of poetic inspiration as a kind of frenzy or enthusiasm, is the most influential account of the poetic process which has come down to us from antiquity. Since Homer it had been customary to speak of poets as inspired, but throughout the early period this idea was balanced by a belief in the importance of poetic craft. What is new in Plato is the emphasis on the passivity of the poet and the irrational nature of his inspiration, which is quite incompatible with any notion of craft or technique. 'The poet', he says in an early dialogue, 'is a light creature, winged and holy, and is unable to compose until he is possessed and out of his mind, and his reason is no longer in him' (*Ion* 534). This image of the inspired poet remains substantially unchanged in his last work, the *Laws* (719C) where he refers to what purports to be an old story that 'the poet, whenever he sits on the Muse's tripod, is not in his senses, but like a spring lets whatever comes into his head flow freely.' In fact Plato's view of poetic inspiration is remarkably consistent: throughout his work he insists that the poet, when composing, is in a frenzy and out of his mind; he creates by divine dispensation, but with no knowledge of what he does.

Plato may not have invented the notion of inspiration as a kind of enthusiasm (we find it already in Democritus), but he was its most influential exponent, and he does seem to have been the first to connect poetic inspiration with madness (*mania*). In the *Phaedrus* Socrates makes the paradoxical statement that our greatest blessings come to us through madness, if that madness is sent by the gods. There are, he suggests, four types of divine madness: prophetic madness which comes from Apollo; telestic or ritual madness whose patron is Dionysus; poetic madness inspired by the Muses; erotic madness caused by Aphrodite and Eros. This is the context of Plato's classic statement of the doctrine of '*furor poeticus*':

Third is the possession and madness which comes from the Muses. It takes hold of the tender and untouched soul, rousing it up and exciting it to frenzy in lyric and other kinds of poetry [. . .] But whoever comes to the gates of poetry without the Muses' madness, persuaded that art will make him a good poet, is ineffectual himself, and the poetry of the sane man is eclipsed by that of the mad.

(245A)

Despite the potency of the imagery and the extravagance of the language we should not be seduced into thinking that the poet is deemed to be literally mad, in the sense of being what we would call clinically insane. For Plato stresses that this form of madness is divine, and later on in the same dialogue (265A) he specifically contrasts two kinds of madness, one of which is divine in origin, while the other results from disease. In drawing an analogy between the prophet, the Bacchant, the poet and the lover, Plato is, of course, stressing the irrational nature of their activities; but it is the temporary mental state of the inspired poet which interests him rather than his permanent disposition, the poetic process rather than the poetic personality.

Plato's account of poetic inspiration is deliberately ambiguous, for, by using the language of divine possession he maintains a link with the traditional concept of inspiration, but turns that concept upside down. In early Greek literature the divine origin of poetry is used to guarantee its truth and quality, but for Plato the principal implication of the idea of divine inspiration is that poets have no knowledge or understanding, an implication which can hardly be complimentary. So whilst praising poets in the most fulsome terms, he is able to undermine their authority without explicitly attacking them in any way.

Aristotle clearly alludes to Plato's idea of inspiration as a kind of madness in chapter 17 of the *Poetics*. In his discussion of poetic imagination he says that the poet will write most convincingly if he is himself able to feel the emotions which he wants his characters to express: 'That is why poetry is the work of a *euphuēs* (a man endowed by nature) rather than[18] a *manikos* (a madman); the former are adaptable, whereas the latter are out of their minds (*ekstatikoi*).' Despite the brevity of the statement and the complexity of the context in which it occurs, Aristotle is clearly contrasting two types of poet, the *manikos-ekstatikos*, that is the inspired poet (in the Platonic sense of the word) and the *euphuēs-euplastos*, one endowed by nature to be adaptable or versatile. This is the first explicit formulation in Greek literature of a distinction between inspiration and natural endowment (to call it 'genius' as many commentators do is probably stretching the term too much) as alternative sources of poetic creativity.

As we have seen, the earliest Greek poets do not themselves distinguish between the temporary and permanent aspects of the Muses' inspiration. It is only in Pindar's poetry that a distinction is implied between inspiration which provides the immediate source of a poem and natural talent as the permanent quality which the poet has. But although he seems to recognize inspiration and natural talent as separate ideas, Pindar nowhere implies that they are alternatives to each other: throughout his work poetic creativity appears to spring from a combination of the two; and both, in his view, are god given. Plato too, on the one occasion when he uses *phusis* (nature) in the context of poetry, places it alongside the idea of inspiration: 'And I soon realized that the poets did not compose their poems through wisdom, but by nature, and that they were inspired like seers and soothsayers' (*Apology* 22 B–C). Once again nature and inspiration are presented as joint rather than alternative elements in poetic creativity. Aristotle's distinction between the two has to be read in the light of a long history of speculation about the sources of the poet's gifts.

A text which elucidates Aristotle's brief statement in the *Poetics* and which is of central importance to any study of the history of the idea of genius, as Klibansky, Panofsky and Saxl have shown,[19] is the pseudo-Aristotelian

Problems 30.1. The passage begins with the question, 'Why is it that all those who are outstanding (*perittoi*) in philosophy, politics, poetry or arts (*technai*) are melancholic?' Some *perittoi*, we are told, are melancholic to such an extent that they are affected by diseases caused by black bile, a predominance of black bile being, of course, the chief characteristic of the melancholic, according to the ancient theory of humours. Many of the heroes were of this type, including Heracles, Lysander, Ajax and Bellerophon: Heracles suffered from epilepsy, which was said to have been a common affliction of the melancholic; both he and Lysander were covered in sores before death (also a characteristic melancholic disease); Ajax went completely out of his mind (*ekstatikos*); Bellerophon became a recluse who avoided all contact with others. In later times, the author tells us, Empedocles, Plato and Socrates were melancholic in temperament, as were many other distinguished people including the majority of poets.

There then follows a detailed discussion, the basis of which is a comparison between the effects produced by wine and by black bile, these substances being similar in that they are both full of breath or air (*pneuma*). In most people black bile arising from daily food does not change their character, it merely produces melancholic diseases. But those people in whom black bile predominates by nature (that is, those who are melancholic) immediately develop different characteristics according to their various constitutions:

For example, those in whom there is a lot of cold black bile become sluggish and stupid, but those who are full of hot black bile become frenzied (*manikoi*) or brilliant (*euphueis*) or amorous or easily moved to anger and desire, and some become more talkative. Many too, if this heat approaches the seat of the intellect, are affected by fits of frenzy or possession (*nosēmasin manikois ē enthousiastikois*) which accounts for Sibyls and soothsayers and all inspired people, when they are affected not by disease, but by natural temperament. Maracus the Syracusan was even a better poet when he was out of his mind.

A modern reader will be struck by the fact that the ancient world already postulated a relationship between mania and depression, but the particular point I wish to note here is that black bile, the characteristic constituent of outstanding men, also causes inspiration of the ecstatic variety. In general, the discussion continues, those people in whom there is a small quantity of black bile are normal; but those who have a large proportion of black bile are quite unlike the majority of men.

The passage as a whole is significant not only because it envisages a coherent relationship between inspiration and a certain kind of temperament, the melancholic, but also because it formulates for the first time the notion, which was later to become so influential, that genius is akin to madness. Black bile, when it is present in the right quantity and at the right temperature, is the cause of outstanding achievement, but, if the balance is upset or the bile changes temperature, it causes morbid conditions such as those of mania or depression. A man who is melancholic by temperament, therefore, is fitted for outstanding achievement, but he is constantly at risk: a change in the quantity or temperature of the black bile in his body might lead to mania, depression or madness. In other words, there is a direct relationship between genius and madness.

Plato had already described poetic creativity in terms of *mania*, but it is important to remember that he used the word *mania* of poetic inspiration. As we saw, his chief concern was to demonstrate the irrationality of the poetic process; he was not interested in the nature of poetic genius. The author of *Problems* 30, however, replaces Plato's mythical explanation of the poetic process with a quasi-scientific notion of the melancholic character of genius. Poetry is produced not by divine inspiration, but by men who are melancholic in temperament, and so-called inspiration is merely the result of the black bile in their bodies becoming heated.

In the *Problems* there is a clear distinction between temperament, a man's permanent disposition, and the temporary state of inspiration, and the relationship between them is carefully worked out. But often the two are confused. Take, for example, Horace's words in the *Ars Poetica* (295–8): 'Because Democritus thinks natural talent (*ingenium*) is a greater blessing than wretched art and bans sane poets from Helicon, a good many don't bother to cut their nails or beards, but seek solitary places and avoid baths.' What Horace does here is to conflate the notion of natural talent (*ingenium*) with the idea of manic inspiration to produce the figure of the mad poet. As far as we know, Democritus never said that poets are actually mad any more than Plato did; he simply described inspiration as 'enthusiasm' (*enthousiasmos*). The figure of the mad poet crops up again at the end of the *Ars Poetica* (453–66):

Sensible men are afraid to touch a mad poet (vesanum [. . .] poetam) and avoid him like the plague [. . .] If whilst he's wandering around pouring forth his sublime verses he should fall into a well or a pit, no one will bother to pull him out however long he cries for help. But if someone were to let down a rope, I'll say, 'How do you know that he didn't throw himself down on purpose? Maybe he doesn't want to be saved?' And I'll tell him about the death of the Sicilian poet: Empedocles, wanting to be thought an immortal god, coolly jumped into blazing Etna. Let poets have the right to destroy themselves.

The story about Empedocles (who is here treated as a poet rather than as a philosopher) is introduced as an example to illustrate the poet's madness. In these lines, as C. O. Brink points out, Horace interprets the Democritean-Platonic idea of inspiration with 'malicious liberalism: inspiration is like an infectious or frightening disease'.[20] In doing so he ignores the Platonic distinction between the *theia mania* (divine madness) of inspiration and *mania* as a disease; he also confuses, presumably deliberately, the notions of *ingenium* and inspiration. Whereas Plato used the word *mania* in a quasi-metaphorical way to emphasize the irrationality of the poetic process, Horace transfers the concept of madness to the poetic personality: he depicts the poet as literally mad.

In fact there is no linguistic distinction in Greek or Latin between madness and inspiration: both *mania* and *furor* have a wide semantic range covering a variety of non-rational states including anger, passion, inspiration and insanity. The ambiguity of the Latin word is nicely illustrated in Statius' pertinent characterization of Lucretius' poetry as the product of the 'lofty *furor*' of its learned author ('docti furor arduus Lucreti', *Silvae* 2.7.76), where *furor* must allude to poetic inspiration; but misinterpretation of the word may well have fostered the tradition, so beloved of romantic readers of Lucretius, that the poet was mad.[21] Indeed failure to distinguish between inspiration and madness clearly contributed to the ever-popular notion of genius as a form of madness, an idea which reached its zenith in the nineteenth century in the works of, for example, Cesare Lombroso, Professor of Legal Medicine at the University of Turin, who described genius as a degenerative psychosis of the epileptoid group, and traced this idea back to antiquity, to the works of Aristotle, Plato and Democritus.[22]

The *Problems* passage on melancholy is unusual in a number of respects, not least in elevating practitioners of *technai* (arts and crafts) on to the same level as poets and philosophers. The word *technē*, of course, covers anything from painting, pottery and sculpture to shoemaking, carpentry and shipbuilding, there being no linguistic or conceptual distinction in the Greek world, or indeed in antiquity generally, between crafts and the fine arts. From Homer onwards the products of craftsmanship were highly valued and greatly admired, as we can see from the many literary descriptions of marvellous handiwork, and from the prestige attached to works of art in Greece and Rome alike. But the status of the craftsman himself is less clear.[23] In philosophical works, at least, there is a long and enduring tradition that the activity of the craftsman, forced to earn his living by working with his hands, is 'banausic', unworthy of the philosopher and incompatible with the life of moral and political virtue to which the free man should aspire. This attitude is reflected in authors as diverse as Xenophon, Plato, Aristotle, Cicero, Seneca and Plutarch. To take an example, it is not surprising that we should find an author such as Lucian, whose imaginative life was lived through the literature of an earlier age, describing the horrors of the banausic life in terms reminiscent of Xenophon and Plato. In *The Dream*, a supposedly autobiographical account of his youth, he recalls how the figures of Sculpture and *Paideia* (Education or Culture) appeared to him in a dream, each trying to persuade him of the merits of their respective life styles. *Paideia*'s words epitomize the whole tradition of prejudice against the manual arts. If you become a sculptor, she says, 'you will be nothing but a workman, one of the common people, cowering before your superiors [. . .]. Even if you were to become a Phidias or a Polyclitus and produce many wonderful works, everyone would praise your craftsmanship, but no-one in his senses would want to be like you. For whatever you might be, you would be regarded as a *banausos*, a manual labourer who earns his living by working with his hands' (*The Dream* 9).

How far this tradition reflects the actual social status of artists and craftsmen is a complex and controversial question to which there can be no simple answer. In any case it would be absurd to assume that their situation was identical in all places and in all periods of antiquity. So far as classical Greece was concerned, Herodotus (2.167) states it as a fact that, with the exception of Corinth, craftsmen were universally considered to be lower in the social scale than people who have no connection with manual work. On the other hand there are certain indications that earlier attitudes to craftsmen were not as uncompromisingly negative as the literary evidence I have considered so far would suggest. In Homer (*Odyssey* 17.382–5) the craftsman, together with the seer, the healer and the bard, is classed as one of the *dēmioergoi*, 'public workers' who have specialized skills which are of use to the community at large.

In fact the economic importance of craftsmen in ancient society was never denied: even Plato and Aristotle recognize that craftsmen, however banausic they may be, are essential to the economic and cultural life of the *polis*. Craftsmen themselves, to judge from the number of inscriptions and signatures of the sort 'so and so made me', which appear on pottery and sculpture from the seventh century BC onwards, were proud of the objects they made. According to Aristotle (*Politics* 3.1278a) the majority of artisans were rich, an observation which is confirmed by inscriptional evidence. But whatever the economic prosperity enjoyed by individual craftsmen, it is clear that as a group they had no political status; at Athens, for example, a large proportion of craftsmen were metics, resident aliens who were not citizens. It is indeed one of the great paradoxes of Greek culture, as P. Vidal-Naquet has observed, that Greece, particularly in the fifth and fourth centuries BC, was a *'civilisation de l'artisan'*; but the ideology of the dominant class, expressed in the literature of the period, denied the importance of the craftsman, banishing him to the shadows and condemning him to be nothing but *'l'héros secret de l'histoire grecque'*.[24]

The paradoxical situation of the craftsman is reflected even within the literary-philosophical tradition itself. Plato, ambivalent in this as in so many other respects, frequently uses imagery associated with craftsmanship and clearly finds much that is admirable in the activity of the so-called *banausoi*: in the *Timaeus*, for example, one of the central images is that of the demiurge or creator as craftsman, fashioning the universe with the careful precision of the artisan. In Lucian's *Dream*, quoted above, the figure of Sculpture counters *Paideia's* strictures on the banausic nature of the sculptor's life by holding up the examples of Phidias, Polyclitus, Myron and Praxiteles, 'men who receive homage second only to the gods' (8). On the mythical level the plurality of technical divinities and the number of legendary figures such as Daedalus and Prometheus who fall into the category of *prōtos heuretēs*, 'first discoverer', reveal a deep concern with craft and technology. But the ambiguous role of crafts in Greek society is encoded in these mythical prototypes: Hephaestus, admired for his wonderful technical ability, is nevertheless deformed and misshapen, a god, but one who is not the equal of the Olympian deities whom he serves.[25]

Despite the ambiguous state of artists and craftsmen in general, it is of course true that certain outstanding individuals did achieve positions of great honour and prestige. One has only to think of the conspicuous economic wellbeing of Phidias, friend of Pericles and universally renowned, of Zeuxis displaying his wealth in the gold lettering embroidered on his cloak, of Parrhasius, decked in purple robes and golden crown, proclaiming himself prince of painters and progeny of Apollo, or of Apelles, favourite of Alexander the Great. However apocryphal the legends that surround these figures, the mere fact of their existence suggests a certain elevation of the artist's status, at least at the time when these legends first arose: as F. Coarelli points out, the 'myth' of the great fifth-century artist, though largely the result of Hellenistic speculation, nevertheless clearly owed something to contemporary attitudes.[26] During the Hellenistic period itself, when art was no longer a function of the *polis*, but an expression of the power of monarchs, there was a growing appreciation of the artist's value. Indeed the situation of artists like Apelles and Lysippus at the court of Alexander may not have been so very different from that of their counterparts in the courts of Renaissance Europe.

Nevertheless it remains true that in antiquity the concept of the artist was never fully detached from that of the artisan, and it is symptomatic of ancient attitudes to art that there is no tradition associating artists with inspiration. In his chapters on the history of art (*Natural History* 35) Pliny speaks of the *ingenium* (natural talent) of individual painters (as in the Renaissance, painting was considered the least banausic of the manual arts), but nowhere mentions inspiration. When discussing Apelles, in his opinion the greatest painter of all, Pliny acknowledges that his works have a certain quality, *venustas* (charm), which distinguishes them from all others, but for the most part he concentrates on the extraordinary lifelike accuracy of Apelles' paintings. There is little evidence in Pliny or anywhere else to suggest that anything other than great technical ability was thought necessary for the creation of what we would call works of art. Poets were inspired, but artists were not.

Yet another manifestation of the ambivalent status of artists in antiquity lies in the enduring distinction made between the artist and his work. Scholars point out that already in Homer technical ability is regarded as a divine gift and therefore separable from the artist or craftsman who uses it. Many centuries later we find the same distinction, albeit more explicitly drawn, between the maker and his product in Lucian's *Dream* (quoted above), or again in a well-known passage in Plutarch's *Life of Pericles* (2.1) where the products of virtue are contrasted with works of art. The contemplation of noble deeds inspires us to act virtuously, he says, whereas the pleasures afforded by art have no such effect: 'No gifted young man wants to be a Phidias or a Polyclitus because he has seen the Zeus at Olympia or the Hera at Argos, nor an Anacreon or a Philetas or an Archilochus because he enjoys their poems. For if a work delights us for its charm it does not necessarily follow that its maker merits our serious attention.'

What is not so often observed is that the distinction between the maker and his product applies as much to poetry as to any other form of art. In the *Iliad* (2.594–600) the bard Thamyris actually has his gift of song taken away by the Muses because he dared to challenge them to a contest. Plato's doctrine of *furor poeticus* makes the poet's productions entirely separate from the poet himself, who becomes merely a mouthpiece of the Muses. Lucian makes the same point in a characteristically facetious way in his *Dialogue with Hesiod* in which the poet disclaims all responsibility for his work: 'None of my poetry is my own work. It's all composed by the Muses, and they are the only ones who can tell you why they have put in one thing and left out another.' Both poets and artists are therefore dissociated from the works which they produce; but poets, by claiming to be divinely inspired, stress their traditional connection with the gods and thus achieve a status denied to the painter or sculptor. It was not until the Renaissance that artists were fully emancipated from their association with manual labour and able to take their place alongside poets as the recipients of divinely inspired power.[27]

Of course the many anecdotes about painters and sculptors recorded by Pliny and others might be taken to suggest an interest in such people as individuals, but in practice they reveal very little about the personalities they purport to describe. Indeed ancient biography as a whole is somewhat disappointing from the modern point of view: the ancient writers show none of that concern with the wellsprings of personality which we have come to expect of biography, nor do we find anywhere the idea, so prevalent in the modern world, that achievement can be explained in terms of personality. Whatever the many and various motives there may have been for writing about the lives of famous men, the notion that an examination of a man's life will somehow illuminate his work was not one of them. If we look to the ancient *Lives of the Poets* hoping to discover something about how and why poets wrote we shall be disappointed; for they consist largely of an amalgam of stock, often romantic, themes thought appropriate to poets in general, for example, miraculous portents surrounding the poet's birth, and of material derived from the particular poet's work. Indeed one of the most salient features of these ancient *Lives* is their curious inversion of the biographical fallacy: rather than seeking to interpret the work of art in terms of the artist's life, the life was invented out of the work. So, Homer was said to have been a pupil of Phemius who appears as a bard in the *Odyssey*; Pindar was supposed to have had a twin brother who was an athlete; because Aeschylus portrayed drunkards on the stage, he was said to have written his tragedies while drunk; many of the lyrics in Euripides' plays describe the sea, a fact which gave rise to the well-known story that the poet lived in a cave by the sea, and so on. In fact the ancient *Lives* offer no independent insight into the literary works of their subjects or into the nature of the creative personality.[28]

Although ancient biography as a whole has little to offer on the subject of genius, the stories and legends that accrued around one particular figure should have a place in any discussion of the development of the idea of genius. Socrates has a special significance not so much because he is portrayed by both Plato and Xenophon as a unique and extraordinary individual, but rather because of his *daimonion*, the divine sign, unique to him, which guided him at various points in his life and which seems to have formed the basis of the charge against him that he acknowledged 'strange gods', *daimonia kaina*. In the *Apology* (31C–D) Socrates explains why he has never taken part in political life: 'I experience a certain divine or daimonic something, which in fact Meletus has caricatured in the indictment. It began in childhood and has been with me ever since, a kind of voice, which whenever I hear it always turns me back from something I was going to do, but never urges me to act. This is what has prevented me from taking part in politics.'[29] In choosing to describe this experience in rather vague and imprecise terms as 'something divine and daimonic' (elsewhere he calls it 'the daimonic sign', 'the sign of the god', 'the customary sign') Socrates implies that it is mysterious and beyond his control, emanating from a source which he himself does not fully understand; but he does not ascribe this experience specifically to the action of a *daimon* nor does he connect it with any general belief about the nature of *daimones*.

In Homer the term *daimon* covers that whole range of supernatural phenomena and religious experience which cannot be attributed to or explained in terms of the Olympian gods. As Walter Burkert puts it, '*Daimon* does not designate a specific class of divine beings, but a peculiar mode of activity.'[30] But already in Hesiod (*Works and Days* 121–6) *daimones* are more precisely categorized as dead men of the Golden Age who act as beneficent guardians of men on earth, a myth which gave rise to the belief that great men should be honoured after death as *daimones*. Plato describes *daimones* as, amongst other things, intermediaries between gods and men (*Symposium* 202D) and guardian spirits allotted to each man at birth (*Phaedo* 107D), but it was later Platonists rather than Plato himself who connected these with Socrates' mysterious inner voice. So, in Plutarch's treatise on *Socrates' Sign* (588C–589F) the voice which Socrates heard is interpreted as the unspoken communication of a *daimon*, perceptible only by rare and exceptional men such as Socrates, whose minds are pure, freed from the disturbances of the body, and who are themselves holy and daimonic. Similarly for Apuleius (*On the God of Socrates* 155–7), Socrates' sign was the voice of the *daimon*, that disembodied and invisible spirit attached to each one of us, which will guide us in the right way through life if only we will cultivate and revere it as Socrates did his. Apuleius' description of this tutelary *daimon* sounds very like an account of the Roman *genius*, but in fact he distinguishes between this disembodied *daimon*, which he compares with the Roman *Lar* (157), and another kind of *daimon*, the spirit or soul which inhabits each man: 'In our language [. . .] you could call it *Genius* because this god which is the soul of each man, although it is immortal, is in a certain way born with a man' ('*Eum nostra lingua* [. . .] *poteris Genium vocare, quod is deus, qui est animus sui cuique, quamquam sit immortalis, tamen quodam modo cum homine gignitur*').

Later ages saw in Socrates an example of the daimonic man, an extraordinary being who embodies in himself that mysterious power which is traditionally attributed to divinity. The irrational nature of his experience combined with its uniqueness provided at least one eighteenth-century thinker with the starting point from which to develop a new concept of genius which would challenge the rationality of the Enlightenment. Johann Georg Hamann's *Sokratische Denkwürdigkeiten (Socratic Memoirs)*, published in 1759, the same year as Young's *Conjectures on Original Composition*, was to influence both Herder and Goethe, and heralded that cult of the daimonic man so characteristic of the Romantic era.[31] And in the nineteenth century, by a curious irony, we find Socrates the subject of the first 'pathography' or clinical history of genius, when Louis-Francois Lélut published his *Du Démon de Socrate* (1836) in which he claimed that the hallucinations from which Socrates suffered in the shape of his inner voice proved that he was mad.[32]

To Plato and his followers Socrates was an exceptional individual, remarkable both for his unique personality and for his total dedication to the life of philosophy, but they would not have called him a genius. Similarly Homer, though traditionally regarded as divinely inspired, the source not only of all poetry and eloquence but also of wisdom and knowledge, did not become a genius until the eighteenth century. For it was only then that the modern idea of genius as an extraordinary creative power embodied in man was first formulated.

It has often been observed that a key feature in the development of this idea was the fusion between the two accounts of poetic creativity which have been at the centre of my discussion in this chapter.[33] That fusion between divine inspiration and natural talent or innate ability is nowhere more apparent than in Edward Young's *Conjectures on Original Composition*, 'perhaps the most concentrated manifesto for original genius', as Jonathan Bate reminds us in chapter 4 of this book. When Young describes how an original composition springs up plant-like from the hidden depths of the mind he attributes to genius characteristics which were traditionally associated with inspiration: 'An *Original* may be said to be of a *vegetable* nature; it rises spontaneously from the vital root of Genius; it *grows*, it is not *made*;' or again, 'What, for the most part, mean we by Genius, but the Power of accomplishing great things without the means generally reputed necessary to that end? A *Genius* differs from a *good understanding* as a magician from a good architect: *that* raises his structure by means invisible; *this* by the skilful use of common tools. Hence Genius has ever been supposed to partake of something Divine.' Miraculous creative power, once attributed to divine inspiration, is here seen to emanate from the mind of the genius himself. For Young, man is the source of his own creative powers, and genius is, as it were, innate inspiration: 'Learning we thank, Genius we revere; That gives us pleasure, This gives us rapture; That informs, This inspires and is itself inspired; for genius is from heaven, learning from man [. . .] Learning is borrowed knowledge; Genius is knowledge innate, and quite our own.'[34]

The factors which led to the formulation of the concept of genius in the eighteenth century were many and complex, as we shall see in subsequent chapters of this book, but it is clear that the influence of classical antiquity played a decisive part in shaping the early stages of its development, as Edgar Zilsel long ago pointed out in his fundamental study on the origins of the concept of genius.[35] In a general sense the image of the poet as an inspired being is an ancient analogue to the modern notion of genius in that both share a basic belief in the inexplicability of the creative act. But it is not a simple question of continuity in terms of the history of ideas. What is striking is the extent to which the eighteenth-century discourse on genius grew out of a rediscovery or reinterpretation of various aspects of classical antiquity. The meteoric rise of Longinus, the image of Pindar as a poet of wild fervour and uncontrollable natural force, above all the centrality of Homer in the literature of the period bear eloquent witness to the seminal and creative influence of the classical tradition on the growth and development of the new conception of genius.

Notes

1 R. Klibansky, E. Panofsky and F. Saxl, *Saturn and Melancholy* (London, 1964).
2 Ibid., p. 42.
3 See S. H. Monk, *The Sublime: A Study of Critical Theories in Eighteenth Century England*, 2nd edn (Ann Arbor, 1960); D. A. Russell, *'Longinus': On the Sublime* (Oxford, 1964); J. Schmidt, *Die Geschichte des Genie-Gedankens 1750–1945* (2 vols, Darmstadt, 1985), vol. 1, pp. 54–9 and bibliography there given.
4 See further, P. Murray, 'Poetic Inspiration in Early Greece', *Journal of Hellenic Studies*, 101 (1981), 87–100.
5 See R. Buxton, 'Blindness and Limits: Sophocles and the Logic of Myth', *Journal of Hellenic Studies*, 100 (1980), 22–37; P. Murray, 'Homer and the Bard', in *Aspects of the Epic*, eds T. Winnifrith, P. Murray and K. Gransden (London, 1983), pp. 1–15.
6 J. S. Mill, 'Two Kinds of Poetry' in *Early Essays by John Stuart Mill*, ed. J. W. M. Gibbs (London, 1897), p. 221.
7 See R. Harriott, *Poetry and Criticism Before Plato* (London, 1969), pp. 109–12; B. Gentili, *Poesia e Pubblico nella Grecia Antica* (Bari, 1983), pp. 203–31.
8 See A. Kambylis, *Die Dichterweihe und ihre Symbolik* (Heidelberg, 1965), pp. 52–61; M. West, *Hesiod: Theogony* (Oxford, 1966), pp. 158–61.
9 Cf. the myth of Alcmaeon, son of the seer Amphiaraus, himself said to be descended from Apollo; Alcmaeon married Manto, the daughter of the Theban seer, Teiresias. And see Herodotus 9.92–5 for Deiphonus, seer son of the seer Evenius.
10 West, *Hesiod*, p. 187.
11 See F. Solmsen, 'The Gift of Speech in Homer and Hesiod', *Transactions of the American Philological Association*, 85 (1954), 1–15. West's suggestion (*Hesiod*, pp. 44, 181–2) that the passage as a whole is inserted for the benefit of the king or kings before whom the poem was performed seems to me the most convincing

interpretation of these problematic lines. But even if there is some truth in the suggestion, first put forward by E. A. Havelock, *Preface to Plato* (Oxford, 1963), pp. 107–11, that the passage reflects a once intimate connection between poets and kings, the nature of Hesiod's poetic gift is nevertheless quite different from the gift of eloquence bestowed on kings.

12 See, for example, G. M. A. Grube, *The Greek and Roman Critics* (London, 1965), p. 9: 'Pindar claims inspiration from the Muses [. . .] but he was not the man to think of himself as a passive instrument; with him inspiration is a permanent state rather than a temporary "possession" by a god; it is nearly identified with inborn talent, which is then directed by the poet himself.'

13 Bruno Snell, *Die Ausdrücke für den Begriff des Wissens in der vorplatonischen Philosophie* (Berlin, 1924), pp. 1–20, and 'Wie die Griechen lernten, was geistige Tätigkeit ist', *Journal of Hellenic Studies*, 93 (1973) 178–9.

14 See P. Wilson, 'The Knowledge and Appreciation of Pindar in the Seventeenth and Eighteenth Centuries', unpublished D.Phil. thesis (Oxford, 1974); J. Schmidt, *Die Geschichte des Genie-Gedankens*, vol. 1, pp. 179–92.

15 *The Spectator*, 160 (3 September 1711), ed. D. F. Bond (5 vols, Oxford, 1965).

16 Edward Young, *Conjectures on Original Composition* (London, 1759), p. 30. For G. J. Vossius (1577–1649), see further J. E. Sandys, *A History of Classical Scholarship* (3 vols, Cambridge, 1908), vol. 2, pp. 307–9.

17 In D. A. Russell and M. Winterbottom (eds), *Ancient Literary Criticism* (Oxford, 1972), p. 494.

18 I agree with those scholars who insert the word *mallon* here on the authority of the Arabic text. If it is omitted, as in the manuscripts, the sense is 'poetry is the work of a man endowed by nature *or* of a madman.' See further G. F. Else, *Aristotle's Poetics: The Argument* (Harvard, 1957), pp. 496–502; D. W. Lucas, *Aristotle: Poetics* (Oxford, 1968), pp. 177–9 and S. Halliwell, *The Poetics of Aristotle* (London, 1987), pp. 145–8.

19 Klibansky, Panofsky and Saxl, *Saturn and Melancholy*; see also H. Flashar, *Melancholie und Melancholiker* (Berlin, 1966); Bennett Simon, *Mind and Madness in Ancient Greece* (Ithaca, 1978), pp. 228–37.

20 C. O. Brink, *Horace on Poetry: the 'Ars Poetica'* (Cambridge, 1971), p. 422.

21 See C. Bailey, *Titi Lucreti Cari: De Rerum Natura* (3 vols, Oxford, 1947), vol. 1, pp. 8–12.

22 C. Lombroso, *Genio e Follia* (Pavia, 1864), translated anonymously into English from the 5th edn as *The Man of Genius* (London, 1891), pp. 359 and 2–3. On genius and madness see the chapter by Neil Kessel in this volume; A. Storr, *The Dynamics of Creation* (London, 1972), pp. 203–16; G. Becker, *The Mad Genius Controversy* (Beverly Hills, 1978); R. Porter, *A Social History of Madness* (London, 1987), pp. 60–81 with bibliography on pp. 240–1.

23 See A. Burford, *Craftsmen in Greek and Roman Society* (London, 1972) and the very useful collection of essays edited by F. Coarelli, *Artisti e Artigiani in Grecia* (Bari, 1980).

24 Quoted by F. Frontisi-Ducroux, *Dédale. Mythologie de l'artisan en Grèce ancienne* (Paris, 1975), p. 25.

25 See ibid. and J.-P. Vernant, *Mythe et pensée chez les Grecs*, 2nd edn (Paris, 1985),

pp. 263–322. On the 'first discoverer' *topos* see A. Kleingünther, Πρῶτος εὑρετής *Philologus, Supplementband* 26, 1 (1933).

26 Coarelli, *Artisti e Artigiani in Grecia*, p. xii.

27 See M. Kemp, chapter 2 in this volume and 'From "Mimesis" to "Fantasia": the Quattrocento Vocabulary of Creation, Inspiration and Genius in the Visual Arts', *Viator*, 8 (1977), 347–98; R. and M. Wittkower, *Born under Saturn* (London, 1963).

28 See J. Fairweather, 'Fiction in the Biographies of Ancient Writers', *Ancient Society*, 5 (1974), 230–75; M. R. Lefkowitz, *The Lives of the Greek Poets* (London, 1981).

29 Trans. W. K. C. Guthrie, *History of Greek Philosophy* (Cambridge, 1971), vol. III, p. 402. For other references to the divine sign see e.g. *Apology* 40Λ–C; *Euthydemus* 272E; *Republic* 496C; *Theaetetus* 151A, and in general P. Friedländer, *Plato: an Introduction*, trans. H. Meyerhoff (New York, 1958), pp. 32–44.

30 W. Burkert, *Greek Religion*, trans. J. Raffan (Oxford, 1985), p. 180.

31 See P. Grappin, *La Théorie du génie dans le préclassicisme allemand* (Paris, 1952), pp. 188ff.; J. Schmidt, *Die Geschichte des Genie-Gedankens*, pp. 97–103; H. M. Jones, *Revolution and Romanticism* (Cambridge, Mass., 1974), pp. 261–95 on 'The Doctrine of Romantic Genius'.

32 See G. Becker, *The Mad Genius Controversy*, p. 28.

33 See e.g. Logan Pearsall Smith, 'Four Romantic Words' in *Words and Idioms* (London, 1925), pp. 98–100; P. Kaufman, 'Heralds of Original Genius' in *Essays in Memory of Barrett Wendell* (Cambridge, Mass., 1926) pp. 196–7; W. Ringler, 'Poeta Nascitur Non Fit: Some Notes on the History of an Aphorism', *Journal of the History of Ideas* 2 (1941), 502; M. H. Abrams, *The Mirror and the Lamp* (New York, 1953), pp. 198–200.

34 Edward Young, *Conjectures on Original Composition* (London, 1759), pp. 12, 26–7 and 36.

35 E. Zilsel, *Die Entstehung des Geniebegriffes. Ein Beitrag zur Ideengeschichte der Antike und des Frühkapitalismus* (Tübingen, 1926).

2

The 'Super-artist' as Genius: The Sixteenth-Century View

Martin Kemp

You painted yourself, Dürer, in your Melancholy,
And your genius in tears, taking pity on you,
Has personified you in your creation.
I do not know what could be more admirable in this world,
More full of dreaming and deep anguish
Than this great seated angel . . .
(Théophile Gautier, 'Melancolia')[1]

To the Romantic era no image seemed more perfectly to embody the notion of artistic genius than Albrecht Dürer's masterful engraving of *Melencolia I* (plate 1). The great, gloomy figure, paralysed by dark meditations on sublime mysteries, proved to be perfectly in tune with Romantic notions of the pathology of genius. A great artist such as Dürer came to be regarded as one who was sanctified through his gifts of transcendent melancholy, achieving a level of insight denied the normal person. But it was an insight achieved at the cost of inner torment and, not infrequently, the languishing of the artist's physical constitution. The sanctifying of the creative genius is nowhere more clearly seen than in the designs by Schinkel for the hall in which the Dürer festival was to be celebrated in 1828.[2] The focal point was a great altarpiece at the centre of which stood an image of the 'divine' artist himself. In Germany at least, and increasingly elsewhere in Europe, Dürer had entered the hallowed ranks of the true geniuses. He was, as Schlegel exclaimed, the 'Shakespeare of painting'.[3]

Modern scholarship, exhibiting no less a fascination with Dürer's *Melencolia I,* has striven to achieve a more historical understanding of the system of values expressed in the engraving, searching amongst Renaissance sources for texts and images relating to the Saturnine temperament, in

Plate 1   Albrecht Dürer, *Melencolia I*, engraving, 1514, Glasgow University, Hunterian Art Gallery

order to unlock the precise meaning of the print as a whole and in its carefully conceived parts. The classic treatment by Klibansky, Panofsky and Saxl, drawing upon the writings of such authors as Ficino and Agrippa, showed the extent to which Dürer's image was a profound and detailed expression of ideas derived from Renaissance astrology, humoural medicine and what may be broadly described as Platonizing philosophy.[4] Part of their historical case was that Dürer's image bore witness to the genesis of the modern concept of genius and that the artist's own writings expressed precocious ideas of inner creativity and inspiration that were only to reach maturity in the Romantic period. Their statement that 'the depression of *Melencolia I* reveals [. . .] both the obscure doom and the obscure source of creative genius' would not have provoked dissent from even the most thoroughgoing Romantic of the nineteenth century.[5] However, as a number of subsequent scholars have emphasized in various ways, a rereading of the writings of Dürer suggests that we should at least hesitate before we too readily claim to be witnessing the birth of the modern notion of genius in this engraving.[6]

If we are to look amongst Dürer's own works for a perfect expression of the creative powers to which he aspired, the harmonious engraving of *St. Jerome in his Study* (plate 2) seems to me to be a better candidate than the *Melencolia*. The Saint, seated in his spacious and tranquil study, is deeply engaged in productive creation as his hand obeys the will of his inspired mind. The *St Jerome* is a moving statement of the fertility of the human intellect under divine guidance, and, as such, stands in direct contrast to the paralysis of earthbound imagination in the *Melencolia*. In the words of Ficino, 'those who escape the baneful influence of Saturn, and enjoy his benevolent influence, are not only those who flee to Jupiter but also those who give themselves over heart and soul to divine contemplation.'[7] Alternatively we could look at Joseph the carpenter in the woodcut of the *Holy Family in Egypt* for an image of the artisan working according to the principles of divine analogy to produce works that reflect, albeit in a minor key, the creative power of the Almighty himself.[8] Indeed, I hope to show that such images of divinely guided productivity possess a wide relevance for notions of genius in the visual arts in the sixteenth century and provide a corrective for overly romantic interpretations of the visual and written evidence relating to those whom I am calling the 'super-artists' – the Dürers, Michelangelos, Raphaels, Titians, etc. In the following investigation I will, so to speak, be keeping Saints Jerome and Joseph no less clearly before my eyes than the much-vaunted *Melencolia*.

Reading the written evidence in conjunction with the visual requires caution not only with respect to the general issue of the way in which later stances precondition our response but also in relation to our handling of the vocabulary used in the period itself. We should certainly not assume that the relevant terms, *ingenium* or *ingegno* and *genio* (or *genius* in its Latin form) should be translated or interpreted as 'genius' in the romantic or modern sense.[9] We also need to be alert to the possibility that less obvious words, such as *virtù* and *divino*, might have carried some of the modern connotations of genius. These terms in Renaissance writing also need to

Plate 2 Albrecht Dürer, *St Jerome in his Study*, engraving, 1514, Glasgow University, Hunterian Art Gallery

be interpreted in close relation to a cluster of words which came to be loaded with particular significance in discussions of artistic productivity in the literary and visual arts. A series of key terms, annexed with lesser or greater directness from classical criticism of literature and to some degree from medieval poetics, came to be inseparably associated with what we would call artistic creativity. These include *fantasia*, *invenzione*, *excogitare* (in Latin), *inteletto*, *spirito* and *furore*, all relating to the inspirational origins of artistic processes and often juxtaposed with terms which referred to the physical production of works, *manus* (hand) and *ars* (skill). These clusters of technical terms need themselves to be set in the context of the broader conceptual framework of attitudes towards the imitation of nature, the role of the individual and of individual style, the sources of knowledge and the character of inspiration.[10] These attitudes were in turn articulated within specific social and institutional settings, particularly when we enter the era that witnessed the birth and rise of the academies of arts. A comprehensive review of these extensive and complex factors clearly lies outside the scope of this essay, but we should remain alert to their implications for our analysis of the written and visual evidence relating to the concept of genius.

During the course of the fourteenth and fifteenth centuries, with the birth of humanist criticism of the visual arts, we can witness two parallel phenomena in the use of the vocabulary adopted from the literary arts. On one hand there was an increasing likelihood that a humanist author would openly or tacitly acknowledge that it was proper to use the term *ingenium* or *ingegno* when referring to the practice of the visual arts in general, while on the other it became more common for an individual artist to be credited with this attribute on his own behalf. The artist around whom these developments arose was the great Florentine painter and designer, Giotto, who was credited from the time of Boccaccio with having revived the art of painting which had been slumbering since classical antiquity.[11]

It became increasingly common for the classic formulation of the relationships between *ingenium*, invention and memory in Cicero's theories of oratory to be adapted to the humanist praise of art and artists. In such usages, however, we should remember that *ingenium* refers to a high level of inborn talent and does not necessarily imply the possession of transcendent genius in the modern sense. It may also be the case that the title of *ingegno* was accorded to a named artist on account of his remarkable qualities as a man – transcending the limited nature of his calling – rather than carrying an implication that the practice of the visual arts in general necessarily requires the exercise of an *ingegno* to match that of poets or orators.

Whereas the example of Giotto remained relatively isolated in fourteenth-century writing – his had become more-or-less the obligatory name when any author wanted to cite a famed artist of the modern era – he was joined by a growing band of 'super-artists' during the course of the fifteenth century. Filippo Brunelleschi was earliest and most spectacular. His supreme inventive skills, culminating in the astonishing dome of Florence Cathedral, earned him an epitaph from Carlo Marsuppini in which the humanist Chancellor of the City lavished praise on the recently deceased master: 'how valiant the architect was in this Daedalian art is documented both by the wonderful vault of this celebrated temple and the many machines invented by his *divino ingenio*.'[12] We might note, in passing, that this image of the architect-engineer-inventor as a 'divine Daedalus' may be more readily aligned with Joseph in Dürer's *Holy Family* than with *Melencolia* in her contemplative melancholy.

By the latter part of the century a number of artists had emerged whose social status and widespread reputation was reflected in written testimony to their supreme talents. Mantegna and Perugino, two of the artists pestered by Isabella d'Este, are outstanding in this respect. Indeed, the way in which Isabella persistently attempted to solicit works from masters with leading reputations throughout Italy reflected the rise of a small elite of 'super-artists' who needed to be treated with more deference than was due to mere craftsmen. Mantegna's position at the Gonzaga court in Mantua, where he was granted a title and lived in some style in a Renaissance *palazzo* of his own design, can be vividly illustrated by letters to and about him in the orbit of the North Italian courts. It is clear that he was regarded as a difficult character, quick to take offence and slow to meet obligations. Even his immediate masters, the successive Gonzaga Marquisses, recognized that he required careful handling. Federigo went as far as to remind the Duchess of Milan that 'normally these excellent masters are capricious (*hanno del fantastico*).'[13]

Francesco Gonzaga made a decree in 1492 to confer benefits on Mantegna. The document opens with a series of classical references to the way in which the great men of antiquity secured renown by their patronage of great masters:

For Hiero, King of Syracuse, the friendship of Archimedes was no mean illustration of his fame [. . .] Alexander [. . .] is above all glorious for not having desired any painter other than Apelles or any sculptor other than Lysippus. Augustus gained glory and honour for having shown so much favour to Vitruvius, whom he raised from a base condition by enobling him. In the light of these circumstances, what rank could we accord to Andrea Mantegna, this man of true merit (*virtutis virem*), without argument the most remarkable of all those who profess painting through the diversity of their talents (*ingenij*)?[14]

Although this preamble is in the nature of a rhetorical flourish, it does suggest the degree to which an enlightened patron was taking seriously

Alberti's advice about the ability of art to confer immortality upon those involved in the making and commissioning of works of art.

It is perhaps more surprising to us to find Perugino numbered amongst the 'super-artists', given his present-day image as a conservative maker of well-made images who was to be surpassed in every respect by the young Raphael. However, in the late *quattrocento* he was accorded (and expected to be accorded) the very highest rank. Many of the documents associated with Perugino testify to his stature. One of the most remarkable, in that it appears in an unexpected context, is a laudatory poem appended to the 1488 contract for the Fano altarpiece. The poem opens with a confident assertion that Perugino is the first painter in all the world, and continues with classical references of the by-now conventional kind:

> Another Parrhasius and Lysippus, you who both
> through the *ingenium* of the ancients and *arte* of the moderns
> use and employ your own *ingenium*
> to paint Mary[15]

The artist with whom Perugino was coupled in this eulogy was the frame-maker, Joachim, a pairing which may seem to take something of the lustre away from the honour, but we should remember that the frames of major altarpieces were architectural and sculptural achievements of great magnificence and expense.

One point that should be made very firmly with respect to the fifteenth-century usage of *ingenium* in the visual arts is that it is invariably conjoined, implicitly or explicitly, with the concept of manual skill (*arte*) and with the mastery of those rational rules (known collectively as *dottrina* or *disciplina*) which govern such matters as imitation, composition and decorum. There is a general distrust in 'art theory' of the kind of fervent and spontaneous inspiration which may be categorized as 'poet's madness'.

The key points of reference for this concept were to be found in Plato's writings, including the famous passage in the *Timaeus* in which he describes how *fantasmata* can arise during sleep, illness or under divine inspiration. These 'fantasms' can be utilized by the intellect to provide access to prophecies and otherwise unperceived truths.[16] This idea was developed by Cicero into the doctrine that poetry was composed under the influence of a special kind of frenzy (*furor*), and Seneca went so far as to assert that 'there has never been any great *ingenium* without some touch of madness' – a formula quoted in the Renaissance by Petrarch.[17] To this formula was added the Aristotelean association of *ingenium* with melancholy. In the hands of Ficino the resulting equation was developed into the fully fledged doctrine of the Saturnine temperament, which predisposed those under its influence to the melancholy madness of the seer – at once uniquely endowed with Platonic *furor* and yet damned by the dark awareness that comes from an incomplete insight into the profound truths of the universe.[18] The melancholic walks a precarious tightrope over the slough of despond and the turbulent rapids of insanity.

There is no indication in the fifteenth-century sources that any practitioner of the visual arts was or wished to be regarded in this light, but it has been suggested that the cluster of concepts exploited by Ficino came into increasing play in the sixteenth century, both with respect to individual artists and in relation to more general theories of art. Certainly, if we are to discover something more momentous than the increasingly regular possibility that an artist – almost any artist of merit – would be credited with *ingenium*, we will need to look for characteristics resembling those described by Ficino and his followers. My strategy in undertaking such a search will be to concentrate on the literature surrounding the most spectacularly lauded of the 'super-artists' in North and South Europe, Dürer and Michelangelo.

There is no doubt that Dürer for his part considered that the painter required an inborn talent in order to operate at the highest level in 'this great, far-reaching and infinite art of painting'.[19] 'He who wishes to be a painter must have a natural aptitude for it.'[20] Painting 'is worthy because God is accordingly honoured when it is seen that he has bestowed such understanding on one of his creatures in whom is such art'.[21] The terms used by Dürer, *gesick*, *vernunft* and *verstand* indicate that some special kind of insight must be possessed as an innate gift from on high. This gift takes the form of an inner spark which can be the source of great things: 'I will ignite a small fire, but if you all contribute to it with expert perfection there may with time burst out of it a great fire which will light the whole world.'[22] The echo of Christ's words in the Gospel of St Luke – 'I am come to send fire on the earth' – is no doubt intended, in much the same way that he intended the hieratic frontality and riveting gaze of his Munich *Self-Portrait* to carry resonances of the imitation of Christ.[23] The process through which artistic products were forged in this creative fire was characterized in Platonic terms: 'a good painter is inwardly full of figures and if it were possible for him to live for ever, he would have, from the inner ideas of which Plato writes, always something new to pour out in his works.'[24] This statement, as Panofsky has shown, fuses the conception of God's creativity expressed by Seneca with Ficino's characterization of the melancholic's capacity for generating new ideas.[25]

The special gifts of the true artist accounted for the peculiar potency exhibited in even a slight sketch by a great master:

An artist of understanding and experience can show more of his great power and art in small things, roughly and rudely made, than many another in his great work. Powerful artists alone will understand the truth of this strange remark. For this reason a man may often draw something with his pen on a half-sheet of paper or engrave it with his tool on a block of wood and it will be fuller of art and better than another's great work at which he has laboured for a whole year. And this gift is wonderful. For God sometimes grants to a man an understanding of how to make something the like of which, in his day, could not have been found.[26]

This gift does not alone, however, provide a guarantee of good art. Dürer shares the *quattrocento* insistence on the need for rational learning and practical discipline. Indeed he paid more attention than any of his predecessors to the way in which the native talents of the youth should be schooled according to the true doctrines of art. The training embraced the whole man, both his mental and physical constitutions, which for Dürer, given his belief in humoural medicine, were inseparably associated. One of his instructions warns us that 'if the child works so hard as to fall under the hand of melancholy, he should be seduced away from it by happy music which can charm his blood.'[27]

The tone of these remarks has obvious consequences for our interpretation of *Melencolia I*. The general alignment of Dürer's image with the ideas of melancholy in Ficino's *De vita triplici* and in Henry Cornelius Agrippa's *Occulta philosophia* remains convincing, in spite of later challenges to Panofsky's famous interpretation. What is not acceptable is the exaggerated weight that has been placed on this image as a form of 'spiritual self-portrait', as the romantics were the first to have us believe. For all that Dürer was obviously fascinated by the theory of melancholy and recognized a propensity within himself (as with all great artists) to fall under its influence, his favoured model of creative 'genius' can at best be seen as a pendant to the *Melencolia* and more reasonably as a sharp antidote to its destructive forces. The fact that Dürer chose to distribute his engraving of *St Jerome* with the *Melencolia* strongly suggests that he had just such an interpretation in mind. The model of divine insight represented by St Jerome, which relies as much upon the assumptions of medieval hagiography as Ficinian metaphysics, has, I believe, a wide relevance for sixteenth-century ideas of the inspired artist, not only in Northern Europe but also in Italy. The epithet *divino*, associated most spectacularly with Michelangelo, may in this sense be seen as a more significant term than *ingegno*.

Dürer's centrality for our present theme extends far beyond his own theories and works of art. His ideas continued to live in the writings of a group of distinguished humanists who were concerned to perpetuate his fame. The eulogy by Pirckheimer published in 1528 in the first edition of the *Treatise on Human Proportions* perfectly sets the tone:

Benign Fortune bestowed on Dürer all her favours,
Genius (*ingenium*), beauty and impeccable faith [. . .]
Go hence, our adornment, but not beyond reach, glory of our race,
With Christ as your guide, enter the celestial realms!
For there you will forever enjoy unchallenged renown,
Receiving as your desserts, o blessed man, rewards worthy of your gifts.[28]

For the Latin edition of the same treatise in 1532 Camerarius provided a compelling humanist portrait of his friend which is designed to affirm Dürer's 'singular skill and genius as an artist and as a man'.[29] *Ingenium*, for Camerarius, is inseparably associated with the artist's learning: 'he had brought painting into the fixed track of rule and recalled it to scientific principles.' It was through Dürer's intellectual insight into these principles that his hand was able to express his genius: 'after his hand had, so to speak, attained its maturity, his sublime and virtue-loving genius became discoverable in his best works [. . .] The nature of the man is never more certainly and definitely shown than in the works he produces as the fruit of his art.' 'Nature had specially designed him as a painter,' as was reflected not only in his works of art but in his whole person. His physical characteristics and temperament bore equal witness to the favours of God. Although he was given to profound study, 'he was not of a melancholy severity nor of a repulsive gravity; nay, whatever was conducive to pleasantness and cheerfulness, and was not inconsistent with honour and rectitude, he cultivated all his life.'

There is every reason to think that the characterizations of Dürer's genius by Pirckheimer and Camerarius were entirely consistent with those favoured by the artist himself. As it happens, Camerarius elsewhere undertook an informative *ekphrasis* of the *Melencolia*. He recognized that the artist has represented 'the emotions of a deep and thoughtful mind which he called the melancholic [. . .] in whom the black bile, as the physicians call it, is superabundant [. . .] Such minds commonly grasp everything' but 'they are frequently carried away into absurdities.'[30] Camerarius's text nowhere suggests that Dürer's own being is to be read into the image. Rather he treats it as a supreme demonstration of the artist's intellectual and manual gifts. The *ekphrasis* specifically opens with praise of Dürer's 'divine hand' and closes with a reference to his magisterial technique. The implication is that it was *ars et ingenium* that allowed Dürer to portray melancholy so brilliantly, not the artist's self-identification with the gloomy angel.

For the generation of Dürer and his humanist friends there was no question that *ingenium* could only bear fruit if it achieved expression through a detailed cultivation of rational rules. The artist's prodigious labours to master the geometrical secrets of human proportion – so admired by his humanist colleagues – reflected the weight placed on the science of art in this equation. It was precisely this aspect of Dürer's work that encountered the sharpest criticism in the second half of the century, particularly at the hands of Michelangelo and those writers who considered themselves to stand in his succession. The criticism, expressed in its canonical form by Federigo Zuccaro, centred on the Michelangelesque dictum that the artist must possess 'compasses in his eyes rather than in his hands'.[31] As Francis Bacon was to say, 'the painter must do it by a kind of felicity [. . .] not by rule.'[32] The attitude behind this conviction signals that the balance was beginning to shift towards a different sort of insight from that envisaged by Dürer and his contemporaries.

We would not expect Michelangelo, whose piety yielded nothing in intensity to that of Dürer, to place a lesser emphasis than his German predecessor upon the divine sources of the artist's creative potency. But the way in which the divine gift could find expression was viewed in a distinctively different light by the great sculptor.

Like Dürer he did not doubt that the artist was born not made:

> As a trustworthy guide in my vocation,
> When I was born I had a gift for beauty,
> In both the arts my lantern and my mirror.[33]

> . . . my eyes were made
> By my bright star to see
> The difference between beauties[34]

> Since I've the beautiful art, that those who bear it
> From Heaven use to conquer Nature with,
> Even if she can resist everywhere,
> If I, not blind and deaf, was born for it,
> A true match for my heart's fire-setting thief,
> He is to blame who fated me to fire.[35]

The last of these three excerpts from three of his poems already hints that Michelangelo's view of his own gifts, which destined him both for supreme ecstasy and profound discontent, embraces more of the tortures of *Melencolia*'s mind than Dürer himself was prepared to admit into his own psychology. To overcome the potentially negative effects of his unaided eyes and intellect Michelangelo consistently sought spiritual and transcendentally inspirational sources for true beauty:

> All beauty that we see here must be likened
> To the merciful Fountain whence we all derive,
> More than anything else, by men with insight.[36]

> While toward the beauty that I saw at first
> I bring my soul, which sees it through my eyes,
> The inward image grows, and this first withdraws,
> Almost abject, and wholly in disgrace.[37]

And in the most famous of all his sonnets on his own art, '*Non ha l'ottimo artista alcun concetto*', addressed to his spiritual guide, Vittoria Colonna:

> The best of artists never has a concept
> A single block of marble does not contain
> Inside its husk, but to it may attain
> Only if hand follows the intellect.
> The good I pledge myself, bad I reject.
> Hide, O my lady, beautiful, proud, divine,
> Just thus in you, but now my life must end,
> Since my skill [*arte*] works against the wished effect [. . .]
> If at the same time death and pity
> Are present in your heart, my lowly insight [*basso ingegno*]
> Burning, can grasp nothing but death from it.[38]

From a relatively early stage of his career Michelangelo manifested a powerful sense of the ultimate inadequacy of his own mental and physical gifts (*ingegno* and *arte*) in capturing the sublime ideas towards which he strove – an awareness which corresponds closely to Saturnine melancholy as characterized by Ficino. His pessimism is partly personal:

> As in hard stone, a man at times will make
> Everyone else's image in his own likeness
> I make it pale with weakness.[39]

– using imagery which exploits the commonplace that 'every painter paints himself.'[40] But during the later phases of his career his pessimism centred increasingly upon the insufficiency of art itself, however well conceived and realized:

> So that the passionate fantasy which made
> Of art a monarch for me and an idol,
> Was laden down with sin, now I know well,
> Like what all men against their will desired [. . .]
> There's no painting or sculpture now that quiets
> The soul that's pointed toward that holy love
> That on the cross opened Its arms to take us.[41]

This sentiment is made all the more poignant when we realise that the recipient of the sonnet from which these passages are drawn was Giorgio Vasari, whose *Lives* of the artists represented the ultimate affirmation of the Renaissance confidence in the untrammelled power of individual artists and of Michelangelo's *ingegno* in particular.

For Michelangelo's commentators in the sixteenth century, it was not his ultimate pessimism which attracted attention so much as his somewhat earlier affirmation that the individual soul might aspire to ascend towards the divine source of grace through the contemplation of beauty on earth. The classic instance is Benedetto Varchi's humanist commentary in 1547 on '*Non ha l'ottimo artista alcun concetto*'.[42] The *concetto*, for Varchi, is the mental vehicle which may transport the artist to the heights or to the depths according to the nature of the *ingegno* from which it arises:

Men, either brilliant [*ingegniosi*] or good, we say to have beautiful, good, elevated or great conceptions [*concetti*]; that is good thoughts, brilliant fancies [*ingegnose fantasie*], divine inventions or discoveries [. . .] On the other hand we speak of bad, clumsy and ugly imaginings [*immaginazioni*], tasteless inventions, disgusting fantasies [*fantasie*] and unworthy thoughts.[43]

Varchi makes it clear that if love can find expression at the highest level through the intellective rather than the vegetative or sensitive faculties of the soul, it can aspire to an elevated and even divine vision of true beauty: 'the whole and sound intellect ascends by means of the eyes to high beauty.' It was this kind of ascent that Michelangelo had himself expressed in some of the sonnets dedicated to Tommaso de' Cavalieri and depicted in the highly finished drawing of the *Rape of Ganymede* presented to this young nobleman, who was the recipient of his idealized love.[44]

Not surprisingly it was the affirmatory image of Michelangelo's *alto ingegno* – capable of transcending the limitations of the earthbound *fantasia* with which normal men are endowed – which dominated the remarkable obsequies organized in 1564 by the Florentine Academy to mark the return of the corpse of the newly deceased artist to the city of his birth. The publication of the commemorative volume – *Esequie del divino Michelangelo Buonarroti* – was itself a remarkable testimony to the stature which the greatest artists might now aspire to attain.[45] The obsequies for the Emperor Charles V in Piacenza and Bologna provided the only direct precedent. The volume contains full descriptions of the designs conceived by the artists of the recently founded Academia del Disegno for the temporary decorations and catafalque, together with glowing humanist testimonials to Michelangelo's *virtù* in the form of laudatory poems. References to the artist's divinity – he was inevitably *Angelo Michel divino* – became virtually commonplace. His *virtù* – embodying his inherent greatness of moral and intellectual stature (translated by Wittkower not altogether misleadingly as 'genius') – was paraded with an insistence that was in danger of becoming monotonous. One of the many verses attached to his sepulchre will give a flavour of the tributes:

> Lo, here are the ashes of Buonarroti. Astonished nature found
> That through his genius [*ingenio*] art is now her equal.
> His works for all to see bear witness to this truth.
>
> (Paolo del Rosso)[46]

The same author noted that 'with his divine brush every subject became poetry also.'

The intimate concord of Michelangelo's Christian virtue and artistic genius was affirmed visually on his catalfalque by flanking figures executed by the sculptor Vincenzo Danti. On one side stood Christian Charity trampling Vice, while on the other was represented,

A slender youth, wholly animated with an air of beautiful liveliness, standing for *ingegno*, with two wings on his temples, as may sometimes be seen in paintings of Mercury; and under this youth was a very finely made figure with ass's ears, standing for ignorance, the mortal enemy of *ingegno*.[47]

One of the temporary paintings showed Michelangelo in conversation with a woman who signified sculpture and who held in her hand a tablet inscribed, '*Simili sub imagine formans*' – quoting Boethius's *Consolatio philosophiae* to the effect that God formed the world according to a beautiful image in his mind – thus unambiguously implying that Michelangelo's creative processes should be regarded as analagous to those of God.[48]

The recorded effect of the creations of Michelangelo's transcendent talent upon spectators was to overcome their minds with wonder. As David Summers has shown, terms such as *stupendo*, *stupore* and *meraviglia* began to be used in connection with his works in order to suggest that their effects lay beyond rational comprehension and the descriptive powers of language.[49] The products of his art were assigned to a supra-rational realm to which only the most sublime works of literature had previously been admitted, most notably Dante's *Divina commedia*.

All this admiration for Michelangelo's divine powers does not mean that contemporaries failed to recognize at least something of the problematical side of his 'genius' that had so occupied Michelangelo himself. Vasari was aware that 'he had so perfect an imagination that the things propounded in his thought [*idea*] are of a kind that the hands cannot express such great and awesome concepts [*concetti*], and thus he often abandoned his works.'[50] A similar kind of discontent was attributed by Dolce to Leonardo, who 'possessed an *ingegno* so elevated that he was never satisfied with anything that he was making'.[51] Such sentiments are intimately linked with the increasingly enthusiastic appreciation of unfinished works and rough sketches amongst commentators and connoisseurs during the second half of the century.

For almost all the Italian authors on art during this period, whether or not they were unqualified admirers of Michelangelo, it was he who provided the point of reference when they wished to discuss creative 'genius' at the very highest level. His fellow Tuscan, Vasari, provides the most obvious source, not only in his life of Michelangelo but also for the way in which he refracts his criticism of other artists through the lens of Michelangelo's qualities. Paolo Uccello, overcome with the obsessive study of perspective, becomes an example of someone who has allowed 'a fertile and spontaneous talent' to mutate into something 'sterile and laboured'.[52] The harsh style of Verrocchio, the master of Leonardo, was 'the product of endless study rather than a gift or facility from nature'.[53] The moral is that 'an artist's talent can only truly express itself when prompted by his intellect and when he is in a state of inspired rapture: it is then that he demonstrates his divine *concetti*.'[54] Of the artists of the earlier eras, only Donatello measured up to the highest standards, transcending the limits of his period: 'in him was conjoined invention, design, skill, judgement, and every other quality that can possibly be expected of a divine genius [*ingegno divino*].'[55] And in Vasari's notable justification of the spontaneous roughness of finish in Donatello's *Cantoria*, compared to the polish of Luca della Robbia's companion-piece, he is moved to note that as 'poems given by *furore poetico* are true and good, and are better than the laboured, so the works of men excellent in the arts of design are better when they have been made in one go, by the force of that *furore*, than when they are refined little by little with toil and labour.'[56] Donatello was, in a sense, a Michelangelo before his time.

For Vasari, Michelangelo was the supreme talent, brought by God into nature to provide an exemplar as an artist and as a man for all lesser mortals. Near the opening of Michelangelo's *Vita* he is at pains to show the way in which heaven had uniquely favoured the future artist, in that the hour of his birth – when Mercury and Venus were in the house of Jupiter and 'peaceably disposed' – preordained him 'to fashion sublime and magnificent works of art'.[57] Vasari was conscious that some of the obsessive and antisocial traits in his hero's character laid him open to charges of being less than exemplary in behaviour. Michelangelo's taste for melancholic solitude was wholly defensible in Vasari's eyes: 'those who attribute to him fantastic or strange propensities are mistaken, because whoever wishes to work well must distance himself from all cares and burdens; because his *virtù* requires thought, solitude and opportunity so as not to lead the mind into error.'[58] And in defending the painter's nude figures from contemporary charges of lasciviousness, he relies on the argument that Michelangelo's moral *virtù* is such as to preclude any possibility that he could give birth to lascivious creations.[59]

Authors outside Florence were no less alert to the way in which Michelangelo had come to provide the touchstone. Aretino and Dolce, both writing in Venice, and the Milanese Lomazzo all provide striking witness to the overwhelming force of Michelangelo's reputation. Although the dominant purpose in Lodovico Dolce's *Dialogue on Painting* [. . .] *Entitled 'L'Aretino'* is to exploit Pietro Aretino as a spokesman for the all-round merits of Raphael and the excellence of Titian, the extraordinary quality of Michelangelo is fully recognized. Dolce's 'Aretino' does not deny 'that Michelangelo is a rare miracle of art and Nature'.[60] We also know from Aretino's own writings that he had no hesitation in agreeing with Ariosto in according Michelangelo the epithet *divino* – indeed one of Aretino's letters to the artist is specifically addressed 'To the divine Michelangelo', and in a letter to Vasari he refers to the Medici tombs as being 'carved by the God of sculpture'.[61] However the Aretino of Dolce's dialogue is not prepared to accept 'Fabio's' sweeping judgement that 'Michelangelo's excellence is such, that without going beyond the truth, one may suitably compare it with the light of the sun, which by a long way overwhelms and extinguishes all other lights.'[62] Aretino argues that there can be more than one artist of the highest talent, and that the artists of his own day bear witness to this fact.

Dolce's 'Aretino' describes both Raphael and Titian as *divino*.[63] His reluctance to set one talent definitively above all others is typical of an increasing willingness in the later half of the century to acknowledge that there may be many different kinds of 'genius' in a single art, all of equal excellence in their own particular ways and in their special spheres of operation.[64] The true painter is a 'child of nature', like the poet, and each painter's inborn individuality means that there cannot be, as some believe, 'only one form of perfect painting'.[65] Michelangelo's 'genius' in figure style, particularly with respect to foreshortenings, is acknowledged by Dolce no less than by his contemporaries, but there remained areas of art in which his talents were ineffectual. Thus when Aretino gazes out of his *palazzo* across the Grand Canal at a ravishing sunset, he recognizes that Titian's brush alone could rival Nature's own painting of the skies: 'with light and shades she gave deep perspective and high relief to what she wished to bring forward and set back, and so I, who knows how your brush breathes with her spirit, cried out three or four times, "Oh Titian, where are you?" '[66] The painter is being invited to participate in the poet's *afflatus* or *furor* in the presence of Nature's wonders.

The individuality of the genius of each artist would not only manifest itself in forms of 'specialized' expression but also in fallibilities and flaws. Aretino makes it clear, most notably in his increasingly exasperated correspondence with Michelangelo, that even the greatest geniuses may err in the most serious way. The great creator must be 'gifted with poetic talent when still in his swaddling clothes', but the inborn qualities may also embrace less admirable propensities.[67] This can be the only explanation for Michelangelo's extraordinary lapses of taste in his Sistine Chapel *Last Judgement*: 'is it possible for a man who is more divine than human to have done this in the foremost church of God? [. . .] His work would be more permissible on the walls of a voluptuous brothel.'[68] The relish with which Aretino corruscates Michelangelo's obscenities gives the impression that the waywardness of the artist actually sharpens our sense of his particular genius. Such a sense had appeared in biographical writings earlier in the century. Paolo Giovio's life of Cesare Borgia provides a striking example, in which all Cesare's physical, intellectual and moral propensities bear vivid witness to an *ingenium* which is deeply flawed yet highly fascinating.[69]

The most developed expression of the individuality of artistic genius in the sixteenth century occurs in the writings of Giovanni Paolo Lomazzo, most particularly in his *Idea del tempio della pittura (1590)*.[70] Underpinning Lomazzo's theory of art was an elaborate system of astrological predeterminations. He followed Ficino in believing that as the human *spiritus* descended to earth it was irrevocably influenced by the configuration of planets in the lunar realms through which it passed. When he came to assign seven 'governors' to the temple which he erected for the worship of painting, each was identified with the dominant influence of a particular planetary deity. This scheme explained why the *genii* of the individual governors are 'in their manners all dissimilar amongst themselves, but in such a way that in the part of painting to which they have been inclined by nature, and to which they have been directed by their art and industry, none may desire greater excellence'.[71] Michelangelo, we will not be surprised to learn, exhibited the melancholic temperament of Saturn. Lomazzo's estimate of the qualities in Michelangelo's personality and art that reflect his planetary affinity correspond closely to those attributed to the melancholic by Ficino, and share much in common with Dürer's darkly contemplative *Melencolia*. Michelangelo's art, in its sombre grandeur and fury of conception, reflects the deep duality of the melancholic's soul.

However, we should not take Lomazzo to be saying that the Saturnine temperament is *the* requisite for genius in the arts. The less perturbed temperament of Raphael, who was born under the influence of Venus, finds expression in works of a beauty which are no less elevated for all their apparent ease and sweetness. Similarly, each of the other governors of the temple of painting manifest their planetary temperaments in no less admirable if different ways. Lomazzo also reminds us, not least in his *Trattato* (1584), which should be read in conjunction with his more emblematic *Tempio*, that the possession of inborn gifts is not in itself sufficient to ensure the production of great art.[72] However much he may emphasize the power of *genio*, with its qualities of poetic furor and imaginative inspiration, he shares the universal insistence of all art theorists during the fifteenth and sixteenth centuries that rational learning, studious application and manual discipline are absolutely essential if inborn talent is to reach fruition. We should recall that the whole drift of art theory in the newly emergent academies of art was to insist on the intellectual teachability of the principles of art in an institutional context. The dominant social motivation of the academies was that the artist should be accepted as a member of a high echelon in society. This social aspiration worked powerfully against any acceptance of the idea that the gifted individual was necessarily bizzare in behaviour.

If we chose to look back from this late sixteenth-century viewpoint at the two images which we juxtaposed at the start of this study, the *Melencolia* and the *St Jerome* by Dürer, we would be justified in saying that the qualities of *Melencolia* had come increasingly into the foreground in the characterization of artistic 'genius' but not in such a way that the divine virtues of Jerome assumed a subsidiary role. We are still some way from the autonomous genius of the Romantic period, accountable only to itself and disdainful of normality. However, if it is necessary to slough off the anachronisms that come from an overemphasis upon the idea of melancholy in the sixteenth century as equivalent to modern conceptions of genius, we should not underrate the magnitude of the shift of attitudes towards art and artists that occurred during the Renaissance. A few supremely gifted individuals, whom I have called 'super-artists', were seen as having achieved a near-immortal status through their transcendent talents. The terms in which writers and patrons referred to Dürer, Michelangelo and their fellow 'deities' of art make even the remarkable praise of Giotto during the thirteenth century seem constrained. Practitioners of the visual arts who in earlier centuries would have been regarded as high-level artisans could now, if their talent and devotion were of the necessary order, be hailed as the possessors of a divine *virtù* to rival that of poets and princes. Aretino obviously felt no incongruity in the fact that he should be addressing 'the divine Michelangelo' in terms no less effusive than those he used when writing to 'the divine King of England'.[73] The transformation in attitudes towards the inherent worth of the great artist had been remarkable.

Notes

1 *Oeuvres, I. Poésies complètes* (Paris, 1882), pp. 217–20. See also U. Finke, 'Dürers Melancholie in der franzosischen und englischen Literatur und Kunst des 19. Jahrhunderts', *Zeitschrift des Deutschen Vereins für Kunstwissenschaft*, 30 (1976), 63–81.
2 See the excellent treatment of this and other themes with respect to Dürer's critical fortune by J. Bialostocki, *Dürer and his Critics* (Baden-Baden, 1986), pp. 123ff. Also T. DaCosta Kaufman, 'Hermeneutics in the History of Art: Remarks on the Reception of Dürer in the Sixteenth and Early Seventeenth Century', in *Nüremberg, A Renaissance City, 1500–1618. A Symposium* (Austin, 1985).
3 F. Schlegel, *Ansichten und Ideen von der christlichen Kunst*, ed. H. Eichner (Munich, 1959), p. 60.
4 R. Klibansky, E. Panofsky and F. Saxl, *Saturn and Melancholy* (London, 1964), pp. 284ff.
5 Ibid., p. 341.
6 See, amongst others: F. Yates, *The Occult Philosophy in the Elizabethan Age* (London, Boston and Henley, 1979), pp. 49–59; K. Hoffmann, 'Dürers "Melencolia"', in W. Busch, R. Hausherr and E. Trier (eds), *Kunst als Bedeutungsträger* (Berlin, 1978); D. Pingree, 'A New Look at Melencolia I', *Journal of the Warburg and Courtauld Institutes*, 43 (1980), 257–8; P. Sohm, 'Dürer's Melencolia I: the Limits of Knowledge', *Studies in the History of Art*, 9 (1980), 13–32; T. Lynch, 'The Geometrical Body in Dürer's Engraving, *Melencolia I*', *Journal of the Warburg and Courtauld Institutes*, 45 (1982), 226–32; and T. Brunius, 'Albrecht Dürers Melencholia I', in E. Ullmann (ed.) *Von der Macht der Bilder. Beiträge des C.I.H.A.-Kolloquiums 'Kunst und Reformation'* (Leipzig, 1983), pp. 212–15.
7 M. Ficino, *De vita triplici*, III, 22, in *Opera omnia* (Basel, 1576), I, pp. 564ff., quoted by Klibansky, Panofsky and Saxl, *Saturn and Melancholy*, p. 272.
8 See C. Hahn, 'Joseph as Ambrose's "Artisan of the Soul" in *The Holy Family in Egypt* by Albrecht Dürer, *Zeitschrift für Kunstgeschichte*, 47 (1984), 515–22.
9 In addition to the general literature on 'genius', see especially, for the visual arts in the Renaissance, E. Panofsky, 'Artist, Scientist, Genius: Notes on the Renaissance-*Dämmerung*' in *The Renaissance: Six Essays* (New York, 1962), pp. 121–82; M. Baxandall, *Giotto and the Orators* (Oxford, 1971); M. Kemp, 'From "Mimesis" to "Fantasia": the Quattrocento Vocabulary of Creation, Inspiration and Genius in the Visual Arts', *Viator*, 8 (1977), 347–98; and D. Summers, *Michelangelo and the Language of Art* (Princeton, 1981).
10 See D. Summers, *The Judgement of Sense* (Cambridge, 1986); and M. Kemp, '"Equal Excellences": Lomazzo and the Explanation of Individual Style in the Visual Arts', *Renaissance Studies*, 1 (1987), 1–26.
11 Baxandall, *Giotto and the Orators*.
12 Kemp, '"Mimesis" to "Fantasia"', 394.
13 P. Kristeller, *Andrea Mantegna* (London, 1901), doc. 36. A useful discussion of Mantegna's fame is provided by A. Chastel, *A Chronicle of Italian Renaissance Painting* (New York, 1983), pp. 104ff.

14 Kristeller, *Mantegna*, doc. 52; and Chastel, *Chronicle*, pp. 256–7.

15 E. Battistelli, 'Notizie e documenti sull'attività del Perugino a Fano', *Antichità viva*, 13 (1974), 67; and Chastel, *Chronicle*, p. 260.

16 Plato, *Timaeus*, 71E–72A. Cf. *Ion* 534, *Phaedrus* 245 and above, chapter 1. See also P. Murray, 'Poetic Inspiration in Early Greece', *Journal of Hellenic Studies*, 101 (1981), 87–100.

17 Cicero, *De Oratore*, 2.46.194 and *De divinatione*, 1.37.80; Seneca, *De tranquillitate animi*, 17.10–2; and Petrarch, *De secreto conflictu curarum mearum*, in *Francesco Petraca Prose: La letteratura italiana*, 7 (1955), 174.

18 Klibansky, Panofsky and Saxl, *Saturn and Melancholy*, pp. 254ff.

19 M. Conway (ed.), *Literary Remains of Albrecht Dürer* (Cambridge, 1889), p. 171; and H. Rupprich (ed.), *Dürer. Schriftliche Nachlass* (3 vols, Berlin, 1956), vol. II, pp. 91–2.

20 *Literary Remains*, pp. 181 and 204; and *Schriftliche Nachlass*, vol. II, p. 99.

21 *Literary Remains*, p. 172; and *Schriftliche Nachlass*, vol. II, p. 92.

22 *Schriftliche Nachlass*, vol. II, p. 100. See B. Decker, 'Dürers Selbstbildnis', in *Dürers Verwandlung in der Skulptur zwischen Renaissance und Barock* (Frankfurt, 1981), pp. 405–16.

23 *Luke*, XII, 49.

24 *Literary Remains*, p. 243; and *Schriftlicher Nachlass*, vol. II, pp. 109–10.

25 E. Panofsky, *Idea. A Concept in Art Theory*, trans. J. Peake (New York, 1968), pp. 123–5.

26 *Literary Remains*, p. 244; and *Schriftlicher Nachlass*, vol. II, pp. 109–10.

27 *Literary Remains*, p. 171; and *Schriftlicher Nachlass*, vol. II, pp. 91–2.

28 W. Pirckheimer in *Schriftlicher Nachlass*, vol. I, p. 303; and Bialostocki, *Dürer and his Critics*, pp. 23–5. See H. Rupprich, 'Pirckheimers Elegie auf den Tod Dürers', *Anzeiger der Österreichischen Akademie der Wissenschaften, phiklos.-hist. Klasse*, 93 (1956), 136–50.

29 J. Camerarius in *Schriftlicher Nachlass*, vol. I, p. 307; and Bialostocki, *Dürer and His Critics*, pp. 21–2. See P. W. Pershall, 'Camerarius on Dürer: Humanist Biography as Art Criticism', in F. Baron (ed.), *Joachim Camerarius (1500–1574). Beiträge zur Geschichte des Humanismus im Zeitalter der Reformation* (Munich, 1978), pp. 11–29.

30 J. Camerarius in *Schriftlicher Nachlass*, vol. I, p. 319; and Bialostocki, *Dürer and his Critics*, pp. 29–30. See W. Hescher, 'Melancholia (1541). An Essay in the Rhetoric of Description by Joachim Camerarius (1500–1574)', in Baron (ed.), *Camerarius*, pp. 31–120.

31 See Summers, *Michelangelo*, pp. 332–79.

32 F. Bacon, *Essays*, ed. S. Reynolds (Oxford, 1890), p. 34.

33 Michelangelo Buonarroti, *Rime*, ed. E. Girardi (Bari, 1960), no. 164; and *Complete Poems and Selected Letters of Michelangelo*, trans. G. Gilbert (Princeton, 1980), no. 162. See also, R. J. Clements, *The Poetry of Michelangelo* (London, 1966). I have, for the sake of consistency, generally adhered to the translations of Gilbert.

34 *Rime*, no. 173; *Poems*, no. 171.

35 *Rime*, no. 97; *Poems*, no. 95.

36 *Rime*, no. 83; *Poems*, no. 81.

37 *Rime*, no. 44; *Poems*, no. 42.
38 *Rime*, no. 151; *Poems*, no. 149. For an analysis of this important poem, see Summers, *Michelangelo*, pp. 203–33.
39 *Rime*, no. 242; *Poems*, no. 240.
40 M. Kemp, ' "Ogni dipintore dipinge se": a Neoplatonic Echo in Leonardo's Art Theory', in C. Clough (ed.), *Cultural Aspects of the Italian Renaissance. Essays in honour of Paul Oskar Kristeller* (Manchester, 1986), pp. 311–22.
41 *Rime*, no. 285; *Poems*, no. 283.
42 B. Varchi, *Due lezzioni di M. Benedetto Varchi, nella prima delle quali si dichiara un Sonetto di M. Michelangelo Buonarroti* [. . .] (Florence, 1549). For a good discussion of Varchi's commentary, see Summers, *Michelangelo*, pp. 203ff.
43 Varchi, *Due lezzioni*, p. 23; quoted by Summers, *Michelangelo*, p. 211.
44 A version of the *Rape of Ganymede* is in the Royal Library, Windsor. Generally considered a high-quality copy, it may be original; see *Drawings by Michelangelo*, exhibition catalogue, British Museum (London, 1975). For a Platonizing interpretation of its meaning, see E. Panofsky, *Studies in Iconology* (New York, 1962), pp. 223–5.
45 *Esequie del divino Michelangelo* (Florence, Jacopo Giunti, 1564). See R. and M. Wittkower, *The Divine Michelangelo* (London, 1964), for a facsimile and translation.
46 Wittkower, *The Divine Michelangelo*, p. 79.
47 Wittkower, *The Divine Michelangelo*, p. 98.
48 Wittkower, *The Divine Michelangelo*, p. 103; Boethius, *Consolatio philosophiae*, III, ix, 8.
49 See Summers, *Michelangelo*, pp. 171–6.
50 G. Vasari, *La vita di Michelangelo nelle redazioni del 1550 e del 1558*, ed. P. Barocchi, (5 vols, Milan-Naples, 1962), vol. I, p. 117.
51 M. Roskill, *Dolce's 'Aretino' and Venetian Art Theory of the Cinquecento* (New York, 1968), p. 180.
52 G. Vasari, *Le vite de' più eccellenti pittori, scultori ed architettori*, ed. G. Milanesi, (8 vols, Florence, 1906), vol. II, p. 203. See Kemp, 'Equal Excellences', 15.
53 Vasari, *Le vite*, vol. II, p. 357.
54 Vasari, *Le vite*, vol. II, p. 204.
55 Vasari, *Le vite*, vol. II, p. 425.
56 Vasari, *Le vite*, vol. II, p. 171.
57 Vasari, *La vita di Michelangelo*, vol. I, pp. 4–5.
58 Vasari, *La vita di Michelangelo*, vol. I, pp. 117–18.
58 Vasari, *La vita di Michelangelo*, vol. I, p. 121.
60 Roskill, *Dolce's 'Aretino'*, p. 86.
61 P. Aretino, *Lettere*, ed. F. Flora (Milan, 1960), letter of 15 Sept. 1537. See also, F. Pertile and E. Camesasca (eds) *Lettere sull'arte di Pietro Aretino* (3 vols, Milan, 1957–60); and L. Palladino, *Pietro Aretino: Orator and Art Theorist* (Ph.D thesis, Yale University, 1981, University Microfilms, Ann Arbor, 8210748). I have quoted from the convenient translations by G. Bull, *Aretino. Selected Letters* (Harmondsworth, 1976).
62 Roskill, *Dolce's 'Aretino'*, p. 86.
63 Roskill, *Dolce's 'Aretino'*, pp. 160 and 180.

64 Kemp, 'Equal Excellences', pp. 14ff.

65 Roskill, *Dolce's 'Aretino'*, p. 158.

66 Aretino, *Lettere*, May 1544.

67 Aretino, *Lettere*, 25 June 1537 to Lodovico Dolce.

68 Aretino, *Lettere*, July 1547.

69 Paolo Giovio, *Elogia virorum bellica virtute illustrium* (Florence, 1551), p. 181.

70 G. P. Lomazzo, *Idea del tempio della Pittura*, ed. R. Klein, (2 vols, Florence, 1974). See Kemp, 'Equal Excellences', pp. 18ff.

71 Lomazzo, *Idea del tempio*, p. 33.

72 The *Trattato* is conveniently available in *Scritti sull'arte*, ed. R. Ciardi, (2 vols, Florence, 1974).

73 Aretino, *Lettere*, 1 Aug. 1542.

3
The Second Homeric Renaissance: Allegoresis and Genius in Early Modern Poetics

Glenn Most

In his autobiography, Goethe, reflecting on his poetic youth from a dispassionately ironic perspective, singles out one literary event in particular as having been of decisive importance not only personally, but also culturally: the rediscovery of Homer. Having inveighed against the artificialities of the Neo-Classical aesthetic, dominant in Germany during his youth, and no less so against the various exoticisms to which he had turned in protest, Goethe goes on to write,

But my aesthetic sense was destined to be protected against all these anti-artistic spectres by the most splendid of forces. Happy is ever that literary epoch, when great works of the past surface again and are added to the agenda, for it is then that they produce a fresh effect. For us, Homer's sun rose again, and just as was required by the age, which strongly favoured such an appearance: for nature had been pointed to so often that we had finally learned to consider the works of the ancients too from this perspective. What various travellers had contributed towards the elucidation of Scripture, others provided for Homer. Guys started the ball rolling, Wood gave it a push. A review, published in Göttingen, of the original, which at first was quite rare, acquainted us with its design and let us know to what degree it had been fulfilled. No longer did we see in those poems a strained and bloated heroic world, but rather the reflected truth of a primordial present, and we tried to draw this to ourselves as much as possible. To be sure, at the same time we could not quite bring ourselves to believe the claim that, in order to understand Homeric nature correctly, we would have to familiarize ourselves with savage peoples and their customs, as depicted by the travel-writers of the New World: for it could not be denied that both Europeans and Asians were represented in the Homeric poems as being at a high cultural level, perhaps indeed at a higher one than the times of the Trojan War might have enjoyed. But that principle was nevertheless in harmony with the dominant nature credo, and to that degree we were willing to grant it validity.[1]

Despite the tone of slightly rueful mockery, Goethe's words do capture something of the aura of extraordinary excitement which had surrounded the figure of Homer a generation earlier. Young Werther, who refused to read anything but Homer as long as he was relatively healthy[2] – as he gradually sickened, he lapsed first into Klopstock and then, irreversibly, into Ossian[3] – and who consoled himself for his expulsion from polite society by driving into the countryside and reading of the hospitality the swineherd showed Odysseus,[4] might seem to us, in this regard as in others, a bit drastic, but Goethe himself was not above insisting, on the day before Christmas, that a country parson go and fetch him a copy of the *Odyssey* so he could check a passage,[5] and years later the sight of a park in Palermo reminded him so forcefully of the island of the Phaeacians that he ran out of the park, bought a copy of the poet, and in great excitement spontaneously translated the passage for his companion.[6] It will be noted that Homer, as this last episode demonstrates, can lead one not only towards nature but also away from nature: nature without Homer is not fully nature because it is mere nature, nature as the bald antithesis to art, and Goethe must leave the park because it is not authentically the park unless it can be made to contain within itself, as a reflective miniature, Homer's *Odyssey*. We may take this scene of a northern poet who forsakes the not quite artless beauties of Sicily in the spring only so as to return to them and declaim within them a German version of a Latin translation of the Greek original, to the improvement of his companion (and no doubt the amusement of the locals), as emblematic of the complexities of a century that had begun by confidently finding, like Pope's Virgil, that 'Nature and Homer were [. . .] the same,'[7] but had then gone on to ask what on earth that was supposed to mean.

Goethe speaks of the rediscovery of Homer as a second dawn, and in fact, this second modern Homeric Renaissance, the eighteenth century's discovery of Homer as a natural poet of original genius, was far more significant, not only for the modern understanding of Homer's poetry but, beyond that, for the development of Western culture as a whole, than the first rediscovery of Homer in the West that had come with the diffusion of Greek studies in the early Renaissance. For although that first Renaissance had indeed given Western Europe, for the first time in almost a millenium, the capacity of reading its founding poet in his native language, it is astonishing how little that capacity was exploited for several centuries. Petrarch may have cried out in frustration at the manuscript of Homer he treasured but could not read, '*O magne vir, quam cupide te audirem!*' ('O great man, how eagerly would I hear you speak!').[8] But even long after Europe had begun to learn Homer's language, he remained more a vague figure of conventional veneration, still Dante's '*Omero poeta sovrano*' ('sovereign poet Homer'),[9] than an intimately and widely cherished interlocutor. The reasons for this are many and complex. The early Renaissance was in general more concerned with Latin, its living language, than with Greek; when it measured Homer against Virgil and found him wanting, this was at least in part because Virgil was considered the founder of modern Italian poetry, and the chances for a specifically national literary tradition had to be protected.[10] In this first period, the Greek texts that tended to attract the most attention were the sources of occult wisdom, from Plato to Hermes Trismegistus, rather than Homer: as we shall see shortly, the general verdict of late antiquity, according to which the poet was in fact proffering that very same wisdom, but covered over with the veil of allegory, must have inclined scholars to prefer the texts in which they could look upon beauty bare. As more texts, inscriptions, coins and other artefacts became known, scholars turned from the few literary authors who had been the core of pre-Renaissance philology to what we have learned to call the ancillary disciplines: straightening out ancient history, chronology, law, the *Realia* in general sufficed to occupy the time and strength even of such giants as Scaliger and Casaubon. It was only with the Reformation that, for the first time since the Middle Ages, a single Greek text once again became central to Classical philology: but now it was not Homer, but the New Testament, upon whose editing and interpretation careers and cultures rose and fell.[11]

Until the eighteenth century Homer was edited rarely,[12] and though he was translated rather more often, into Latin and later into the vernacular, a detailed knowledge of his poetry remained the uncontested property of a few scholars and poets.[13] From the end of the seventeenth century on, however, first in France, then in England and Germany, controversy about Homer's merits and vices becomes one of the dominant modes of public discussion of literary and, beyond that, of cultural values. Through the Age of Reason, writers swarm to Homer 'as thicke as flies in spring / That in a sheepe-cote (when new milke assembles them) make wing / And buzze about the top-full pailes.'[14] The very massiveness of the eighteenth century discussion of Homer is one of the reasons why it is quite difficult to provide a brief general account of the motives and structure of this second Homeric Renaissance;[15] but there are others as well; a second one resides in the fact that writers of opposite views often shared many of the same key terms, such as nature and talent, without recognizing that these were being used antonymically; and, third and finally, many of the writers of this period, even the most systematic ones, tend irritatingly to slide back from their most original and penetrating insights into conventional formulations. Hence this article can only offer a deliberately schematic account of what was at stake in one of the most complex transformations of modern European culture, and its procedure will be of necessity paradigmatic.

In Book 17 of the Odyssey, Odysseus, accompanied by the swineherd Eumaeus, approaches his house for the first time in twenty years. Before he enters, his aged dog Argus recognizes him through his disguise and tries to greet him; but the effort proves to be too much for him, and he dies. In this celebrated and affecting scene,[16] Homer's description emphasizes the dog's decrepit state, which, for all its pathos, is also an indispensable narrative device, for otherwise the suspense created by this potentially dangerous premature recognition could not be dissipated:

δὴ τότε κεῖτ' ἀπόθεστος ἀποιχομένοιο ἄνακτος
ἐν πολλῇ κόπρῳ, ἥ οἱ προπάροιθε θυράων
ἡμιόνων τε βοῶν τε ἅλις κέχυτ', ὄφρ' ἂν ἄγοιεν
δμῶες Ὀδυσσῆος τέμενος μέγα κοπρίσσοντες·
ἔνθα κύων κεῖτ' Ἄργος ἐνίπλειος κυνοραιστέων.

(17.296–300)

While his master was away, he was lying then, despised, upon a lot of dung of mules and cows which lay piled up in heaps in front of his gates until Odysseus' servants could carry it off in order to manure a big field; there lay the dog Argus, full of dog-smashers.

The dog's abandonment symbolizes the household's neglect in its master's absence and is emphasized both by his placement on heaps of dung (Odysseus' estate, for all its wealth, remains provincial, in contrast for example to Nestor's and Menelaus' more sophisticated palaces[17]) and by his infestation with ticks, prosaic pests for which, in the absence of a proper epic term, Homer ingeniously coins the hapax κυνοραιστής ('dog-smasher') on the analogy of θυμοραιστής ('spirit-smasher').

The scholia on this passage and Eustathius' commentary indicate clearly which aspects of the text drew the most attention from ancient and medieval philologists.[18] Their approach is largely linguistic. Hapaxes (ἀπόθεστος ['despised']: Σ 296, Eust. 296; κυνοραιστέων ['dog-smashers']: Σ 300, Eust. 300) are glossed, sometimes falsely;[19] unusual usages of words (non-sacral τέμενος ['field']: Σ 299, Eust. 298) are explained; the use of the future participle to indicate intention (κοπρίσοντες ['in order to manure']: Σ 299) is pointed out; the spelling and meaning of technical terms (κοπρήσσοντες ['in order to manure']: Σ 299, Eust. 298) is clarified. The periphrasis in κυνοραιστέων ('dog-smashers') obviously causes the most trouble: the greatest ancient scholars had argued in vain about just what kind of insect Homer had had in mind, dog-flies, ticks, or some other kind of pest for which this would be the technical designation (Σ 300); one branch of the scholia cuts the knot by declaring the insects identical with those called τζιβίκια in ordinary spoken medieval Greek.

Evidently, Homer is being used, in part at least, as a textbook to

introduce students to a foreign language: the poetic idiom of Classical
Greek literature, mastery of which continued to be a prerequisite for a
successful career in later Greek society for many centuries after spoken
Greek had evolved into a language with a very different pronunication
and even a somewhat different grammar. Late antique and Byzantine
study of the ancient classics seems to have been intended primarily as a
training ground in the complex artificialities of pseudo-Attic Greek for
future state and Church bureaucrats. Homer, as the first author read in
school (and probably the last one read by many students), was an
elementary thesaurus of ancient Greek – a view which, to be sure, tended
quickly to lead to absurdities, since after all it was not Homeric Greek, but
rather the Classical Attic of the great fourth-century prose writers like
Plato and Demosthenes that later Greeks were being taught to imitate.
More than one Byzantine scholar claims that Homer wrote an early
version of the Attic dialect or exemplifies Attic usages from the Homeric
Kunstsprache.[20]

There is an implicit recognition of historical change in these ancient
commentaries, but since diachronic progression is being conceived
essentially on the model of linguistic difference, and since the purpose of
the instruction is to minimize such difference as far as possible, that
change is obscured by taking the form of translation. Thereby Homer's
continuing validity is protected from ever being put into doubt. Moreover,
as the foundation of education, he can be considered not only as a treasury
of pure Greek but also as the ultimate source of all human knowledge.
After all, if most students may end up never going on to study Aristotle,
Ptolemy, and Galen, then at least they will have derived the benefit from
their primary education of having become acquainted with the text from
which those later writers had derived whatever truths they knew about
cosmology, astronomy and medicine. Already in such ancient texts as
Heraclitus' *Homeric Allegories* and Pseudo-Plutarch's *On the Life and Poetry
of Homer* we find the insistent claim that all the sciences derive ultimately
from Homer;[21] and this strategy of curricular legitimation continues
largely uncontested throughout the Byzantine period. Eustathius begins
his Homeric commentaries by taking up the old cliché that, just as all
rivers have their ultimate source in Ocean, so too all sciences have theirs
in Homer.[22]

At first glance, to be sure, Homer might not seem to have much to teach
us about physics and the other sciences. The claim that, on the contrary,
he did, had to be supported by a technique which required the student to
move beyond that first glance – especially since that same first glance was
all too likely to discover episodes in which Homer, who was supposed to
provide the straight path towards proper action and correct knowledge,
instead seemed to be scattering obstructions in the form of flagrant

violations of social decorum, moral virtue, philosophical doctrine, and even Christian belief. Did the gods laugh when Hephaestus found Ares in bed with Aphrodite? Homer was not at all indulging in a frivolous entertainment or an impious sacrilege: rather, he was demonstrating that when the craftsman adds grace to his ironworking, the result is delightful.[23] Allegorical interpretation preserved Homer's privileged place in the educational curriculum not only by permitting the clever teacher to show that all other subjects were already contained in this one, but also by defusing the potential objections to this use of a text that had in fact been composed for very different purposes and for a very different audience. In both regards, the veil of allegory impeded the recognition of historical difference.

But how could a single poet, a mere mortal, have possibly become master of the knowledge of all things human and divine? The Greeks were in no doubt on this score: Homer was divinely inspired, in his poems the voice of a superhuman wisdom spoke of things hidden from the ignorant masses and revealed only to the initiated few. The language of the mystery religions accompanies allegorical interpretation, probably from its very beginnings and certainly through the Middle Ages, and provides the cultic equivalent for the biographical legends of Homer's miraculous birth and childhood; both are found as late as Eustathius.[24] What must be stressed in this context is that the doctrine of Homer's divine inspiration and the technique of the allegorical interpretation of his poems, so far from being in conflict with one another in Greek culture, in fact depended upon one another: if Homer had not been divinely inspired, one could not pretend to explain all the wisdom allegoresis uncovered in his poetry, and conversely, the best evidence for his inspiration was furnished precisely by allegoresis. Thus Longinus at one point can liken Homer to the Pythian priestess at Delphi, possessed by a divine vapour and uttering prophecies as one inspired, and at another can declare that the Battle of the Gods, sublime and terrifying as it is, must be rejected as blasphemous unless it is interpreted allegorically.[25] And the Neoplatonist Proclus identifies as being the most inspired parts of Homer's poetry those very ones which most urgently require allegorical interpretation.[26]

When Homer migrated West during the early Renaissance, he carried with him as part of his luggage this profound conceptual bond between allegoresis and inspiration, and the Italian scholars who welcomed the one did not think of questioning the other. Thus the notes Politian appended to his translation of the *Iliad* in the 1470s freely mix praise for the inspired rhetoric of Homer's poetry with allegorical interpretations of its details; for the latter, Politian cites with approval ancient Neoplatonist commentators who described Homer as 'like some immense and boundless ocean'.[27] The Florentine Neoplatonists are celebrated as early and enthusiastic proponents of both doctrines; but views like theirs in this regard persisted for centuries. In the mid-sixteenth century, Jean Dorat's celebrated allegorical lectures on Homer at the Collège de Coqueret and at the Collège Royal were praised by one student as the products of 'Homer's only and best interpreter'.[28] Erasmus repeated the oceanic image of Homer's encyclopedism, calling him 'as it were the ocean of all fields of knowledge', and claimed that, 'just as Holy Scripture does not bear much fruit if you remain stuck on the letter, so too the poetry of Homer or Virgil can only be useful for you if you conceive it wholly as an allegory.'[29] As late as 1704, Gerhard Croese was claiming, in his significantly entitled *ΟΜΗΡΟΣ ΕΒΡΑΙΟΣ sive HISTORIA HEBRAEORUM ab HOMERO Hebraicis nominibus ac sententiis conscripta in ODYSSEA & ILIADE* ('*JEWISH HOMER, or HISTORY of the JEWS written by HOMER in the ODYSSEY & ILIAD with Jewish names and doctrines*'), that Homer's poetry was an allegory of sacred history, an 'image of Holy Scripture': the *Iliad* narrated the Israelites' siege and destruction of the city of Jericho and the *Odyssey* recounted the life of the patriarchs, Lot's escape from Sodom and the death of Moses; Homer had merely altered the times and places and inserted a few poetic episodes.[30]

But history had already passed Croese by. In the same year as Croese published his theological lucubrations in Dortrecht, Jonathan Swift, in the anonymous first edition of *A Tale of a Tub*, ridiculed views of Homer's encyclopedism by complaining that 'having read his writings with the utmost application usual among *modern wits*, I could never yet discover the least direction about the structure of that useful instrument, a *save-all*,' and pointed out the poet's 'gross ignorance in the *common laws of this realm*, and in the doctrine as well as discipline of the Church of England'.[31] Indeed, already a century earlier, Bacon had cast doubt upon the allegorical interpretation of Homer:

in many the like encounters, I do rather think that the fable was first, and the exposition devised, than that the moral was first, and thereupon the fable framed. For I find it was an ancient vanity in Chrysippus, that troubled himself with great contention to fasten the assertions of the Stoics upon the fictions of the ancient poets [. . .] (notwithstanding he [Homer] was made a kind of Scripture by the later schools of the Grecians), yet I should without any difficulty pronounce that his fables had no such inwardness in his own meaning.[32]

The crucial development affecting views of Homer from the fifteenth through the seventeenth centuries was the gradual decline in the validity attributed to allegorical interpretation. There were many reasons for this: the gradual emancipation of Renaissance classical philology from its Byzantine inheritance in matters as diverse as the pronunciation of Greek and ancient chronology; the development of new philosophical schools which lessened the attractiveness of Stoic and Neoplatonic versions of Homer; the spate of discoveries in the sciences which made Homer's anticipation of Aristotelian physics and Hippocratic medicine uninteresting; and, perhaps most important of all, the general critique of allegorical methods associated with the Protestant Reformation. The seventeenth century witnessed not only the rise of hermeneutics but also, in tandem with this, the decline of allegoresis.[33]

It was the absence of allegoresis that made the Quarrel of the Ancients and Moderns that broke out in France at the end of the seventeenth century different from anything that had preceded it. Already in antiquity there had been controversies in which those who liked only the most ancient poets had opposed those who defended modern writers: Horace's *Epistle* 2.1 to Augustus, in which the modernist case is forcefully presented, shows that, appearances notwithstanding, Perrault and Fontenelle were authorized by ancient precedent.[34] And in the Renaissance, contrasting Greek poets, especially Homer, and more modern poets, like Virgil, and criticizing the former for their violations of the taste and decorum preserved by the latter, was a literary-critical *topos*, one well illustrated, for example, in the poetic theories of Vida and Scaliger.[35] But as long as allegoresis remained a generally viable method, Homer's stature was insulated from any of the dangers to which such discussions might have exposed it. To be sure, not every Homeric lapse could be allegorized away; but not every one needed to be: the fact that the most flagrant and celebrated scandals could be successfully defended as the occult promulgations of inspired wisdom meant that lesser embarrassments could be left to take care of themselves without endangering the value of the whole. Thus Eustathius sees no difficulty in accepting the *Odyssey*'s reference to dunghills in front of the palace as typical of Homer's habit of inserting into his poetry some elements of lifelike realism (κατὰ βιωτικὴν οἰκονομίαν, Eust. 17.298). And the same casualness with regard to vulgar language and cruder objects is displayed by English translators of Homer through the seventeenth century. Consider for example Chapman's translation of this passage:

> But, his King gone, and he now past his parts,
> Lay all abjectly on the Stable's store,
> Before the Oxe-stall and Mules' stable dore,
> To keepe the clothes cast from the Pessants' hands,
> While they laide compasse on Ulysses' Lands,
> The Dog with Tickes (unlook'd to) over-growne.[36]

The fact that Chapman wanders so far away from the meaning of the original might be mistakenly attributed to some sense of decorousness on his part and not recognized for what it really is, a straightforward mistake quite typical of him, did not his Odysseus go on in the next lines to complain, 'That such a Dog as this should have his laire / On such a dunghill';[37] and neither of his seventeenth-century successors, Ogilby[38] and Hobbes,[39] seems to display the least diffidence with regard to such thoroughly Anglo-Saxon monosyllables as 'dung', 'ticks', and 'fleas'.

That, after the Quarrel of the Ancients and Moderns, things could no longer be so simple, is shown by a glance at the translation of this passage by Alexander Pope, who, despite his strong disagreement with Perrault's strictures, feels nonetheless compelled to elevate Argus to mellifluous Latinate polysyllables:

> Now left to man's ingratitude he lay,
> Un-hous'd, neglected, in the publick way;
> And where on heaps the rich manure was spread,
> Obscene with reptiles, took his sordid bed.[40]

What has happened in the meantime?

Perrault's *Parallèle des anciens et des modernes* nowhere denies that Homer is a poet of genius – on the contrary, Perrault concludes the first volume of his work with a poetic epistle to Fontenelle entitled '*Le Génie*' ('Genius'), a veritable hymn to '*ce feu, cette divine flamme, / L'Esprit de son Esprit & l'Ame de son Ame. / [. . .] / Une sainte fureur, une sage manie, / Et tous les autres dons qui forment le Génie* ('this fire, this divine flame, / The Spirit of his Spirit and the Soul of his Soul. / [. . .] / A holy rage, a wise madness, / And all the other gifts that form Genius'), exemplified at greatest length and in most detail by Homer himself, of whom Perrault writes that, despite his many faults, '*En tous lieux on l'adore, en tous lieux ses écrits / D'un charme inévitable enchantent les esprits*' ('Everywhere he is adored, everywhere his writings / With an inescapable charm bewitch men's spirits').[41] What in fact is missing from his *Parallèle* is any sense whatsoever that allegorical interpretation might be fruitfully applied to Homer's poetry. In the first volume, the Abbé, the spokesman of the radical modernists, mocks the tendency of those who have a boundless veneration for the ancients to take refuge in allegories: 'It is amusing to see in what allegories these Interpreters take refuge when they lose their heads; sometimes they go so far as to claim that the secret of the philosophical stone is concealed beneath the wise and mysterious shadows of their allegories' (1.15 = 104). But if we have been expecting the President, the champion of the ancients, to haul out this weapon when he is backed into a corner, we shall be gravely disappointed. Only once does the President dare invoke allegoresis to justify a Homeric embarrassment:

The Abbé: [. . .] let us go on to examine the sentiments and thoughts with which Homer has embellished his two Poems. In the first book of the Iliad, Vulcan says to his mother Juno that he is afraid Jupiter will beat her. That is scarcely worthy either of Gods, or of Homer.

The Chevalier: The peasants would be quite happy to know this passage and to see that they resemble Jupiter when they beat their wives.

The President: Don't you know, Monsieur l'Abbé, that there is a mystery in these words?

The Abbé: So they say: that Homer meant by that that the thunder beats the air and shakes it up with great violence; for Jupiter is the God of thunder and Juno is the Goddess of the air.

The Chevalier: When it rains and is sunny at the same time, the children say that the Devil is beating his wife; and when it thunders, Homer says that Jupiter is beating his. In my opinion, there's not much difference. And so, Monsieur l'Abbé, let's move on to something else.

(3.55–6 = 297–8)

In point of fact, neither does Homer's Hephaestus worry that Zeus might beat Hera, nor does any ancient scholar seem to have proposed anything along the lines of the President's curious meteorological interpretation. But this makes no difference: the Chevalier's contemptuous dismissal of allegorical explanation as no better than the fancies of children is overwhelmingly effective; the President does not take up the challenge, and never again tries to defend a passage in this way.

For allegoresis is by now a dead letter, something even the most hardy defenders of the ancients no longer treat seriously, at least not in Paris. But if embarrassments can no longer be explained away by reference to a divine afflatus which lifts Homer out of his human context and associates him with the secrets of the gods, the immediate consequence is that Homer is brought back into human history: no longer the repository of a timeless wisdom, one universally and eternally valid, he and his age become part of the same historical continuum of which modernity is simply a later segment. All points on that continuum are subject to the same rules: both Perrault's Ancients and his Moderns agree that true Nature, the ultimate ground of all human experience, is always and everywhere the same.[42]

Hence it is superficial to reduce the Quarrel to a debate over whether ancient poets or modern ones should be preferred, whether modern poets must follow the rules derived from ancient models or should be free to work out their own canons. To be sure, the Quarrel was also that, but more fundamentally, it was a controversy about the structure of human history, opposing to one another two visions of the relation between nature and human freedom.

For the proponent of the ancients, history was a falling away from a unique incarnation of natural order. Nature in its regularity provided the only possible model for geniune human success: since in the great Classical poets the order of nature had fully coincided with the order of man, in them artistic perfection, the seamless identity of product and rule, had already been achieved. A historical caesura divided their effortless success from the moderns' strenuous exertions: across the gulf that separated past from present, the bridge thrown over by the latter's imitation could alone restore unity to human time and hence was not only an aesthetic preference but a moral imperative. In history, chronology was destiny: only for the ancients did freedom of will and the necessities embodied in Nature's laws entirely coincide; to live later meant differentially to be free to choose not to follow the ancients, if one were indeed so foolish, or, if one preferred to imitate them, of necessity to fall short of their accomplishment. It was no accident that Madame Dacier, who saw herself as the champion of the ancients in the Homeric war that broke out a generation after Perrault's *Parallèle*, wrote a book entitled *Des Causes de la corruption du goust* ('*On the Causes for the Corruption of Taste*').

The proponents of the moderns shared the view that only Nature could guarantee success; but in their secularized vision of history, the realization of that success was withdrawn from a single moment of the past and projected instead into the future as the attainable goal of human action. Theirs was a faith not so much in perfection as in perfectability:[43] it is not surprising that in consequence they emphasized technolgy and the sciences, since the progress that had been made in those fields since the Renaissance was incontrovertible. Whereas their opponents interpreted the doctrine of the eternal identity of Nature morally as entailing the universal validity of the rules derived from Nature, the modernists interpreted it causally: if Nature was always the same, then so too must be man, Nature's effect. Hence success was always possible: at the very least, the present had a status in no way inferior to that of the past. To come later need not be worse than to come earlier, and indeed, in at least one regard, could be better: for the community of modernists could choose, not to imitate the ancients, but to build upon their accomplishments in those cases in which cumulation was possible, to repeat their successes and avoid their mistakes, in order thereby to hasten the attainment of perfection.[44] Symbolically, Perrault fired the opening shot of the Quarrel in a poem he read before the Académie Française, of which he was a member.

Who won the Quarrel of the Ancients and Moderns? Scholars tend to claim that either one side or the other was victorious (they were not sure which);[45] but in fact both positions were untenable. The party of the ancients was hampered not only by their ability to offer any effective counter-argument to the modernists' prize example, technological and scientific progress; nor were the claims of the modernists weakened only by their failure to distinguish between the sciences and the humanities, to recognize that progress in the one did not entail progress in the other. The true problem lay deeper. The unavailability of allegoresis, which both sides presupposed, meant that Homer must be fully intelligible within human history. But if his wisdom was therefore not timeless, but local, how could the proponents of the ancients justify the claim that his artistic achievement was so universally valid that it could only be imitated, not criticized? As Perrault's discussion of Argus reveals, violations of decorum could no longer be casually accepted:

The Abbé: This dog was on a dunghill in front of the door of Ulysses' palace.
The Chevalier: A dunghill in front of the door of a palace!
The President: Why not? Since the greatest wealth of the princes of those days consisted in land and animals, there is nothing odd about their having lots of dung in front of their doors.
The Chevalier: I suppose: but agree with me that the princes of those days were very similar to the peasants of these.[46]

By defending the piles of manure in front of Odysseus' palace as characteristic of '*ce temps-là*' ('those days'), the President himself has thereby already reduced Homer's content to the effect of primitive conditions, once superseded in the modern world (in Paris at least, if not yet among the peasants). And if the content is primitive, what reason is there to think the form any different? The President makes no response to the objections of the Chevalier and the Abbé; for, within the terms of his argument, no response is possible. Yet the modernists are in fact in no less difficulties. For if Nature is always the same and success is always possible, why need human history improve? The accumulation of knowledge and the steady amelioration which the modernists canonized were in fundamental contradiction with their premise that the cause of human excellence was a non-human factor exempt from historical change. If genius was always possible, then Homer was a genius, and so was Perrault: but if the claim that Perrault was the greater genius was to be defended at all, then only in terms of the improvement that social conditions had experienced between the Homeric and Perraultian ages. But if that was accepted as a decisive factor, how could ever-changeless Nature be alone determinant?

The dead end to which the terms in which the French Quarrel between the Ancients and the Moderns inevitably led did not prevent the issue

from continuing to animate the French salons for generations – on the
contrary. But it did mean that genuine progress in the controversy could
only be achieved by its transpositon across the English Channel. For the
English differed from the French in having had both a Shakespeare and a
Newton; and if Addison offered 'our countryman Shakespeare' as the only
English instance, to be set next to Homer and the Old Testament, of the
first and greatest kind of genius, natural genius, 'those few [. . .] who by
the meer Strength of natural Parts, and without any assistance of Art or
Learning, have produced Works that were the Delight of their own Times,
and the Wonder of Posterity',[47] so too James Thomson did not hesitate, in
his eulogy 'To the Memory of Sir Isaac Newton', to ask

> Did ever poet image aught so fair,
> Dreaming in whispering groves, by the hoarse brook!
> Or prophet, to whose rapture heaven descends?
> Even now the setting sun and shifting clouds,
> Seen, Greenwich, from thy lovely heights, declare
> How just, how beauteous the refractive law

and to conclude with the prayer,

> oh, look with pity down
> On humankind, a frail erroneous race!
> Exalt the spirit of a downward world!
> O'er thy dejected country chief preside,
> And be her Genius called! her studies raise,
> Correct her manners, and inspire her youth.[48]

In eighteenth-century England, the value of the national achievement,
in both poetry and science, was never seriously at issue; so too, since it was
largely taken for granted that in both fields progress was possible and
genius was necessary, for the first time it became possible to thematize
and compare the differences between the humanities and the sciences.[49]
Hence the English were at liberty to extract certain elements from the
French controversy and to reformulate them in terms of their own
interests. Those Englishmen who chose to draw upon the arsenal of the
champions of the ancients abandoned the neo-classical insistence upon
artistic rules and the imitation of canonical models and instead retained
only the conviction of gradual cultural decline; even when they were not
consciously opposed to the modernists, their real allegiance was revealed
in their certainty that when one was born did make an essential difference,
that culture could have a withering effect upon nature, that therefore
modernity had fallen away from an original natural greatness. The
English modernists, on the other hand, neglected their French counter-

parts' larger cultural views in favor of their more narrowly focused revolt against Neo-classical aesthetics. Longinus' vision of a poetry of genius which broke the rules at its own risk, failing wretchedly on some occasions but rising on others to incomparable heights, proved an ancient precedent for the view that ancient precedents were not only unnecessary, but harmful: the true poet imitated not other poets, but nature itself, and such imitation could be performed at any moment in human history, for, while literary models were not always available, natural ones were. Thus, while the English heirs of the champions of the ancients were hypersensitive to issues of cultural evolution and historical change, the English epigonoi of the modernists tended to view them with equanimity, at most invoking culture as a secondary factor which could play some role in modifying, but could not profoundly affect, natural genius. The difference in attitudes becomes clearest if we ask how the English theorists dealt with the question of the allegedly primitive circumstances of the Homeric age: while the former group regarded Homer's cultural inferiority as an enabling condition which was crucially responsible for permitting him to compose a certain kind of poetry, the latter tended to invoke it as an exculpatory explanation to excuse otherwise troubling features.

What both groups shared, and what set them firmly apart from their French predecessors, was a novel conception of Nature. For the French, the only Nature that had counted as Nature had been that Nature which could be taken as identical with the laws of reason: inalterable, incontrovertible, axiomatic – in the words of the young Pope, 'Nature methodized:

> First follow Nature, and your judgment frame
> By her just standard, which is still the same;
> Unerring Nature, still divinely bright,
> One clear, unchanged, and universal light.[50]

But in the course of the eighteenth century, Nature came more and more to mean the factually given, the empirically verifiable, not the general but the individual, not the universal but the local, not the eternally unchanging but the constantly different. The immediate consequence was that Nature ceased to be the rule, and became instead the exception to the rule, not the straight roads by which rationality partitioned and domesticated the world, but the luxuriant undergrowth which stretched out on all sides and was constantly pushing up through cracks in the asphalt. The change can be traced clearly in Pope's later usage, for example in the Preface to his translation of the *Iliad*:

Homer is universally allow'd to have had the greatest Invention of any Writer whatever. The Praise of Judgment *Virgil* has justly contested with him, and others may have their Pretensions as to particular Excellencies; but his Invention remains yet unrival'd. Nor is it a Wonder if he has ever been acknowledg'd the greatest of Poets, who most excell'd in That which is the very Foundation of Poetry. It is the Invention that in different degrees distinguishes all great Genius's: The utmost Stretch of human Study, Learning, and Industry, which masters every thing besides, can never attain to this [. . .] Art is only like a prudent Steward that lives on managing the Riches of Nature [. . .] As in the most regular Gardens, however Art may carry the greatest Appearance, there is not a Plant or Flower but is the Gift of Nature [. . .] Our Author's [*viz.* Homer's] Work is a wild Paradise, where if we cannot see all the Beauties so distinctly as in an order'd Garden, it is only because the Number of them is infinitely greater.[51]

Though Pope's language is not free from ambiguities, the shift it marks is nevertheless remarkable: art is now the attempt to confine nature, and nature the sufficient ground of poetry. Thus, although the dictum with which Kant summed up a hundred years of aesthetics – '*Genie ist die angeborene Gemütsanlage* (*ingenium*), *durch welche die Natur der Kunst die Regel gibt*' ('Genius is the innate disposition [*ingenium*], through which nature gives rules to art')[52] – remained true for the whole of the eighteenth century, during that period the meaning of 'Nature' had evolved significantly, and with it the conception of the poetic genius at whom asymptotically nature and art were said to coincide. That is why, in the eighteenth century, for the first time, genius could come to replace allegoresis as a way of dealing with poetic unintelligibility.

Pope's version of the Longinian theory of the sublime remained the most important eighteenth-century English expression of what I have called the modernist view of Homer, and, just as his translation remained standard through the century, so too formulations from the Prefaces and Notes recur in many later writers. For this conception, the best proof of Homer's genius lay precisely in his violations of Neo-classical decorum – as though to be right was human, to err divine. For as long as Homer followed the rules, the reader's judgement was eager to confirm the poet's success, but when Homer violated them, the reader had no choice but to submit to the poet's coercion. Passages like the following invoke the fundamental dramatic plot of the Longinian sublime, the rape of the reader:[53]

It is to the Strength of this amazing Invention we are to attribute that unequal'd Fire and Rapture, which is so forcible in *Homer*, that no Man of a true Poetical Spirit is Master of himself while he reads him [. . .] the Reader is hurry'd out of himself by the Force of the Poet's Imagination, and turns in one place to a Hearer, in another to a Spectator [. . .] Exact Disposition, just Thought, correct Elocution, polish'd Numbers, may have been found in a thousand; but this Poetical *Fire*, this *Vivida vis animi*, in a very few. Even in Works where all those are imperfect or

neglected, this can over-power Criticism, and make us admire even while we disapprove. Nay, where this appears, tho' attended with Absurdities, it brightens all
the Rubbish about it, 'till we see nothing but its own Splendor.

(224–5)

Argus' dunghill and fleas are just such 'rubbish', and Pope's response to
Perrault's criticisms of them, contained in his note to the passage in his
translation, is highly instructive.

This whole Episode has fallen under the ridicule of the Critics; Monsieur *Perrault*
in particular: 'The Dunghill before the Palace (says that Author) is more proper
for a Peasant than a King; and it is beneath the dignity of Poetry to describe the
dog *Argus* almost devour'd with vermin.' It must be allow'd, that such a familiar
Episode could not have been properly introduced into the *Iliad*: It is writ in a
nobler style, and distinguish'd by a boldness of sentiments and diction; whereas
the *Odyssey* descends to the Familiar, and is calculated more for common than
heroic life. What *Homer* says of *Argus* is very natural, and I do not know any thing
more beautiful or more affecting in the whole Poem: I dare appeal to every
person's judgment, if *Argus* be not as justly and properly represented, as the
noblest figure in it. It is certain that the vermin which *Homer* mentions would
debase our Poetry, but in the Greek that very word is noble and sonorous,
κυνοραιστέων: But how is the objection concerning the Dunghill to be answer'd?
We must have recourse to the simplicity of manners among the Ancients, who
thought nothing mean that was of use to life. *Ithaca* was a barren Country, full of
Rocks and Mountains, and owed its fertility chiefly to cultivation, and for this
reason such circumstantial cares were necessary. 'Tis true such a description now
is more proper for a Peasant than a King, but antiently it was no disgrace for a
King to perform with his own hands, what is now left only to Peasants. We read of
a Dictator taken from the plough, and why may not a King as well manure his
field as plow it, without receding from his dignity? Virgil has put the same thing
into a Precept: *Ne saturare fimo pingui pudeat sola.*[54]

It is a profoundly ambiguous response, postulating a difference in level
between the *Iliad* and the *Odyssey*, claiming that, while the object is mean,
the language with which Homer describes it has a special beauty,
returning to the President's futile excuse in terms of primitive manners,
and finally capping it all with a Virgilian tag no modernist need have been
impressed by. If I am right in suggesting that Pope is ultimately the
English heir of Perrault, this ambiguity is easily explained. But the most
striking and original part of Pope's defence is his suggestion that Homer's
description 'is very natural' – which here can only mean that it describes
with veristic realism a highly specific scene from quotidian life – and the
implication that this is just why this passage is so affecting – not just
effective, but no less deeply moving than the most heroic moments in the

epic. Pope's praise of Homer as an observer of Nature in its changeful specificity recurs throughout the Notes on his translation, for example in his justification of a Homeric simile:

There are nowhere more finished pictures of nature than those which Homer draws in several of his comparisons. The beauty, however, of some of these will be lost to many, who cannot perceive the resemblance, having never had opportunity to observe the things themselves. The life of this description will be most sensible to those who have been at sea in a calm.[55]

Half a century later, it will be just this prejudice that will send Robert Wood out to the Middle East, 'to read the Iliad and the Odyssey in the countries where Achilles fought, where Ulysses travelled, and where Homer sung', and to discover that 'the nearer we approach his country and age, the more we find him accurate in his pictures of nature, and that every species of his extensive Imitation furnishes the greatest treasure of original truth to be found in any Poet, ancient or modern.[56]

This is the one branch into which views of Homer in eighteenth-century England split: for such writers, Homer was validated as the poet who best described Nature's fleas and dunghills – in Woods's words, again, because of 'that exactness, which runs through his descriptions of every kind [. . .] in the great province of Imitation he is the most original of all Poets, and the most constant and faithful copier after Nature' (4–5). The other branch was that of the primitivists, for whom Homer did not so much depict Nature as rather embody Nature; and these, as I have suggested, were the heirs of the French proponents of the ancients. Vico's 'discovery of the true Homer' had already revealed that the poet, properly understood and freed from the mistakes of allegorical interpretation, was indistinguishable from the Greek people as a whole in the course of their progress from monstrous savagery to some degree of culture, and that the poetic wisdom which formed the starting point for the evolution of the Homeric epics was the expression of the primitive state of their earliest phase, so that the epics could be considered as 'two great store-houses of the natural law of the Greek peoples'.[57] Thomas Blackwell's arguments that the causes for Homer's genius were not divine, but natural,[58] provided support for the English primitivists who were soon to discover in Ossian an authentically English Homer and in Homer the great bard of the state of nature. It is easy, and correct, to point out the extraordinary confusions the primitivists labored under, and the variety of anthropologically quite diverse cultures they thought they could subsume under a single category.[59] But we should not neglect the extraordinary pathos, the deep nostalgia, which characterized the primitivists and which provided one of the impulses that pushed England out of the eighteenth century and into Romanticism.

But only one of the impulses: for since the primitivists were convinced that the best poetry could only be written before the beginning of civilization, they themselves were capable of conceiving of poetry only in the mode of loss. The last chapter of Duff's *Essay on Genius* bears the title, 'That original poetic genius will in general be displayed in its utmost vigour in the early and uncultivated periods of society which are peculiarly favourable to it; and that it will seldom appear in a very high degree in cultivated life';[60] and the poems that correspond are weighted down by the maudlin elegiac tone of Gray's laments for dying Celtic bards and of Crabbe's and Goldsmith's eulogies for the loss of the English countryside. such poems were not so much the morning star of Romanticism as rather the evening star of the eighteenth century. When Romanticism did dawn, in Wordsworth's and Coleridge's *Lyrical Ballads* of 1798, it found its most authentic voice in the description, precise, unillusioned, yet deeply empathetic, of the smallest and least conventionally impressive experiences of ordinary nature. 'I have at all times endeavoured to look steadily at my subject,' wrote Wordsworth in the 'Preface',[61] and in poems like 'The Thorn', 'Lines left upon a seat', 'The Leech-Gatherer', and 'Michael', that endeavour was rewarded by a new and profoundly influential voice. To be sure, as he aged, Wordsworth was to end up relapsing behind his early radical insights, becoming the ponderous Victorian moralist we regret in the survivor of his youth (just as, even after the *Lyrical Ballads*, Cowper could persist in the Popian tradition of euphemistic Homer translators[62]). But the young Wordsworth, who was capable of beginning a poem with the stanza,

> There is a Thorn – it looks so old,
> In truth, you'd find it hard to say
> How it could ever have been young,
> It looks so old and grey.
> Not higher than a two years' child,
> It stands erect, this aged Thorn;
> No leaves it has, no prickly points;
> It is a mass of knotted joints,
> A wretched thing forlorn.
> It stands erect, and like a stone
> With lichens is it overgrown.

(2.240–1)

or who could hang a deeply moving, almost Biblical story of trust and betrayal from 'a straggling heap of unhewn stones' which a traveller 'might pass by, / Might see and notice not' ('Michael' 2.81), had learned his lesson from just such descriptions as Homer's of Argus. This is the voice to which modern English and American poetry has not ceased to respond.

Notes

Revised version of a lecture delivered on 22 April 1987 at the University of
Warwick. I am grateful to Tony Grafton and David Quint for their suggestions.
Unless otherwise indicated, all translations are my own.

1 J. W. Goethe, *Dichtung und Wahrheit* = *Gedenkausgabe der Werke, Briefe und
  Gespräche*, ed. E. Beutler (24 vols, Zürich, 1948–64), 10.588–89. This edition is
  cited hereafter as GA.
2 13. Mai = GA 4.272.
3 12. Oktober = GA 4.343. Compare the comment of the older Goethe, as
  reported by H. C. Robinson: 'He spoke of Ossian with contempt and said: No
  one remarked that while Werther is in his senses he talks about Homer and
  only after he grows mad is in love with Ossian' (*Gespräche* 13.8.1829 = GA
  23.605).
4 15. März = GA 4.333.
5 To Carl August 24.12.1775 = GA 18.299. Until the *Odyssey* arrived, poor
  Goethe had to make do with the Bible. Fortunately for all concerned, the text
  came the next day: to Carl August 25.12.1775 = GA 18.301.
6 *Italienische Reise*: Palermo 15.4.1787 = GA 11.263.
7 Alexander Pope, 'An Essay on Criticism', 1.135.
8 Francesco Petrarca, *Familiarum Rerum* 18.2.10, cited from V. Rossi (ed.),
  Francesco Petrarca, Le Familiari (Florence, 1937), vol. 3, p. 277. Cf. also 24.12.1ff.
  = V. Rossi and U. Bosco (eds) (Florence, 1942), vol. 4, pp. 253ff.
9 *Inferno* 4.88.
10 This is especially clear in Vida's *De Arte Poetica*, 1527 edition, 2.549–62,
   reprinted in R. G. Williams (ed.), *The De Arte Poetica of Marco Girolamo Vida*
   (New York, 1976), pp. 78–80.
11 Cf. Rudolf Pfeiffer, *History of Classical Scholarship 1300–1850* (Oxford, 1976),
   p. 76.
12 Though the *editio princeps* of Homer (Florence, 1488) was one of the earliest
   Greek texts printed, no new critical edition of Homer seems to have been
   published between Giphanius's at Strasbourg in 1572 and Barnes's at
   Cambridge in 1711.
13 On the relations between Renaissance epic poetry and contemporary classical
   philology, see especially Guido Baldassarri, *Il Sonno di Zeus. Sperimentazione
   narrative del poema rinascimentale e tradizione omerica* (Rome, 1982) and Michael
   Murrin, *The Allegorical Epic. Essays in its Rise and Decline* (Chicago – London,
   1980).
14 *The Iliads of Homer* [. . .] by Geo. Chapman, 16.594–96; cited from A. Nicoll
   (ed.), *Chapman's Homer* (2nd edition Princeton, 1967), 1.339.
15 For such an account, the reader is well served by such general surveys as G.
   Finsler, *Homer in der Neuzeit von Dante bis Goethe* (Leipzig/Berlin, 1912) and K.
   Simonsuuri, *Homer's Original Genius: Eighteenth-century Notions of the Early Greek
   Epic (1688–1798)* (Cambridge, 1979). Cf. also the interesting discussion in
   Murrin, *The Allegorical Epic*, pp. 173–96.

16 Cf. most recently G. S. Schwartz, 'The kopros motif. Variations of a theme in the *Odyssey*', *Rivista di Studi Classici*, 23 (1975), 177–95.

17 Compare Telemachus' reaction the first time he sees a really sophisticated rich man's house, the palace of Menelaus: *Od.* 4.43–46, 71–75.

18 The scholia on this passage are cited from W. Dindorf (ed.), *Scholia Graeca in Homeri Odysseam* (Oxford, 1855 = Amsterdam, 1962), pp. 644–5, and are indicated in the text by Σ and the line number; Eustathius' commentary is cited from G. Stallbaum (ed.), *Eustathii Commentarii ad Homeri Odysseam* (Leipzig, 1825 = Hildesheim – New York, 1970), 2.147, and is indicated in the text by Eust. and the line number.

19 Thus it is mistaken to derive ἀπόθετος from α—privative + ποθέω; in fact, as πολύθεστε at Callim. *H.* 6.47 shows, it comes from ἀπο— + θέυυαυθαι, cf. R. Pfeiffer, *Callimachus* (2 vols, Oxford, 1949), vol. I, p. 286 on *fr.* 325.

20 Cf. e.g. N. G. Wilson, *Scholars of Byzantium* (Baltimore, 1983), pp. 71, 189. Already in the Hellenistic period Aristarchus claimed that Homer was in origin an Athenian (see T. W. Allen (ed.) *Homeri Opera, V* (Oxford, 1912) pp. 244.13 and 247.8) and already Ptolomaeus Pindarion, a student of Aristarchus', argued that Homer's Greek was the best guide for later speakers and writers (cf. Sextus Empiricus, *Adv. math.* 1.202–8, on which cf. F. Montanari, 'Tolomeo Pindarione, i poemi omerici e la scrittura', *Ricerche di Filologia Classica* 1 (Pisa, 1981) 97–114, here 99ff.).

21 Heraclitus, *Homeric Allegories* 4.4, 22.2, 76; Ps-Plutarch, *De vita et poesi Homeri* 6. Cf. M. van der Valk, *Researches on the Text and Scholia of the Iliad* (Leiden, 1963–4), 1.465ff.

22 Eustathius, *Commentarii ad Homeri Iliadem* (Leipzig, 1827 = Hildesheim/New York, 1970), 1.7f.

23 Heraclitus, *Homeric Allegories* 69.12–16.

24 Eustathius, *Commentarii ad Homeri Iliadem* 1.30ff., Stallbaum, *Eustathii Commentarii ad Homeri Odysseam*, 1713.18ff.

25 Longinus, *On the Sublime*, 13.2, 9.7.

26 Proclus, *Commentary on Plato's Republic*, 6th essay, book 2, chapter 7. The passages in question are translated in *Proclus. Commentaire sur la République. Tome I: Dissertations I–VI*, trans. A. J. Festugière (Paris, 1970), pp. 211–13.

27 Cf. A. L. Rubinstein, 'The Notes to Polizian's "Iliad" ', *Italia Medioevale e Umanistica*, 25 (1982), 205–39, esp. 211–27 on Politian's allegoresis; the passage quoted is on 223.

28 Pfeiffer, *History of Classical Scholarship*, pp. 104, 106. Ms A184 at the Biblioteca Ambrosiana contains a student's notes to a course by Dorat on the *Odyssey* and the Homeric Hymns; the section on the Aeolus episode at the beginning of *Odyssey* 10 is presented and discussed in Geneviève Demerson, 'Dorat, commentateur d'Homère', in *Études Seizièmistes offertes à V.-L. Saulnier = Travaux d'Humanisme et Renaissance*, 177 (Geneva, 1980), 223–34, esp. 227ff. on Dorat's moral and physical allegoresis.

29 Cf. T. Bleicher, *Homer in der deutschen Literatur (1450–1740). Zur Rezeption der Antike und zur Poetologie der Neuzeit* (Stuttgart, 1972), pp. 60, 62.

30 Ibid., pp. 169–70.

31 Jonathan Swift, *A Tale of a Tub and Other Works*, ed. A. Ross and D. Woolley (Oxford, 1986), p. 61.
32 Francis Bacon, *The Advancement of Learning*, book II, cited from H. G. Dick (ed.), *Selected Writings of Francis Bacon* (New York, 1955), p. 246. In the Preface to his *The Wisdom of the Ancients*, on the other hand, published only four years later, Bacon's position is more complicated: though he remains entirely sceptical with regard to those ancients who, 'wishing only to gain the sanction and reverence of antiquity for doctrines and inventions of their own, have tried to twist the fables of the poets into that sense', singling out Chrysippus and the alchemists in particular, nevertheless he himself is convinced 'that beneath no small number of the fables of the ancient poets there lay from the very beginning a mystery and an allegory' (Dick, *Francis Bacon*, p. 404); Bacon's own interpretations here often explain the myths politically, as allegories of civil affairs, particularly of rebellions. An excellent analysis of the complexities of Bacon's attitude to allegoresis against the background of Renaissance thought is provided by Paolo Rossi, *Francesco Bacone. Dalla magia alla scienza* (Torino, 1974), pp. 130–220.
33 I have discussed this matter briefly in my 'Rhetorik und Hermeneutik: Zur Konstitution der Neuzeit', *Antike und Abendland*, 30 (1984), 62–79.
34 Hor. *Epist.* 2.1.18ff.
35 Vida, *De Arte Poetica*, 1.170f., 2.541ff.; Scaliger, *Poetices Libri septem* 1.5, 5.3, cited from F. M. Padelford, *Select Translations from Scaliger's Poetics* (New York, 1905), pp. 37, 73–81.
36 Cited from Nicoll, *Chapman's Homer*, 2.302.
37 Ibid.
38 *Homer his Odysses* translated [. . .] by John Ogilby (London, 1665), p. 247: 'But now he lay in a dejected state, / Upon a dunghill just before the Gate, / That Mules, and Steeds congested with their Dung; / Which Swains on the improving pasturage flung. / There lay poor *Argus*, full of Ticks.'
39 *Homer's Odysses* translated [. . .] by Tho. Hobbes, 2nd edn (London, 1677), p. 209: 'But all the while his Master was away, / The Servants of his keeping took no care, / But on the Dung before the Door he lay, / Which there was heap'd to manure Fields and Leas, / From many Mules and Cattle faln away. / There lay the old Dog *Argus* full of Fleas.'
40 *Homer's Iliad and Odyssey* translated [. . .] by Alexander Pope (London, 1715), cited from J. Butt (ed.), *The Twickenham Edition of the Poems of Alexander Pope*, vol. 10: *The Odyssey of Homer. Books XIII–XXIV*, ed. M. Mack *et al.* (London – New Haven, 1967), pp. 148–49.
41 Charles Perrault, *Parallèle des anciens et des modernes en ce qui regarde les arts et les sciences* (Paris, 1688) 1.29, 31, 32; cited from H. R. Jauss (ed.) (Munich, 1964), pp. 172–3. Future citations from this edition are indicated in the text.
42 This view is expressed most explicity by the Abbé (1.88f. = 123, 3.156 = 323), but the President never disputes it and accepts it e.g. at 3.280–1 = 442.
43 Cf. Perrault, *Parallèle*, ed. Jauss, pp. 25–33.
44 Thus the Abbé can say, 'Once more, Nature is always the same in general in all its productions; but historical periods are not always the same; and all other things being equal, it is an advantage for a historical period to have come after others' (2.280 = 250).

45 Cf. Perrault, *Parallèle*, ed. Jauss, p. 9.

46 3.98 = 308.

47 *The Spectator*, 160 (3 September 1711), ed. D. F. Bond (5 vols, Oxford, 1965).

48 James Thomson, *The Poetical Works* (London, 1862), 2.175–82; cited from G. Buchdahl, *The Image of Newton and Locke in the Age of Reason* (London/New York, 1961), pp. 53, 56.

49 E.g., William Duff, *An Essay on Original Genius* (London, 1767), pp. 91ff., 124ff; Alexander Gerard, *An Essay on Genius* (London, 1774), pp. 318ff.

50 Pope, 'An Essay on Criticism', 1.89, 68–71.

51 N. Ault (ed.), *The Prose Works of Alexander Pope. Vol. I: The Earlier Works, 1711– 1720* (Oxford, 1936), pp. 223–4. Subsequent citations will be indicated in the text.

52 Immanuel Kant, *Kritik der Urteilskraft* § 46.

53 On the rape of the reader in classical theories of the sublime, cf. my 'Sublime degli Antichi, Sublime dei Moderni', *Studi di estetica*, 12 (1984), 113–29.

54 Pope, *Poems*, ed. Butt, vol. 10.

55 On *Iliad* 14.21–8; cited from B. A. Goldgar (ed.), *Literary Criticism of Alexander Pope* (Lincoln, Nebraska, 1965), pp. 141–2.

56 Robert Wood, *An Essay on the Original Genius and Writings of Homer* (London [1775] = Washington, DC, 1973), pp. v–vi. Subsequent citations will be indicated in the text. On Wood see especially the humane and erudite discussion in David Constantine, *Early Greek Travellers and the Hellenic Ideal* (Cambridge, 1984), pp. 66–84.

57 Giambattista Vico, *Principj di Scienza Nuova* (Naples, 1744). *Libro Terzo: Della discoverta del vero Omero. Sezione seconda: Discoverta del vero Omero. Capitolo secondo: I poemi di Omero si truovano due grandi tesori del diritto naturale delle genti di Grecia*. Vico is cited from the edition of F. Nicolini (Rome-Bari, 1978).

58 Cf. Simonsuuri, *Homer's Original Genius*, 99ff.

59 See e.g. René Wellek, *A History of Modern Criticism: 1750–1950. Volume I: The Later Eighteenth Century* (New Haven/London, 1955), p. 126.

60 Duff, *Essay on Original Genius*, p. 260.

61 E. de Selincourt (ed.), *The Poetical Works of William Wordsworth* 2nd edn. (Oxford, 1952), 2.390. Cf. also 2.386: 'The principal object, then, proposed in these Poems was to choose incidents and situations from common life, and to relate or describe them, throughout, as far as was possible in a selection of language really used by men, and, at the same time, to throw over them a certain colouring of imagination, whereby ordinary things should be presented to the mind in an unusual aspect [. . .] Humble and rustic life was generally chosen, because, in that condition, the essential passions of the heart find a better soil in which they can attain their maturity, are less under restraint, and speak a plainer and more emphatic language.' Subsequent citations from this edition will be indicated in the text.

62 *The Odyssey of Homer* translated [. . .] by the late William Cowper, 2nd edn. (London, 1802), 2.125: 'Forlorn he lay, / A poor unheeded cast-off, on the ground, / Where mules and oxen had before the gate / Much ordure left, with which Ulysses' hinds / Should, in due time, manure his spacious fields. / There lay, by vermin worried to the bone / The wretched Argus.'

4
Shakespeare and Original Genius

Jonathan Bate

According to the *Oxford English Dictionary*, the mid-eighteenth century was an especially important moment in the history of the word genius. In substantiating its fifth definition of genius, the essence of which is 'instinctive and extraordinary capacity for imaginative creation, original thought, invention, or discovery', *OED* states:

This sense, which belongs also to F[rench] *génie*, Ger[man] *genie*, appears to have been developed in the 18th c[entury]. (It is not recognized in Johnson's Dictionary). In sense 4 [natural ability or capacity] the word had come to be applied with especial frequency to the kind of intellectual power manifested by poets and artists; and when in this application 'genius', as native endowment, came to be contrasted with the aptitudes that can be acquired by study, the approach to the modern sense was often very close. The further development of meaning was prob[ably] influenced by association with senses 1 and 2 [spirit, as in *genius loci*], which suggested that the word had an especial fitness to denote that particular kind of intellectual power which has the appearance of proceeding from a supernatural inspiration or possession, and which seems to arrive at its results in an inexplicable and miraculous manner. This use, which app[arently] originated in England, came into great prominence in Germany, and gave the designation of *Genieperiode* to the epoch in German literature otherwise known as the 'Sturm und Drang' period.

The aim of this chapter is to exemplify, though also to modify, this definition in the form of three closely linked claims. Let me begin by stating these as bare assertions:

1 The concept of 'original genius' as the essence of poetry became widespread by the mid-eighteenth century.
2 The full development of this concept was central to the growth of what we now think of as 'Romantic' aesthetics.

3 Shakespeare was the cardinal exemplar of 'original genius' – so much so, that it was above all because of him that the concept was developed and became so widely accepted.

I must immediately qualify the last of these, for Shakespeare was not the only exemplar. Homer also played an important role; so too did Pindar and the sublime of the Old Testament prophets; and in the 1760s Ossian was hailed as the archetypal original genius. While glancing beyond the limits of this chapter, I should also say that I will not be doing anything like justice to the complex two-way relationship between England and Germany at which *OED* hints: I shall not be able to make more than passing reference to the importance of Shakespeare and original genius for the '*Sturm und Drang*'.[1]

My principal modification of *OED* is over the date at which our modern conception of genius became widely accepted. *OED* acknowledges that sense 4 (natural ability) shades into our sense 5 ('poetic' or 'original' genius) prior to the mid-eighteenth century, but gives an invocation in Fielding's *Tom Jones* (1749) as the first usage for sense 5. Considerable weight is attached to the absence of sense 5 from Johnson's *Dictionary* (1755). But is the sense absent from Johnson's *Dictionary?* On the very first page of his Preface Johnson contrasts the drudgery of the lexicographer with the 'conquest and glory' that are achieved by 'Learning and Genius'. In this context, learning and genius serve to represent two poles of literary excellence; to separate them is to divide art from nature, education from inspiration, what may be developed from what is innate. It is to imply that genius may be the opposite of learning. It is to make a distinction which in the seventeenth century was made most frequently when Shakespeare was contrasted to Ben Jonson (the *locus classicus* is the juxtaposition of 'Jonson's learned sock' and 'Sweetest Shakespeare fancy's child, / Warbl[ing] his native wood-notes wild' in Milton's 'L'Allegro').

In his Preface, Johnson also points out that 'Such is the exuberance of signification which many words have obtained, that it was scarcely possible to collect all their senses'; he says that the solution to the difficulties, and the supply of the defects, caused by this profusion of meaning 'must be sought in the examples, subjoined to the various senses of each word, and ranged according to the time of their authors'.[2] In other words, the definitions are incomplete without a full consideration of the illustrative quotations. Now the illustrative quotation for Johnson's second sense of genius, 'A man endowed with superiour faculties', is Addison's 'There is no little writer of Pindarick who is not mentioned as a prodigious *genius.*' Here we already have the association of genius with poetry, and in particular the wild Pindaric ode. But I think that Johnson would also have expected the user of his dictionary to recall, or reacquaint himself with, Addison's fullest attempt to define genius: the well-known essay that was no. 160 in *The Spectator*. In this paper, which is dated 3 September 1711, we find all the essentials of the conception of original genius which, according to the *OED*, is not properly formulated until the middle of the century.

For Addison, the first class of geniuses are those 'who by the meer Strength of natural Parts, and without any assistance of Art or Learning, have produced Works that were the Delight of their own Times, and the Wonder of Posterity'.[3] There is an unquestioned assumption that genius is a term used to praise writers, especially poets, and above all those poets whose strength comes from nature rather than art or learning: 'There appears something nobly wild and extravagant in these great natural Genius's, that is infinitely more beautiful than all the Turn and Polishing of what the *French* call a *Bel Esprit*.' This dissociation from the French term '*esprit*', at a time when French thinking dominated literary theory, implicitly makes genius into a distinctively English category. English criticism of the late seventeenth and early eighteenth centuries sets up an opposition between genius and the rules of art associated with French Neo-Classicism: because of the example of Shakespeare, English theorists reject French strictness. In Addison's first class of geniuses, Shakespeare is a lone Englishman occupying a privileged place beside Homer, Pindar, and the sublime parts of the Old Testament.

Addison is one of many writers in the early eighteenth century who yoke Shakespeare, genius, and originality or naturalness. Again and again, one comes across remarks like the following, which is from a little *Dissertation on Reading the Classics* written in 1709 by one Henry Felton: '*Shakespeare* is a wonderful Genius, a single Instance of the Force of Nature, and the Strength of Wit.'[4] And in the same year as the *Spectator* paper, we find Elijah Fenton making the link with the sense of genius as a 'presiding deity' when he describes Shakespeare as 'the Genius of our Isle'.[5] There is frequently a patriotic impulse at work when Shakespeare is used to make French critical principles look deficient; later in the century, the Germans of the '*Sturm und Drang*' would again deploy Shakespeare in a battle against French cultural domination.

Closely related to Addison's essay on genius are his series of eleven *Spectator* papers on the pleasures of the imagination (nos 411–21). These were enormously influential in both England and Germany; their influence was redoubled in the 1740s when Mark Akenside popularized some of their central ideas in *The Pleasures of Imagination*, one of the key poems of the century. In paper 419, Addison argues that the imagination is particularly pleased by what Dryden had called 'the Fairie Way of Writing', that is to say, writing which comes from invention and fancy, not the observation of nature. The English are said to be especially attuned to this sort of poetry, being 'naturally Fanciful' and disposed to 'Gloominess and Melancholly of Temper'. Here we have one of the seeds of the cult of the gothic, which was to be so important later in the century, and such a formative influence on what we now call Romanticism. Again, Shakespeare is the exemplar: 'Among the *English*, *Shakespear* has incomparably excelled all others. That noble Extravagance of Fancy which he had in so great Perfection, thoroughly qualified him to touch this weak superstitious Part of his Reader's Imagination; and made him capable of succeeding, where he had nothing to support him besides the Strength of his own Genius.' Here, Addison is thinking of Shakespeare's 'Ghosts, Fairies, Witches and the like Imaginery Persons'; the first act of *Hamlet*, *A Midsummer Night's Dream*, *Macbeth*, and *The Tempest* thus come to be seen as his most characteristic achievements. The point had already been made in paper 279: 'It shews a greater Genius in *Shakespear* to have drawn his *Calyban*, than his *Hotspur* or *Julius Caesar*: The one was to be supplied out of his own Imagination, whereas the other might have been formed upon Tradition, History and Observation.' The originality of Shakespeare's supernatural characters, the way in which they seemed to embody the creative power of imagination, was perhaps the single most important factor in the English rejection of Neo-Classical theory. Caliban and Ariel, the fairies and the witches, are an affront to the creed of mimesis; in the second half of the eighteenth century, they will provoke the claim that 'True Poesy is *magic*, not *nature*.'[6]

We should however pause for a moment on the note of Addisonian reason in the phrase 'this weak superstitious Part of his Reader's Imagination'. While recognizing the link between imagination, genius, and the supernatural, Addison views it with an air of detachment and superiority. His own poetic works, such as the widely admired tragedy *Cato*, are in a vein of high classicism that bears none of the marks of the Shakespearean supernatural. Addison may sow the seeds of the cult of imagination, but the fruit is not born in poetic practice until the 1740s. A similar split between theory and practice may be seen in Pope. Shakespeare's originality and inspiration are extolled in Pope's Preface to his edition of the plays, and the *Essay in Criticism* asserts that

> Great Wits sometimes may *gloriously offend*,
> And *rise* to *Faults* true Criticks *dare not mend*;
> From *vulgar Bounds* with *brave Disorder* part,
> And *snatch* a *Grace* beyond the Reach of Art[7]

yet Pope's own poetry is perhaps the most artful, ordered, and 'French', the most un-Shakespearean, in the language.

The split in fact goes back to Dryden's twin roles as the father of both

English literary criticism and English Neo-Classical poetic practice. In Johnson's words, Dryden 'refined the language, improved the sentiments, and tuned the numbers of English poetry'; he instituted a poetry in which, as Thomas Warton put it, 'imagination gave way to correctness, sublimity of description to delicacy of sentiment, and majestic imagery to conceit and epigram.'[8] In crude terms, Dryden replaced Shakespearean imagination and original genius with French art and learning. Yet in his poetic theory, he could not go along with a French-style condemnation of Shakespeare for breaking the rules of art. In 1692 Thomas Rymer launched his vigorous and ruthlessly Neo-Classical attack on Shakespearean tragedy; Dryden responded by claiming that Shakespeare's genius outweighed his deficiencies:

we know, in spite of Mr R—, that genius alone is a greater virtue (if I may so call it) than all other qualifications put together. You see what success this learned critic has found in the world, after his blaspheming Shakespeare. Almost all the faults which he has discovered are truly there; yet who will read Mr Rym[er] or not read Shakespeare? For my own part, I reverence Mr Rym[er]'s learning, but I detest his ill nature and arrogance. I indeed, and such as I, have reason to be afraid of him, but Shakespeare has not.[9]

Dryden's own learning and concern for decorum lead him to acknowledge the truth of some of Rymer's claims, but his heart is with Shakespeare, as may be seen from the metaphor of blasphemy which implicitly makes the playwright into a god. Dryden also knows where the hearts of the people are: who will not read Shakespeare because of Rymer? As far as the people were concerned, Shakespeare's genius was never in question; it was what Rymer took to be the inferior judgement of the people that led to his attack on Shakespeare in the first place (he claimed that his position was a matter of aesthetic principle, but it is more likely that he had a grudge against popular judgement because his own play *Edgar, or the English Monarch* never reached the stage). Subsequent critics profited from Rymer's discomfiture: they knew that however much one demanded decorum, learning, art, the unities, and so on, English readers would retort with the example of Shakespeare. Hence the awkward juggling act performed by such English theorists as John Dennis and Charles Gildon: 'If *Shakespeare* had these great Qualities by Nature, what would he not have been if he had join'd to so happy a Genius Learning and the Poetical Art?'; 'Those scatter'd Sparks of a great *Genius*, which shou'd shine with united Glory, are in the huddle of Ignorance or want of *Art* so dissipated and divided, and so blended with Contraries, that they are extreamly obscur'd, if not entirely extinguish'd.'[10]

Dryden performs the balancing act with the greatest poise. In his *Essay of Dramatic Poesy* (1668) Shakespeare is contrasted to the more learned and classical Ben Jonson: 'I must acknowledge [Jonson] the more correct poet, but Shakespeare the greater wit. Shakespeare was the Homer, or father of our dramatic poets; Jonson was the Virgil, the pattern of elaborate writing; I admire him, but I love Shakespeare.' Dryden made the comparison between Shakespeare and Homer again in his *Discourse concerning the Original and Progress of Satire* (1693), where they are associated with 'a happy, abundant, and native genius' that is lacking in those who have only 'their wretched art'.[11] The distinction between Homer's genius and Virgil's judgement became commonplace in the eighteenth century; the opposition between Shakespeare and Jonson gradually gave way to one between Shakespeare and Milton, as the latter cast his mighty shadow over the eighteenth century.

The split between theory and practice in Dryden is seen most vividly in *All for Love*. In the preface to that play, he writes 'In my style I have professed to imitate the divine Shakespeare' who 'by the force of his own genius perform[ed] so much that in a manner he has left no praise for any who come after him'.[12] It could not be clearer that Shakespeare is the exemplar of original genius and divine inspiration; Dryden's desire to imitate him is so great that for once he disencumbers himself of rhyme. Yet when we read *All for Love* we cannot conceive it as Shakespearean: we have to concur with Leavis's judgement that 'Shakespeare's verse seems to enact its meaning, to do and to give rather than to talk about, whereas Dryden's is merely descriptive eloquence.'[13] As so often, Leavis is following T. S. Eliot, who made a comparison between *All for Love* and *Antony and Cleopatra* in a radio talk printed in *The Listener* of 22 April 1931. Eliot considers the dying words of Shakespeare's Charmian,

> It is well done, and fitting for a princess
> Descended of so many royal kings.
> Ah, soldier!
>
> (V. ii. 325–7)

and Dryden's, 'Yes, 'tis well done, and like a queen, the last / Of her great race: I follow her' (V. i. 505–6). Eliot remarks that in themselves the two lines of Dryden do not seem less poetic or less dramatic than those of Shakespeare. 'But,' he continues,

consider Shakespeare's remarkable addition to the original text of North, the two plain words, 'Ah, soldier'. You cannot say that there is anything peculiarly poetic about these two words, and if you isolate the dramatic from the poetic you cannot say that there is anything peculiarly dramatic either, because there is nothing in them for the actress to express in action; she can at best enunciate them clearly. I could not myself put into words the difference I feel between the passage if these two words, 'Ah, soldier', were omitted and with them. But I know that there is a difference, and that only Shakespeare could have made it.[14]

As Leavis is following Eliot, so Eliot is tracking the steps of Hazlitt who, with Coleridge, was among the first to see that the essence of Shakespeare's uniqueness lies in such details as this. Thus in his essay on *Antony and Cleopatra* in *Characters of Shakespear's Plays* (1817), Hazlitt writes 'Few things in Shakespear (and we know of nothing in any other author like them) have more of that local truth of imagination and character than the passage in which Cleopatra is presented conjecturing what were the employments of Antony in his absence – "He's speaking now, or murmuring – *Where's my serpent of old Nile?*" '[15] It takes a critic of genius such as Eliot or Hazlitt to see that such minutiae constitute the marks of poetic genius.

That *All for Love* is an imitation of *Antony and Cleopatra* raises a further problem. The nature of Shakespeare's genius, according to Dryden and his successors, is that it is original, not imitative. This is untrue of course: Dryden said that Shakespeare needed not the spectacles of books to read nature, but we now know that Shakespeare read nature through the spectacles of many books (Ovid's foremost among them). But it is what Dryden and his successors believed, and it is what prevented strict French Neo-Classicism from ever taking hold in England. The problem lies in the fact that if Shakespeare is an original, not an imitator, then the very act of imitating him makes one unlike him. In my book *Shakespeare and the English Romantic Imagination*,[16] I have argued that this problem was only really solved when the Romantic poets failed in their overt Shakespearean imitations and learnt instead to assimilate his language through allusion and echo. I shall not reiterate that argument here except to say that the most characteristic kind of Romantic Shakespearean allusion, one which summons up a passage in Shakespeare that is especially associated with the imagination, occurs in those poets who throw off the style of Dryden and Pope, and write in a way that, according to Addison's theory in *Spectator* 419, is more authentically English. I am thinking of the rhapsodic poets of the 1740s who rediscovered such forms as the ode, and who may be seen as the harbingers of English Romanticism. Dryden and Pope acknowledged Shakespeare's genius, but did not let it shape their poetic practice. A poet such as William Collins, on the other hand, weaves invocations to Shakespeare into his own poems:

> O more than all in powerful genius blest,
> Come, take thine empire o'er the willing breast!
> Whate'er the wounds this youthful heart shall feel,
> Thy songs support me and thy morals heal![17]

In a moment such as this, *OED*'s senses 4 and 5 of genius are coalescing with senses 1 and 2: Shakespeare is not only a creative genius, but also the presiding genius of the subsequent poet's creation. Collins's short lyrics, which exercised a significant influence on much verse written in the second half of the century, including the songs of William Blake, self-consciously invoke Shakespeare as their presiding deity: they have titles like 'A Song from *Shakespear*'s Cymbelyne' and 'Song. The Sentiments Borrowed from Shakespeare'.

The 1740s also saw the publication of such poems as Joseph Warton's *The Enthusiast: or the Lover of Nature*. The title is indicative of both the rediscovery of nature and the renewed emphasis on inspiration or enthusiasm, as opposed to art. Warton's image of Shakespeare revives and elaborates the native wood-notes of 'L'Allegro':

> What are the Lays of artful *Addison*,
> Coldly correct, to *Shakespeare*'s Warblings wild?
> Whom on the winding *Avon*'s willow'd Banks
> Fair Fancy found, and bore the smiling Babe
> To a close Cavern. (Still the Shepherds shew
> The sacred Place, whence with religious Awe
> They hear, returning from the Field at Eve,
> Strange Whisperings of sweet Music thro' the Air.)[18]

The notion that Shakespeare's inspiration has a divine origin has here led to an almost outrageous identification with Christ, achieved through the juxtaposition of shepherds and birthplace, and the equation of *The Tempest*'s music in the air with the angels heralding the Incarnation.

It is the poetic practice of the artful Addison, *Cato* especially, which Warton dismisses. As I have said, Addison's *theory* of imagination was achieving new life in the 1740s, since it was developed and made more scientific by Akenside in *The Pleasures of Imagination*. When writing of the moment of poetic creation, Akenside introduces a Shakespearean allusion that will be reiterated countless times in the following eighty years. The poet is called 'The child of Fancy': the phrase signals that Shakespeare is the exemplar, for in 'L'Allegro' Milton had famously called him 'fancy's child'. But then there is a more direct allusion:

> By degrees, the mind
> Feels her young nerves dilate: the plastic powers
> Labour for action: blind emotions heave
> His bosom; and with loveliest frenzy caught,
> From earth to heaven he rolls his daring eye,
> From heaven to earth.[19]

Akenside thus bases his image of poetic creation on Shakespeare's own:

> The poet's eye, in a fine frenzy rolling,
> Doth glance from heaven to earth, from earth to heaven;
> And as imagination bodies forth
> The forms of things unknown, the poet's pen
> Turns them to shapes, and gives to airy nothing
> A local habitation and a name.[20]

In the context of *A Midsummer Night's Dream*, this is a critique of the imagination's delusive power, but in the second half of the eighteenth century it was almost universally treated as Shakespeare's own, and therefore the authoritative, definition of poetic creativity. The influence of Akenside's allusion may be seen from a remark in John Gilbert Cooper's *Letters concerning Taste*. Cooper's book was published in 1755, the same year as Johnson's dictionary; the following quotation makes it abundantly clear that, whatever doubts the *OED* may have, the conception of genius as the special property of the poet of imagination was fully enshrined in English culture by this time:

For my Part, I am of opinion, that there is now living a Poet of the most geniune Genius this Kingdom ever produced, *SHAKESPEAR* alone excepted. By poetical Genius, I don't mean the meer talent of *making Verses*, but that glorious Enthusiasm of Soul, that *fine Frenzy*, as SHAKESPEAR calls it, *rolling from Heaven to Earth, from Earth to Heaven*, which, like an able Magician, can bring every Object of the Creation in any Shape whatever before the Reader's Eyes. This alone is Poetry, aught else is a mechanical Art of putting Syllables harmoniously together. The Gentleman I mean is Doctor AKINSIDE, the worthy Author of the *Pleasures of Imagination*, the most beautiful didactic Poem that ever adorned the English or any other Language.[21]

The simile of the magician conjuring up all the forms of creation is used by Akenside in the lines immediately following those I have quoted. It became a favourite figure for the poet's act of imaginative creation. John Gilbert Cooper also published in 1755 *The Tomb of Shakespeare. A Poetical Vision*. It is undistinguished as poetry, but its language is revealing: 'Poetic transports of the madding mind', 'plastic thought that still created new', 'the wizard's arm'.[22] The image of Shakespeare as magician, wild genius with wand in hand, was reiterated in numerous minor poems of the latter part of the century with titles like *The Grove of Fancy* (1789) and *The Genius of Shakspeare, A Summer Dream* (1793). Such poems conceive of genius as a supernatural force and embody it in such characters as Ariel, who thus become Shakespeare's 'genii' in the classical sense.

It was not only minor versifiers who gave a prominent place to the

Shakespearean supernatural. James Beattie's *The Minstrel: or, the Progress of Genius* (1771–4) was one of the most popular poems of the age – it also made a deep impression on the young Wordsworth.[23] According to the poem's preface, Beattie's design 'was to trace the progress of a Poetical Genius, born in a rude age, from the first dawnings of fancy and reason, till that period at which he may be supposed capable of appearing in the world as a Minstrel, that is, as an itinerant poet and musician; – a character which, according to the notions of our forefathers, was not only respectable, but sacred'. The poem is in the high Gothic manner, as a representative stanza will suggest:

> Various and strange was the long-winded tale;
> And halls, and knights, and feats of arms displayed;
> Or merry swains, who quaff the nut-brown ale,
> And sing enamoured of the nut-brown maid;
> The moonlight revel of the fairy glade;
> Or hags, that suckle an infernal brood,
> And ply in caves th' unutterable trade,
> 'Midst fiends and spectres, quench the moon in blood,
> Yell in the midnight storm, or ride th' infuriate flood.
>
> (Bk. i, st. 44)

Shakespeare is explicitly incorporated into this vision, for the lines 'Or hags, that suckle an infernal brood, / And ply in caves th' unutterable trade' is furnished with a footnote:

> Allusion to Shakespeare.
> *Macbeth.* How now, you secret, black, and midnight hags!
>   What is't you do?
> *Witches.* A deed without a name.
>
> *Macbeth. Act iv. Scene 1.*

Although such local effects as this are there to conjure up the Shakespearean supernatural, Beattie's stanza form is self-consciously derived from Spenser. I do not want to give the impression that Shakespeare was a lone influence: the revived vogue for Spenser at this time is also far-reaching in its effect on poetic practice. Thomas Warton's contrast between imagination and correctness, which I quoted when speaking of Dryden, was made in his *Observations on The Faerie Queene* of 1754, a book which broke new ground by undertaking the first full-length critical study of Spenser. Beattie's association of Spenser with the Gothic derives from Bishop Richard Hurd's *Letters on Chivalry and Romance*, first published in 1762, in which the structure of *The Faerie Queene* was

christened 'Gothic' and praised for the very lack of classicism which had
denied it the favour of early eighteenth-century critics. The *Letters on
Chivalry and Romance* is another work which alludes strongly to Shakespeare's
magic:

Shakespear [. . .] with a terrible sublime (which not so much the energy of his
genius, as the nature of his subject drew from him) gives us another idea of the
rough magic, as he calls it, of fairy enchantment.

> I have bedimm'd
> The noon-tide Sun, call'd forth the mutinous winds,
> And 'twixt the green sea and the azure vault
> Set roaring war [. . .][24]

Here a nexus of key terms – sublime, energy, genius – leads into a
quotation from Prospero's speech concerning his 'so potent art'. As
happens so often in Romantic allusions to *The Tempest*, Shakespeare has
become his own magician.[25]

Hurd is one of the many critics of the second half of the eighteenth
century who argues that poetry should not necessarily follow nature, that
the creative imagination may be identified more closely with the
supernatural than the natural. Here there is a marked break from the
aesthetics of the earlier eighteenth century. In the age of Pope and
Addison, Shakespeare may have prevented English critics from becoming
too bound by the Neo-Classical rules, but the fundamental classical
principle of following nature remained dominant. But by the time we
reach Hurd – or indeed John Gilbert Cooper, with his distinction between
the 'mechanical Art of putting Syllables harmoniously together' and the
poetic genius's 'glorious Enthusiasm of Soul' – a definite shift has taken
place. Shakespeare's untamed genius is no longer a slightly embarrassing
exception to classical decorums; it is now the very essence of poetry. In
Cooper's words, 'This alone is Poetry.'

The shift in emphasis accounts for *OED*'s opinion that the period
around 1750 was a turning point. But the almost universal idolatry of
Shakespeare in England throughout the eighteenth century meant that
the cult of genius ante-dated 1750 by a long way; the turning point is in
aesthetic theory, not the assumptions and habits of the reading and
theatre-going public. From the 1740s onwards, the public cult of the Bard
was intensified, mainly thanks to David Garrick, who was proclaimed
(not least by himself) as Shakespeare's high priest on earth. But Garrick
was only building on a pre-existent public taste: Shakespeare was already
the most frequently performed dramatist on the London stage. The
academy, as so often, lagged behind the populus. Hurd recognizes in his
'Notes on the Art of Poetry' (1749) that by rejecting their obsession with
art, the critics are falling in with what the public wants and, it is implied,

already believes: 'There was a time, when the art of JONSON was set above the divinest raptures of SHAKESPEARE. The present age is well convinced of the mistake. And now the genius of SHAKESPEARE is idolized in its turn. Happily for the public taste, it can scarcely be too much so.'[26] It is noteworthy in this respect that the tendency to regularize Shakespeare for the eighteenth-century stage by producing adaptations which adhered to Neo-Classical norms did not extend to three of the four plays that were the most popular in the first half of the century, *Hamlet, Othello* (despite Rymer!) and *1 Henry IV*. The exception, *Macbeth*, which was performed in a version by Sir William Davenant, owed its popularity not to the alterations that made the play more decorous – refinement of the language, excision of the porter – but to the singularly unclassical song and dance routines involving the witches.

The change that is visible in aesthetic theory may be seen from some characteristic titles: around 1700, George Granville (Lord Lansdowne) writes an essay attacking *Unnatural Flights in Poetry*, and around 1720, Charles Gildon codifies *The Laws of Poetry*; from 1750 onwards, books appear with titles like *A Dissertation upon Genius* (William Sharpe, 1755) and *Reflections on Originality in Authors* (Edward Capell, 1766). But no turning point in aesthetic theory is ever absolute. Just as the cult of originality has a life before 1750, so that of correctness survives into the second half of the century. The most famous piece of Shakespearean criticism of the age, Johnson's Preface, was published in 1765, yet it adopts the strategy of balancing merits and faults that was characteristic of earlier years. Equally, Akenside produced not only a forward-looking poem on the imagination, thick with allusions to Shakespeare's creative power, but also a 'Ballance of Poets', a league table that did not gloss over Shakespeare's faults: while the Bard scored top marks (eighteen points out of twenty) for 'Pathetic Ordonnance' and 'Dramatic' and 'Incidental' 'Expression', he only managed ten for 'Taste' and 'Versification', and failed altogether in 'Critical Ordonnance' (for which Akenside gives him nought). Akenside's balance appeared in 1746; it is symptomatic that when a similar 'Poetical Scale' was published twelve years later, a new category was introduced at the head of the list, that of 'Genius', in which Shakespeare alone attained nineteen degrees out of twenty. Akenside explained that his table was based on Roger de Piles's *'balance des peintres'*, which had lain down the rule that twenty points denoted perfection beyond the taste or knowledge of even the greatest critic, that 'The nineteenth Degree is the highest of which the human Mind has any Comprehension, but which has not yet been expressed or executed by the greatest Masters', and that eighteen was accordingly the highest mark attainable. So it was an extraordinary accolade for the 1758 'Poetical Scale' to give Shakespeare nineteen in genius.[27]

A new enthusiasm always provokes a reaction among the more measured or conservative. Thus Johnson wrote in *Rambler* 154 that 'The mental disease of the present generation' is 'a disposition to rely wholly upon unassisted genius and natural sagacity', an insufficient attention to the necessity for imitation and knowledge of the classics. Similarly, Sir Joshua Reynolds said that the purpose of his *Discourses* to the students of the Royal Academy was to caution them 'against that false opinion, but too prevalent among artists, of the imaginary powers of native genius, and its sufficiency in great works'.[28]

Perhaps the most concentrated manifesto for original genius was Edward Young's *Conjectures on Original Composition* of 1759. Dr Johnson was characteristically tetchy about this little book: 'he was surprized to find Young receive as novelties, what he [Johnson] thought very common maxims. [. . .] he believed Young was not a great scholar, nor had studied regularly the art of writing.'[29] They thought differently in Germany: there, where Young's *Night Thoughts on Life, Death, and Immortality* were already immensely popular, its concerns chimed with those of the nascent '*Sturm und Drang*' and within a year two translations had appeared. Together with other British works of the same period and tenor, such as Lord Kames's *Elements of Criticism* (1762) and John Brown's *Dissertation on the Rise* [. . .] *of Poetry and Music* (1763), the *Conjectures* played a significant role in shaping the aesthetics of Herder, and in particular his essay on Shakespeare. Johnson's reaction to Young and that of the Germans are not as divergent as they seem: both are accounted for by the pithiness of the *Conjectures*. Young achieves his effect through the establishment of rigid dichotomies: 'Learning we thank, Genius we revere; That gives us pleasure, This gives us rapture; That informs, This inspires; and is itself inspired; for genius is from heaven, learning from man'[30] (the phrases are held in balance, but genius is always given the stronger epithet; the scale is tipped through the addition of 'and is itself inspired'). Where others were beginning to produce philosophical and psychological tracts about genius, Young crystallized a number of central ideas into maxims that were at once lucid and provocative.

In Neo-Classical poetics, the imitation of ancient authors goes hand in hand with the imitation of nature; Young, in contrast, divides the two practices, confines the term imitation to the imitation of authors, and extols writers who have direct access to nature as originals. '*Originals* can arise from genius only,' he asserts (p. 34). Johnson sees both genius and learning as qualities; Young argues that 'To neglect of learning, genius sometimes owes its greater glory' (p. 29). Dennis argued that Shakespeare would have been even greater if he had added learning to his genius; for Young, he would have been diminished – 'Who knows whether *Shakespeare* might not have thought less, if he had read more?', '*Shakespeare* mingled no water with his wine, lower'd his genius by no vapid imitation' (pp. 81, 78). The *Conjectures*, predictably enough, end with a critique of the frigidity of Addison's artful *Cato*.

Young's metaphors include that of the magician: 'A *Genius* differs from a *good understanding*, as a magician from a good architect; *that* raises his structure by means invisible; *this* by the skilful use of common tools. Hence Genius has ever been supposed to partake of something Divine. *Nemo unquam vir magnus fuit, sine aliquo afflatu divino.*' (pp. 26–7). The allusion to the ancient idea of divine afflatus serves to remind us that the mid-eighteenth century view of genius is by no means new; what is happening is, that of the two very different concepts of poetry bequeathed to the modern world by the ancients – *imitatio* and *inspiratio* (*furor*) – the second is now pre-eminent.

A more novel figure than those of magic and divine inspiration is the following: 'An *Original* may said to be of a *vegetable* nature; it rises spontaneously from the vital root of Genius; it *grows*, it is not *made*: *Imitations* are often a sort of *manufacture* wrought up by those *mechanics, art,* and *labour*, out of pre-existent materials not their own.' (p. 12). It was common in eighteenth-century scientific writing to describe the growth of organisms as spontaneous, but this is the earliest passage I know to use the word 'spontaneously' in the context of poetic production; it is a significant foreshadowing of Wordsworth's famous 'all good poetry is the spontaneous overflow of powerful feelings.' The denigration of mechanical art is commonplace (we saw it in Cooper); the notion that works of art have an organic form has a long history in the Neoplatonic tradition; Young's innovation is in putting the two ideas together. His sharp distinction between organic and mechanic anticipates the principle that will shape the aesthetics of Coleridge and Schlegel. Via aestheticians such as J. G. Sulzer, Young's metaphor was absorbed into the German tradition, where organicism was a central concern of Herder, Kant and many others. The concept was thus sophisticated and generalized until it received its clearest and fullest statement in A. W. Schlegel's lectures, from which Coleridge reimported it into England in the famous formulation:

The form is mechanic when on any given material we impress a pre-determined form, not necessarily arising out of the properties of the material, as when to a mass of wet clay we give whatever shape we wish it to retain when hardened. The organic form, on the other hand, is innate; it shapes as it develops itself from within, and the fullness of its development is one and the same with the perfection of its outward form. Such is the life, such the form. Nature, the prime genial artist, inexhaustible in diverse powers, is equally inexhaustible in forms.[31]

One must not overlook the importance of Shakespeare and genius to this formulation: its context is a discussion of the relationship between genius

and rules which turns on a confutation of Voltaire's abuse of Shakespeare
for not obeying the Neo-Classical unities and decorums ('genial' is,
incidentally, a key Coleridgean word, for 'genial spirits' is a vital
Wordsworthian/Miltonic allusion in his poetry and 'The Principles of
Genial Criticism' a central statement of his aesthetics[32]).

One should not make excessive claims for Young: where he is making a
specific distinction between original and imitated works, Schlegel and
Coleridge introduce the terms mechanic and organic as part of a much
more sophisticated theory of the process of artistic creation. Thus for
Young 'pre-existent materials' mean simply previous books, whereas for
Coleridge 'pre-determined form' means all that is perceived by the senses
as opposed to that which is created anew by the esemplasic power of
imagination – the Coleridgean distinction is closely related to that
between the living, unifying imagination and the mechanical associations
of the fancy. Nor indeed is Young's praise of Shakespeare as unequivocal
as Coleridge's: towards the end of the *Conjectures* the phrase 'in spite of all
his faults' (p. 78) is slipped in, as it never would be in high-Romantic
criticism.

Contemporaneously with Young's *Conjectures*, Scottish Enlightenment
aestheticians were developing a detailed account of the intimate relationship between Shakespeare, genius, and imagination, that nexus of
concerns which was so fundamental to Romanticism. A section in
Alexander Gerard's *Essay on Taste*, also published in 1759, considers 'the
connexion of Taste with Genius'. Gerard argues that 'comprehensiveness
of imagination' is the 'first and leading quality of genius'.[33] For an account
of the operation of genius, he refers the reader to the third book of
Akenside's *Pleasures of Imagination*. In 1758 and 1759 Gerard was working
on a full-length account of genius, which he eventually completed and
published in 1774 with the title *An Essay on Genius*. Together with William
Duff's *Essay on Original Genius* (1767), it exercised a formative influence on
Romanticism largely by way of its popularity in Germany. Gerard's
theory of genius shaped Johann Nicolaus Tetens's theory of *Dichtkraft*;
Tetens's theory of *Dichtkraft* shaped Coleridge's theory of the secondary
imagination.[34] There could be no more vivid example of the movement
from the Scottish Enlightenment to the German '*Sturm und Drang*' to
English Romanticism. Why was Gerard so popular in Germany? An
answer is provided by a very revealing remark about the *Essay on Genius* in
the *Allgemeine deutsche Bibliothek*: 'A splendid book! The gist of this: genius
expresses itself most conspicuously in invention, which is caused by the
imagination, and this in turn depends on the association of ideas [. . .] this
work is a major achievement. Most of the examples are cited from
Shakespeare.' James Engell cites this in his book on *The Creative
Imagination*, and comments, 'Gerard's use of literary authorities was well

accepted, but it was examples from Shakespeare that proved irresistible.'[35]

For Gerard, genius comes from within, not without; it is a power of the mind, not a divine agency. He asserts that 'GENIUS is properly the faculty of *invention*'[36] (by invention he means what we mean by creativity), and asks what power of mind gives a man this faculty – sense, memory, imagination, or judgement? Imagination, he concludes, is the key, though judgement may assist in the completion and ordering of what is invented. Early in the book, it is asserted that Shakespeare's genius places him at the head of the modern poets, although he has as great faults as beauties; his genius is greater than Milton's because of 'the superiority of his invention' (p. 13). The faults of which Gerard speaks are ascribed to Shakespeare's lack of judgement – this is another example of how a seemingly 'Romantic' emphasis on imagination and genius coexists with characteristically eighteenth-century reservations about Shakespeare's indecorums.

For Gerard, then, genius arises from imagination. How does imagination work? Through association: this principle is elaborated in part two of the *Essay*, in chapters with such titles as 'Of the Sources of the Varieties of Genius in the Imagination', 'Of the Influence of the Passions on Association', and 'Of the Predominance of the associating Principles'. It is in these chapters that the case is argued by means of examples from Shakespeare. The chapter on the passions adduces a wide selection of the plays in its examination of how the mind moves under the stress of extreme emotion; then in the analysis of the process of association the language of Mistress Quickly in *Henry IV Part II* and Pompey in *Measure for Measure* is used as primary evidence.[37] Shakespeare's centrality to Gerard's *Essay* is only diminished in part three, which is more concerned with the difference between genius in the sciences and the fine arts.

Duff's *Essay on Original Genius* [. . .] *in Philosophy and the Fine Arts, Particularly in Poetry* is less psychologically sophisticated than Gerard's *Essay*, but more rhapsodic in its claim that poetic originality is the highest form of genius. Duff also sees the plastic, associating imagination as the essential prerequisite of genius; like many before him, he links original genius with the supernatural, and gives Shakespeare supreme position because he is the 'only *English* writer, who with amazing boldness has ventured to burst the barriers of a separate state, and disclose the land of Apparitions, Shadows, and Dreams'.[38] But along with praise for this mark of extraordinary creative genius, goes the criticism that the ruling character of all Shakespeare's compositions is 'An IRREGULAR GREATNESS, WILDNESS, and ENTHUSIASM of Imagination' (p. 162). Most of this is conventional eighteenth-century stuff, but the recurring emphasis on imagination marks Duff out as another precursor of 'Romanticism': a remark like the following smacks to us of Coleridge,

'Imagination is that faculty whereby the mind not only reflects on its own operations, but which assembles the various ideas conveyed to the understanding by the canal of sensation' (p. 6). All that was needed subsequently was the removal of terms such as 'irregular' and the claim that Shakespeare lacked judgement. This development finally took place in the criticism of Schlegel and, above all, in that of Coleridge, where for the first time – thanks to the theory of organic form – the true unity of Shakespeare's plays was demonstrated.

We come here to a paradox. The increasing emphasis on genius as the essence of poetry was fundamental to the rejection of neo-classicism, but too often the criterion of genius was used as an evasion of analysis; it is symptomatic that many eighteenth-century critics found themselves appealing to the *je ne sais quoi* in poetry.[39] In a notebook entry, which T. M. Raysor helpfully entitles 'Shakespeare's Judgment Equal to his Genius', Coleridge castigates such phrases as Duff's 'irregular greatness, wildness, and enthusiasm':

to talk of Shakespeare as a sort of beautiful *lusus naturae*, a delightful monster, – wild, indeed, without taste or judgement, but like the inspired idiots so much venerated in the East, uttering, amid the strangest follies, the sublimest truths. In nine places out of ten in which I find his awful name mentioned, it is with some epithet of 'wild,' 'irregular,' 'pure child of nature,' etc., etc., etc. If all this be true, we must submit to it [. . .] But if false, it is a dangerous falsehood; for it affords a refuge to secret self-conceit, – enables a vain man at once to escape his reader's indignation by general swoln panegyrics on Shakespeare, merely by his *ipse dixit* to treat what he has not intellect enough to comprehend, or soul to feel, as contemptible, without assigning any reason, or referring his opinion to any demonstrated principle.[40]

It is harsh but by no means unfair to accuse some of the Neo-Classical critics of trying to escape their reader's indignation 'by general swoln panegyrics on Shakespeare'. Romantic Shakespearean criticism was new – and remains alive, where so many eighteenth-century essays on the plays now seem dead – because it was simultaneously rhapsodic and analytical. Coleridge and Hazlitt had both the intellect to comprehend and the soul to feel the greatness of Shakespeare; they are the first to track in detail the emotional and poetic movement, the ebb and flow of feeling, that is the fundamental organizing principle of the Shakespearean drama. Paradoxically, the Romantic innovation was to extol not Shakespeare's genius but his art.

This ceases to be a paradox if it is recognized, as the best eighteenth-century critics did recognize, that genius and art are not opposing qualities. It is only false conceptions of art and of originality that lead them to be seen as opposites. True art arises from within, not from the imposition of predetermined rules or forms. Gerard made an advance by proposing that the essense of artistic achievement was genius, not in a vague sense but as a specific though unconscious power of the imagination. Coleridge, synthesizing Tetens (who had learnt from Gerard), Schelling, Kant, and Schlegel, saw the imagination as an organic unifying power. Shakespeare was re-created as both genius and artist, working consciously by a power that is deeper than consciousness.

As for the question of originality, Duff is instructively wrong. His concern for originality led him to publish a sequel to his *Essay* entitled *Critical Observations on the Writings of the Most Celebrated Original Geniuses in Poetry* (1770), in which he claimed that the only three complete original geniuses were Homer, Ossian, and Shakespeare. They are given this status primarily because they are seen as self-originating: Duff takes 'originality' in the sense of 'coming first' to be the ultimate imprimatur of creative originality and hence genius. His position is essentially a primitivist one, arising in large measure from the vogue in the 1760s for James Macpherson's 'translations' of the legendary Gaelic bard Ossian. But this kind of originality does not exist in art: every work depends on prior works and the prior expectations of its audience. Duff's great originals are not originals in his sense: Homer had his predecessors, indeed, Homer may even have *been* his predecessors, if we accept that he was a tradition, not an individual; Ossian can hardly be called an original since he was constructed in the eighteenth century; and Shakespeare's genius did not spring 'out of nature's hand, as *Pallas* out of *Jove*'s head, at full growth, and mature'.[41] Coleridge said that genius may be seen in 'various excellences of translation, selection, and arrangement';[42] modern scholarship has shown that Shakespeare's art depended on the assimilation and refashioning of inherited literary and dramatic traditions.

I do not want to make claims for Coleridge at the expense of eighteenth-century critics; not all of them sloppily invoke 'genius' and 'originality' as qualities that defy analysis. A critic such as Bishop Hurd can be impressively scrupulous, as in the following passage from his 'Dissertation on Poetical Imitation' of 1751, where he is comparing Romeo's

> Look, love, what envious streaks
> Do lace the severing clouds in yonder east.
> Night's candles are burnt out, and jocund day
> Stands tiptoe on the misty mountain tops.
> (III. v. 7–10)

to analogous images in Homer and Virgil:

The reader, no doubt, pronounces on first sight, this description to be *original*. But why? There is no part of it, which may not be traced in other poets. [. . .] the last *image*, which strikes most, is not essentially different from that of Virgil and Homer. [. . .] But the difference lies here. Homer's *expression* of this *impatience* is *general*, *ΩPNYΘ*. So is Virgil's, and, as the occasion required, with less energy, SURGEBAT. Shakespeare's is *particular*: that impatience is set before us, and pictured to the eye in the circumstance of *standing tiptoe* [. . .] This, it must be owned, is one of the surest characteristics of real genius. And if we find it generally in a writer, we may almost venture to esteem him *original* without further scruple.[43]

This analysis should serve to remind us that while the term 'practical criticism' was invented by Coleridge, the technique was practised in the eighteenth century – just as it was practised by Longinus – as a method of making value judgments and determining the precise qualities of genius and originality.

Genius became a Romantic obsession because it was a conception that seemed to guarantee individuality. It is, in Thomas McFarland's words, 'an analogue of the unduplicatibility, always hoped for even if only precariously real, of the individual'.[44] Hamlet may be the archetype of the individual consciousness, but Shakespeare was not Hamlet. If anything, he was the archetype of communality, not individuality. He lived – and lives – in a communality of artists (or, in Hazlitt's term, among an 'aristocracy of letters'). By 'Shakespeare' we mean not an individual, but a body of work, and that body was shaped by many individuals – by Ovid and Shakespeare's other literary precursors, by Marlowe and his other dramatic precursors, by the actors of his company, by the audience without whom no play can be completed. Furthermore, the very value of 'Shakespeare' is that he cannot be restricted to William Shakespeare's lifetime. He is, as his friend Jonson knew, 'Not of an age, but for all time': his communality extends to his *Nachleben*, his place in later cultural life, his influence on the lives of subsequent readers, writers, and playgoers, his status as national poet. He forces the word genius back to its origins, to the idea of a tutelar deity: he presides over both our national identity and our conception of what literature is. Shakespeare has become 'the Genius of our Isle'. He has also become not the artless genius but the genius of art.

Notes

1 See further, in addition to the chapters flanking this one, K. Simonsuuri, *Homer's Original Genius: Eighteenth-century Notions of the Early Greek Epic (1688–1798)* (Cambridge, 1979), and for Germany, Günter Peters, *Der zerrissene Engel: Genieästhetik und literarische Selbstdarstellung im achtzehnten Jahrhundert* (Stuttgart, 1982) and Wendelin Schmidt-Dengler, *Genius: Zur Wirkungsgeschichte antiker*

Mythologeme in der Goethezeit (München, 1978). For early eighteenth-century views on the originality of the divine poetry of Cowley and his successors, see chapter 1 of Patricia Phillips, *The Adventurous Muse: Theories of Originality in English Poetics 1650–1760* (Uppsala, 1984).

2 *A Dictionary of the English Language* (London, 1755), sig. b2ᵛ.

3 *The Spectator* is quoted from the edition of D. F. Bond (5 vols, Oxford, 1965).

4 Quoted from Brian Vickers (ed.), *Shakespeare: The Critical Heritage 1623–1801* (6 vols, London and Boston, 1974–81), vol. ii, p. 215.

5 *An Epistle to Mr Southerne*, Vickers, *Shakespeare: Critical Heritage*, vol. ii, p. 265.

6 Maurice Morgann, *An Essay on the Dramatic Character of Sir John Falstaff* (London, 1777), p. 71.

7 Pope, *An Essay on Criticism* (London, 1711), lines 152–5.

8 Johnson, 'Dryden', *Lives of the English Poets* (1779–81, repr., 2 vols, London, 1906), vol. i, p. 305; T. Warton, *Observations on the Faerie Queene* (London, 1754), quoted from 2nd edn (2 vols, London, 1762) vol. ii, p. 111.

9 Dryden, 'Letter to John Dennis', *Of Dramatic Poesy and other Critical Essays*, ed. George Watson (2 vols, London, 1962), vol. ii, p. 178.

10 J. Dennis, *An Essay upon the Genius and Writings of Shakespeare* (1712), Vickers, *Shakespeare: Critical Heritage*, vol. ii, p. 283; C. Gildon, *The Complete Art of Poetry* (1718), Vickers, *Shakespeare: Critical Heritage*, vol. ii, pp. 322–3.

11 Dryden, *Of Dramatic Poesy*, ed. Watson, vol. i, p. 70; *Discourse concerning Satire*, in Dryden, *Of Dramatic Poesy*, ed. Watson, vol. ii, p. 74.

12 Dryden, *Of Dramatic Poesy*, ed. Watson, vol. i, p. 231. The word 'force', with its suggestions of superhuman strength and perhaps of a divine force that takes over the poet, frequently recurs in discussions of Shakespeare's original genius.

13 F. R. Leavis, *'Antony and Cleopatra* and *All for Love'*, in *The Living Principle: 'English' as a Discipline of Thought* (London, 1975), p. 146.

14 T. S. Eliot, 'Dryden the Dramatist', *The Listener* (22 April 1931), p. 681.

15 *The Complete Works of William Hazlitt*, ed. P. P. Howe (21 vols, London, 1930–4), vol. iv, p. 229.

16 Jonathan Bate, *Shakespeare and the English Romantic Imagination* (Oxford, 1986).

17 *Verses Humbly Address'd to Sir Thomas Hanmer. On his Edition of Shakespear's Works* (1743), 2nd edn (1744), lines 101–4, quoted from Roger Lonsdale (ed.), *The Poems of Gray, Collins, and Goldsmith* (London, 1969).

18 Joseph Warton, *The Enthusiast*, lines 168–75, in Vickers, *Shakespeare: Critical Heritage*, vol. iii, p. 121.

19 Akenside, *The Pleasures of Imagination* (1744), bk iii, lines 380–5, quoted from *The Poetical Works of Mark Akenside* (London, 1845).

20 *A Midsummer Night's Dream*, V. i. 12–17. Shakespeare is quoted from the New Arden edition.

21 J. G. Cooper, *Letters concerning Taste* (London, 1755), p. 101. I owe this reference to Jeremy Maule.

22 J. G. Cooper, *The Tomb of Shakspeare*, lines 39, 44, 56, in Vickers, *Shakespeare: Critical Heritage*, vol. iv, p. 179.

23 'Its success was complete. The voice of every critic was loud in its praise; and before the Second Book appeared (in 1774), four editions of the First had been dispersed throughout the kingdom': Alexander Dyce, in his 'Memoir of

Beattie' in *The Poetical Works of James Beattie* (London, n. d.; I quote the poem from this, the Aldine edition). The influence of *The Minstrel* on the Gothic is apparent from its frequent contributions to Mrs Radcliffe's chapter epigraphs in *The Mysteries of Udolpho* (1794) and to the language of Wordsworth's early poem, *The Vale of Esthwaithe* (1787).

24 R. Hurd, *Letters on Chivalry and Romance* (London, 1762), letter vi, pp. 50–1. The quotation is from *The Tempest* V. i. 41ff.

25 Dryden seems to prefigure this identification in the prologue to *The Enchanted Island* (1670, his and Davenant's adaptation of *The Tempest*): 'But Shakespeare's magic could not copied be, / Within that circle none durst walk but he' (Dryden, *Of Dramatic Poesy*, ed. Watson, vol. i, p. 136).

26 Hurd, 'Notes on the Art of Poetry', in Vickers, *Shakespeare: Critical Heritage*, vol. iii, p. 364.

27 Akenside's 'Ballance' appeared in *The Museum*, 6 December 1746, and the anonymous 'Scale' in *The Literary Magazine*, 3 January 1758, and *The London Chronicle*, 4–7 February 1758; both are reproduced in Vickers, *Shakespeare: Critical Heritage*, vol. iii, pp. 186–90, vol. iv, pp. 326–7.

28 *The Discourses of Sir Joshua Reynolds* (London, repr. 1907), Discourse vi (1774) p. 89.

29 James Boswell, *The Journal of a Tour to the Hebrides with Samuel Johnson* (London, 1785), entry for Thursday, 30th September.

30 Edward Young, *Conjectures on Original Composition* (London, 1759), pp. 36–7. Subsequent page references given in text.

31 S. T. Coleridge, *Shakespearean Criticism*, ed. T. M. Raysor, 2nd edn (2 vols, London, 1960), vol. i, p. 198.

32 For 'genial spirits' see Milton, *Samson Agonistes*, line 594, Wordsworth, 'Tintern Abbey', line 113, Coleridge, 'Dejection: an Ode', line 39; the essays 'On the Principles of Genial Criticism Concerning the Fine Arts' are repr. in S. T. Coleridge, *Biographia Literaria*, ed. John Shawcross (2 vols, Oxford, 1907).

33 *An Essay on Taste* (London, 1759), p. 173. For an eighteenth-century reader, the phrase 'comprehensiveness of imagination' might well have suggested Dryden's famous remark, reiterated in Johnson's Preface, that 'of all modern, and perhaps ancient poets' Shakespeare 'had the largest and most comprehensive soul' (Dryden, *Of Dramatic Poesy*, ed. Watson, vol. i, p. 67).

34 See Thomas McFarland, 'The Origin and Significance of Coleridge's Theory of Secondary Imagination', in *New Perspectives on Coleridge and Wordsworth*, ed. Geoffrey Hartman (New York, 1972), repr. in McFarland, *Originality and Imagination* (Baltimore, 1985), and James Engell, *The Creative Imagination: Enlightenment to Romanticism* (Cambridge, Mass., 1981), pp. 119–28.

35 Engell, *The Creative Imagination*, p. 128.

36 Alexander Gerard, *An Essay on Genius* (London, 1774), p. 8.

37 Gerard acknowledges his debt to a similar account of Mistress Quickly's associations in Lord Kames's *Elements of Criticism* (Edinburgh, 1762).

38 William Duff, *An Essay on Original Genius* (London, 1767), p. 141.

39 For 'Le je ne sais quoi', see M. H. Abrams, *The Mirror and the Lamp: Romantic Theory and the Critical Tradition* (New York, 1953, repr. 1971), pp. 193–5.

40 Coleridge, *Shakespearian Criticism*, vol. i, pp. 194–5.

40 Young, *Conjectures*, pp. 31–2.

41 *Biographia Literaria*, ed. James Engell and W. Jackson Bate (2 vols, Princeton, 1983), vol. i, p. 60 n.

43 Hurd, *Q. Horatii Flacci Epistolae ad Pisones, et Augustum* [. . .] *to which are added Critical Dissertations* (1751), quoted from 5th edn (3 vols, London, 1776), vol. iii, pp. 18–19.

44 McFarland, 'The Originality Paradox', in *Originality and Imagination*, p. 5.

5
Goethe on Genius

Michael Beddow

In mid-eighteenth-century England the idea of genius served two distinct functions. It allowed traditionalists to accommodate the phenomenon of Shakespeare without prejudice to Neo-Classical orthodoxy; and it gave innovators a stick with which to beat that same Neo-Classicism. The first function is found in Addison's well-known 160th number of the *Spectator*, the second in Young's *Conjectures on Original Composition*. Addison tries to concede the achievements of 'natural genius' in Shakespeare, Homer, Pindar and the Old Testament poets without subverting the Neo-Classical ideal of 'artful genius' whose representatives have 'formed themselves by rules, and submitted the greatness of their natural talents to the corrections and restraints of art'.[1] Young performs that very subversion by abandoning the balancing act. Denying that genius has any connection with artfulness, he makes Addison's special case of 'natural genius' into the exclusive paradigm. 'Genius is knowledge innate, and quite our own:'[2] shape and order in art stem from intuitive processes, so the products of genius are radically unlike artefacts made by employing acquired skills in purposive activity.

Both these positions were part of an established critical discourse engaging with a living literary tradition. But in contemporary Germany things were different. The chief critical topic was the absence of a native literary culture and the prospects of creating one. There was a consensus that something was seriously amiss in German cultural life and a general longing, sustained by underlying social and political aspirations, for a German national literature. 'German' in this instance meant a literature in the language of the middle class, as opposed to the francophone culture of the dominant German nobility; and 'national' meant works that would assert the cultural unity of all German-speakers, despite the political division of the nation into numerous sovereign statelets.[3] Alongside the widespread agreement that something needed to be done was an equally general conviction that creating a national literature was a feasible task: it was simply a matter of identifying appropriate measures and carrying them out. But here the agreement broke down, as different conceptions of just what needed to be done were promoted.

Beginning in the early 1730s, Gottsched in Leipzig advocated the imitation of Neo-Classical French drama. He was soon in contention with the Swiss thoreticians Bodmer and Breitinger, whose recipe was to build the regeneration of German literature around a religious verse epic, taking Milton as a model. As the second half of the century began, Lessing came forward, agreeing with Gottsched that the stage must be the medium for the new literature, but passionately condemning his predecessor's advocacy of French Neo-Classical models. Instead, he ostensibly offered Shakespeare as a paradigm closer to the spirit of German culture, though in fact he drew upon elements in the theatre of contemporary France, particularly the work of Diderot, which were English only in so far as they bore the stamp of Richardson's impact on plot and character and theme.

So far these rival panaceas shared an assumption that the key to cultural renewal lay in imitation of one sort or another, and it was here that Young's *Conjectures*, as read first by Hamann then by his disciple Herder, held out a radically different approach. From Young, Herder derived a programme for establishing a German national literature which made assimilation of a foreign model not only unnecessary but actually harmful, so that the advocates of such models could be blamed for the failure of their own attempts to foster national culture. Herder pointed to the poetry of the Old Testament, to Homer, Pindar, Shakespeare (and, of course, Ossian) not as models to imitate but as instances of what emerged when all imitation was shunned. All these examples of original genius had, according to Herder, an uncultured directness: they were natural, untutored expressions of strong feeling. Herder exhorted his fellow-countrymen to abandon attempts at copying foreign achievements, to set aside social and literary conventions, and speak directly from the heart. Herder believed that if the constraints of alien models and stultifying artfulness could be broken, the resulting intense self-expression would regenerate German literature at a stroke. Fearlessly be yourself, Herder proclaimed (where being yourself included being a proud member of your own nation, Herder's most distinctive addition to the notion of original genius) and everything you and your national culture needed would be given unto you in spontaneous utterance, expressing and inspiring fervent enthusiasm. Instead of a pedagogical programme, Herder offered a messianic hope, full of anxious expectation of the original genius who would have the strength of character and will to break through the stultifying bonds of an effete tradition. And Herder found his cultural Messiah in Goethe.

Herder and Goethe met in 1770, when Goethe was a 21-year old law student at the University of Strasbourg who had written a few witty but highly conventional poems. Herder opened Goethe's ears to the power of folk poetry, encouraged him to look in Homer, Shakespeare and the Bible for instances of powerful, apparently unsophisticated expression of intense experience, and to collect folk-songs in the Alsace countryside. For a while, Goethe became an uncritical devotee of Herder's theories, and an equally uncritical imitator of his turgidly rhapsodic prose style. But much more importantly, Herder's praise of original genius and its implications for what was involved in being a poet led Goethe to discover his true talent and find his own poetic voice: in a radically new kind of poetry, he began that creation of a native literary tradition which all the efforts of well-meaning theoreticians had failed to get under way. The first theoretical expression of Goethe's allegiance to Herder's manner and views comes in his essay *On German Architecture* (XIII, 16–26),[4] first published anonymously in November 1772, but probably written, at least in part, in the preceding year, at the same time as the earliest of Goethe's first distinctive lyric poems. It praises original genius in the guise of the architect of Strasbourg cathedral, presented as a supreme example of art arising from the German national soul. Gothic architecture, castigated by Neo-Classical critics as evidence of Teutonic uncouthness, was now appropriated with pride as a manifestation of truly German virtues. Looking back to this piece many years later in his autobiography, Goethe regretted that, 'seduced by the example of Hamann and Herder', he enveloped his thoughts 'in a dustcloud of strange words and phrases, obscuring, to myself and to others, the light that had dawned on me' (X, 556–7). But it was not just Herder's manner that Goethe had adopted. It would be hard to find anything in this essay that Herder himself could not also have said. General principles and artistic traditions, Goethe proclaims, are not only irrelevant, but actually inimical to genius: they 'kill off people of genuine feeling' and 'shackle every power of knowledge and activity' (XIII, 18–19). True art arises from 'intense, unique, individual, spontaneous feeling', which is 'unconcerned about, indeed ignorant of everything alien', and for that very reason is 'whole and vital' and compelling in its effects (XIII, 24). 'German' (i.e. Gothic) architecture and the architecture of the ancient world were both original and 'characteristic' expressions of a national spirit: 'foreign' architecture (and '*welsch*', the word for 'foreign' Goethe uses here, implies, above all, French) is bad because it tries to imitate antiquity without having the courage to be itself.

But it is not just its status as a piece of 'characteristic' national self-expression that identifies Strasbourg cathedral as a work of genius in Goethe's eyes. As well as being 'characteristic' it is also unified. It is this intuited unity which Goethe identifies as the principal hallmark of the work of genius, accounting for the immediate hold which he says the cathedral gained over him the moment he saw it. 'One vast entire impression filled my soul, which, consisting as it did of a thousand harmonizing details, I could indeed savour and enjoy, but which I could not grasp and explain' (XIII, 21). That sentence contains a distinctive argument, or rather refusal of argument, which Goethe's early writings on the subject of genius share with Herder's. From Young, Herder and Goethe derived the belief that true artistic creation was natural, not just because it required no conscious cultivation, but because it partook of Nature's orderliness. Anticipating the Neo-Classical reproof that only conscious, rational organization can impose order upon the works of the imagination, the advocates of original genius claim that the creative imagination is in itself imbued with organizing principles which are spontaneously embodied in its products. However, if we expect some demonstration of what this intrinsic order looks like, we find ourselves fobbed off with a non sequitur. Obviously, form which obeys Neo-Classical canons can readily be identified and described. But it does not follow that form created without conscious artifice necessarily defies description and analysis. The Goethe of these early essays, however, not only assumes but stridently asserts that the formal unity of works of genius can only be apprehended by spontaneous intuition, and makes the alleged ineffability of the formal achievement the index of its worth.[5]

In Goethe's critical writings of this early period rhetorical assertions of emotional response accompany a militant refusal to demonstrate what is rhapsodically claimed. In an essay dating from around 1775, for instance, Geothe returns to the claim that works of genius are characterized by what he calls 'inner form', which he says 'cannot be tangibly grasped, but has to be felt' (XIII, 47–8). The term 'inner form' itself may well come from the aesthetics of Shaftesbury, which Herder also knew and recommended to Goethe. But the association of the genesis and perception of such inner form with the highest pitch of emotional intensity is some way from Shaftesbury's polite urbanity; it is also far from the Aristotelian origins of the notion, for the features of living organisms which led Aristotle to attribute an entelechy to them can be very readily specified and described. Goethe is here continuing the aggressive irrationalism of Young, Hamann and Herder. Such writing had inspirational value to Goethe's contemporaries, but programmatically refusing to ground its enthusiasm, it offers little enlightenment about the nature of genius.

As a theoretician on the subject of genius, the younger Goethe would be of scant interest; his true claim on our attention lies in his emergence, in his contemporaneous creative writings, as the embodiment of the understanding of genius he had assimilated. When Goethe, under Herder's tutelage, began to find his own poetic voice, it could also be called the voice of his nation in the sense that it brought out and extended, for the first time since Luther's Bible translations, the full expressive power of the ordinary German language, unembellished by virtuoso artfulness, rhetorical tropes or ostentatiously learned trappings. Goethe's lyric poems of the first half of the 1770s celebrating love and nature are in truth no more artless than his first drama *Götz von Berlichingen*, which Goethe first wrote in 1771 and then reworked for the revealing reason that his first version was insufficiently spontaneous. They are built around a variety of formal devices which are by no means as indescribable as Goethe the essayist would have claimed, though they owe little or nothing to the standard poetic repertoire of the day. Alongside the love and nature lyrics we find Goethe in the early and mid-1770s writing a series of poems which express his sense of newly unleashed creativity through a series of personae. In *Prometheus* (I, 320–1), the genius as Titan vaunts his autonomous creativity and scorns Zeus's claims to homage, which are heeded only by children, fools and beggars. In *Ganymed* (I, 322) the genius as loving worshipper of Nature abandons himself ecstatically to the embrace of a very different Zeus, imagined now as the immanent divinity within a pantheistically conceived universe. And in a song of praise of Mohammed ('*Mahomets-Gesang*' I, 304–5), which, like the Prometheus poem, was at one stage meant to be part of a drama, the genius as charismatic leader is compared to a mighty river who draws out the potential of the lesser streams, joining their flow with his as he sweeps them on to the all-embracing ocean which is his origin and goal, another metaphor for the immanent divine power which these poems suggest is the driving power behind all creativity, natural or artistic. In other poems of this period, Goethe dons the persona of a painter who sets his private sense of vibrant creativity against the carpings of critics and the philistinism of patrons. In particular, a poem addressed to *Connoisseurs and Art-lovers* (I, 389) expresses the artist's sense of superiority precisely over those who share his sense of nature's vibrant warmth and his joy in great art; for they lack the 'love-filled creator's power' within him, and their response to beauty does not issue in the 'throbbing in the finger-tips' which draws him on to new creation of his own. But Goethe also speaks without adopting such personae, above all in the would-be Pindaric ode 'Wanderer's Storm-Song' (I, 313–17) which sings of the genius's struggle to keep his inner fire of creativity alight in the rain and mud of a spiritually phlegmatic age.[6]

In 1773, Goethe published his revised, more 'spontaneous' version of *Götz von Berlichingen*, a programmatically anti-Neo-Classical drama presenting a panorama of German life in the first quarter of the sixteenth century, loosely built around the life and death of Götz, a teutonic robber-baron with a hand of iron, heart of gold, and a turn of phrase so robust that in later revisions Goethe censored his own text. More than anything else, this play was responsible for unleashing the *Sturm und Drang* movement, a modish cult of original genius which, to Goethe's increasing embarrassment, seemed to spend itself largely in anarchic behaviour, philistine-baiting and the writing of raucous and barely stageable dramas. The following year, 1774, saw the writing and publication of the *Sorrows of Young Werther*, whose central character can be seen as yet another persona through whom Goethe explored a particular partial aspect of genius. Werther himself espouses the cult of spontaneity in all things, inseparable from the notion of original genius. But what makes the novel cast a fascinating light on Goethe's view of original genius is the simple fact that this eschewal of all prudence or rationality does Werther to death. In this essential respect, *Werther* shows Goethe already moving away from Herder, for whom truly natural feeling, consistently cultivated, could neither do nor suffer any genuine harm.

Before Werther encounters Lotte and embarks on the romance which held so much of eighteenth-century Europe in its grip, he writes a number of letters which establish Lotte and his love for her as the occasion rather than the cause of his downfall. The root cause is the particular quality of his sensibility. One of these introductory letters shows Werther passing through a remarkable sequence of emotions. It begins with an expression of serene joy and ends on a note of near despair. And the pivot between these extremes is the point at which intense sensibility is not matched by expressive creativity, where Werther realizes that he cannot give adequate expression to the range and intensity of his feelings. The initial serene joy Werther ascribes to an ecstatic sense of communion with a divinity at the heart of nature. 'I am so happy,' he tells his correspondent, 'so utterly immersed in the sensation of peaceful existence, that my art is suffering. At this moment I could not draw at all, not a single stroke, and yet I have never been a greater painter than at moments like this' (IV, 270). Goethe's first readers would have recognized here an allusion to a much-discussed passage from Lessing's *Emilia Galotti*, the play which, we are told, enigmatically, is open on Werther's desk when he shoots himself. These remarks show Werther initially identifying artistic sensibility with simple receptivity to nature. But then Werther goes on to see his inability to do expressive justice to what he feels, not as evidence of artistic discrimination, but as an affliction, almost an existential threat. 'Oh,' he says, 'if only you could express all this, could breathe on to paper the full, warm life within you, creating there a mirror of your soul, just as your soul is the mirror of the infinite godhead!' (IV, 271). He finds he cannot pass from receptivity to creativity, and the consequence, as he puts it in an abrupt change of emotional direction before the letter breaks off, is that he is being destroyed – *'ich gehe darüber zu Grunde'* – he is being 'overwhelmed by the force of the splendour of all these manifestations'. Intensity of spontaneous feeling here figures as a threat to the stability and integrity of the self, a threat that could be warded off only by channelling sensibility into creativity, a creativity which Werther either does not possess or fails to exercise.

Whether Werther's lack of creativity is meant as a culpable failing or a fateful defect, there is a clear suggestion that sensibility and creativity are not unproblematically part of a single benign process. Creativity appears to be the conscious self's defence against the overwhelming and essentially alien power of receptive sensibility, a notion that goes a long way towards the subversion of the romantic idea of genius performed by Nietzsche's analysis of the Apolline and Dionysiac impulses in creativity. This is not the only point in the novel where we think of Nietzsche: the motif, repeatedly sounded, that happiness is associated with delusion and perception of the truth with misery, culminates in the episode of the madman who was happiest at the time of his most intense derangement and self-alienation '*die Zeit, wo er von sich war*' (IV, 350), literally away from himself as his mother puts it. And some of the metaphors Werther uses to evoke his 'genial' cult of spontaneity have connotations which are anything but unquestionably positive. Respect for 'the rules', he contends at one point, destroys true feeling for nature and the true expression of such feeling:

O my friends! Why does the torrent of genius break out so rarely, so rarely thunder forth in towering waves and shake the depths of your astonished souls? My dear friends, upon both its banks dwell the placid fellows whose summerhouses, tulip beds and cabbage patches would be destroyed and who thus take timely measures to ward off the threatened peril by dams and diversions.

(IV, 277–8)

Werther doubtless intends the river metaphor to embellish his preference for spontaneous feeling over regulated rationality; but it actually qualifies, almost undermines that contention. For what he praises as the manifestation of living nature, the 'torrent of genius', Werther also characterizes through images connoting destruction and death, and what he disapproves of is associated with images of peaceful if unexciting cultivation, growth and life. Genius figures here as an elemental force which those who prefer to live securely rather than perish dramatically do well to defend themselves against. The 'rules' which keep genius in check are here structures needed for survival, not shackles by which the timorous shut themselves off from the Good Life. The force of genius figures as the enemy of discrete selfhood, rather than the straightforwardly benign expression of the individual's true nature. Goethe never again openly portrayed genius in such a questionable light, although the idea that 'the poet' is in some sense the enemy of 'the man' who inhabits the same body figures largely in *Torquato Tasso*, and the proximity of creative energy to destructive power is both implicit in the entire theme of *Faust* and explicit in a number of its episodes. What *Werther* ought to make very clear is that even at the height of his apparently unreserved cult of original genius, Goethe was already concerned with the problem of relating spontaneity to a wider order. It will not do to see the subsequent changes in his views as the familiar pattern of young hothead degenerating into senile reactionary. That view does no justice to any phase of Goethe's development, and it obscures the deeper philosophical implications of Goethe's fascination with genius, to which I shall return later.

During Goethe's first decade in Weimar (roughly 1776–86), the set of questions and answers he associated with the idea of genius underwent a significant shift which was consolidated by his travels in Italy from 1786 to 1788. In essence, that shift involved a revision of the straightforward identification of genius with pure nature and of culture with unnatural stultification. It can perhaps best be traced through his second novel, begun in the mid-seventies as *Wilhelm Meister's Theatrical Mission*, and completed in the mid-nineties as *Wilhelm Meister's Apprenticeship*.

The *Theatrical Mission*, though unfinished, was plainly intended as the fictitious biography of a *Sturm und Drang* original genius. The earliest Wilhelm Meister is a gifted dramatist as well as an aspiring actor and director, and the 'mission' to which the title alludes appears to be nothing less than the regeneration of Germany through the establishment of a national theatre. True, Wilhelm's preoccupation with the theatre is diagnosed as a symptom of what the narrator calls 'unnatural feeling for nature', but this in its turn is presented as the wholly understandable reaction of an individual and a generation 'caught up in urban life, with no sight of nature, no freedom of the heart' (VIII, 549–50). The novel is unsparing about the shortcomings of the contemporary theatrical scene, and does not make light of the obstacles in Wilhelm's way. Yet his vocation to transform the way people live, using powerful drama, energetically performed, to shatter social institutions, is taken wholly seriously. Goethe took the manuscript of the novel with him to Italy, but what he found there made the novel unfinishable in the form he had started it.

Though *Werther* had made him a celebrity throughout Europe and beyond, the Goethe who travelled to Italy was by no means sure that literature was his true vocation. He harboured ambitions to be a painter, and he was about to expand his new-found scientific interests. It was above all the impact of what Italy showed him about sculpture, painting and architecture that changed his conception of the relationship between art and nature, and significantly altered what he understood by genius. A single sentence in a letter written from Rome just before Christmas 1786 encapsulates the change: 'In works of art there is a great deal of tradition: works of nature are always like a freshly uttered divine word' (23 December 1786 to Herzogin Luise: XIX, 45).

Now, of course, 'a freshly uttered divine word' is precisely what Young, Hamann, Herder and the earlier Goethe had discerned in works of original genius, the paradigms of genuine art. But now Goethe is explicitly saying that works of art are essentially different from such pristine utterances of divine spontaneity; they embody 'a great deal of tradition', and this is not a failing but part of their essence and value. Looking at the art of the past and the present all around him as he travelled through Italy and stayed in Rome, Goethe was impressed by the variety of talent, but also by the way that talent was embedded in coherent artistic traditions. He became convinced that there was a collective cultural element in creativity, and that engagement with tradition was not a hindrance to true self-expression but its indispensable medium. The radical individualism of his earlier outlook he now saw as the consequence of Germany's cultural impoverishment,[7] an impoverishment which he held could be remedied by establishing links with a wider European artistic tradition stretching back to antiquity and still alive in the Italian climate. Human creativity, drawing on and enriching such traditions, he now saw as a parallel, or as he once put it, a rival creativity to Nature's: 'a perfect work of art,' he wrote in 1798, 'is a work of the human spirit, and in this sense also a work of Nature' (XIII, 180).

The qualification 'in this sense' marks the essential difference between Goethe's earlier and later views of genius. He no longer holds that the true genius must speak with the original voice of Nature and shun the influences of received culture; genius now involves marrying individual invention with a sense of what human beings have collectively achieved in the development of civilization, creating works which enhance that civilization by intertwining individuality with tradition. The genius consequently needs an informed sense of what others have done and what others need as well as a powerful sense of spontaneous creative energy. Goethe was merely following through this shift of emphasis on the embedding of genius in a tradition when, in the last years of his life, he sometimes spoke as though the true achievements of genius were not so much their actual creations *per se*, but the effect which those creations had on posterity. Eckermann reports how the elderly Goethe spoke in one breath of Napoleon, Mozart and Luther as men of genius because of the inspiration that their accomplishments gave to others, what he termed their 'productivity', not in the sense of personal fecundity, but in the fruits their lives had borne in subsequent generations (XXIV, 673–4).

The extent of the change which Italy brought in Goethe's attitude is visible if we compare what he had written in the essay *On German Architecture* of 1771 with the translation, with intercalated commentary, of the first two chapters of Diderot's essay *Sur la peinture*, which Goethe wrote in 1798. Diderot (writing in 1765, though the French original was published only in 1795) had written that 'there would be no mannerism, either in line or colour, if nature were imitated conscientiously. Mannerism comes from the masters, the academy, the school, indeed even from the Ancients.' These were sentiments that Goethe had unwittingly echoed a few years after Diderot's essay when he proclaimed that 'schools and principles' were shackles to genius. But Goethe now proceeds to take the unfortunate Diderot to task for what had once been a fervently held view of his own, virtually accusing him of corrupting youth:

Are not young people, supposing them endowed with a moderate portion of genius, already too full of themselves? [. . .] And you want to make your young followers sceptical about the schools! Maybe the professors at the Paris Academy of thirty years ago deserved such castigation and discredit, that I cannot judge, but in a general sense, your [. . .] words have not a single true syllable in them. The artist should not only be conscientious towards nature, he should be conscientious towards art as well. The master, the Academy, the schools, the antiquity which you make responsible for mannerism can equally well, if the method is right, propagate a true style, indeed, one may well ask what genius will ever seize upon genuine forms, choose the true style and create for itself a comprehensive method in an instant, merely by observing nature, without any tradition?

(XIII, 226)

This latter notion, the very essence of original genius as he himself had once extolled it, Goethe now dismisses as 'the most vacuous of all [Diderot's] fantasies'.

From this perspective, we can see why *Wilhelm Meister*, the novel that had once been about the pioneering 'Mission' of an original genius, turned into the story of an 'Apprenticeship' and initiation. The Wilhelm Meister of the post-Italian novel is still borne along by a powerful inner sense that he has a part to play in the world different from the one his immediate circumstances make available to him. And the novel continues to take this sense seriously, remaining very much a narrative of self-discovery. But there is a new insistence that spontaneous inclinations are an insufficient guide to the self's true needs and its place in the wider world. Wilhelm's sense of apartness and his quest for a fuller life are not now ascribed simply to an innate trait of character, but are shaped by a contingent childhood influence. And his alienation is not from the world *per se*, but from a particular corner of the world, which has undergone a diversion from a larger and more humane tradition. In passages with no equivalent in the earlier strata of the novel, we learn that the young Wilhelm was fascinated by his grandfather's art collection. This collection, which had stirred the child's aesthetic sensibilities, was sold by Wilhelm's father, who needed the cash to indulge his taste for extravagantly modish living. The trend is continued in Wilhelm's generation by his brother-in-law Werner, who is obsessed with the accumulation of cash, of emphatically abstract wealth. Wilhelm leaves this distasteful environment, which he takes to be 'the' world of bourgeois society, and goes in search of the way that corresponds to his true self; and eventually finds it, not in the threatre where he has long mistakenly sought it, but in marriage into the family of the nobleman who once bought his grandfather's collection, where he refinds his spiritual inheritance, and dedicates himself to transforming the lives of his fellows, not by emotional bombardment from the stage, but through enlightened techniques of estate management.

It is easy to see why some of the early Romantics were disgusted by the direction in which Goethe chose to take Wilhelm's development. It seemed to them as though the quest for beauty had been castigated as a diversion from the true path of utility. But this was not Goethe's intention. Quite the reverse: a good deal of his imaginative and critical writing from his Italian journey onwards is aimed at an understanding of creativity that would encompass the practical and the aesthetic, and so make a distinction between the beautiful and the useful unnecessary and invalid. After Italy, the divergence between the beautiful and the useful replaced the suppression of exuberant spontaneity as the chief malady of modern culture in Goethe's eyes. Had the pre-Italian draft of the play *Torquato Tasso* survived, like the earlier version of *Wilhelm Meister*, we might well have been able to observe a similar shift in emphasis by comparison with the play Goethe wrote shortly after returning from Italy. As it is, there are grounds for speculating that the chief focus of the pre-Italian *Tasso* was the clash between spontaneous genius and over-rigid social convention. What requires no speculation, since the evidence is in the published text, is that the post-Italian *Tasso* subordinates this theme to a much broader set of historical-cultural concerns.

Goethe's *Torquato Tasso* introduced the figure of the misunderstood genius into modern European literature. But although Tasso as Goethe portrays him is certainly a highly self-indulgent character, there is nothing in the least self-indulgent about the way Goethe treats the theme of Tasso's difficulties. Goethe's nostrum against sentimentalizing the afflicted artist is to historicize his predicament. Goethe's Tasso sees a fundamental contrast between classical antiquity and the present age where the status and function of poetry and poets are concerned. In ancient times, Tasso says, poets and heroes, artists and men of action, were equally devoted to the heroic ideal, which they served equally in their respective ways. Heroes performed great deeds; poets, by enshrining those deeds in art, gave them an endurance which the deeds themselves could not have possessed. And beyond that, poets ensured the continuity of the heroic ideal by making available to future generations images of great achievements, which in their turn inspired more heroic deeds. That is why Tasso imagines Alexander the Great entering Elysium and hastening to find both Achilles and Homer: Achilles, whose heroism fired Alexander's exploits many generations later, and Homer, without whose poetry Alexander could never have been inspired by Achilles at all. But Tasso is painfully aware that the world has changed. Men of action are no longer heroes, but diplomats; and poets are regarded by men of practical affairs as no more than the purveyors of entertaining trifles to help them relax in intervals of recreation which punctuate the real business of their lives. This functional view of art is eloquently represented in the play by Antonio Montecatino, chief minister of Alfonso of Ferarra, Tasso's patron. Antonio embodies a world of practical – but not heroic – action which has no room for the kind of art to which Tasso's whole existence is dedicated. Dedicated to the efficient solution of practical problems, Antonio can see no value in anything not demonstrably useful. Rulers may justifiably employ architects, painters and musicians to symbolize the prosperity and the power of the state, and art can provide recreation and relaxation for men of action and help restore their practical energies, but beyond that, art is mere idle embellishment. If Antonio's priorities are correct, Tasso's aims and achievements must be worthless. So firm and radiant is Antonio's self-confidence that it infects Tasso, leads him to view himself through Antonio's eyes, and suffer crippling doubts about the value of his own existence, doubts which underlie his many and various other problems which cannot be explored here.

The historical accuracy of Tasso's vision of a unified ancient culture is in this context neither here nor there. Historical truth or nostalgic myth, it serves as a foil to bring out what Goethe is diagnosing as the chief cultural ill of modern times, the divergence between practicality and beauty. The source of Tasso's torment is not critical rejection of his poetry but his perception that the people who seem to really matter in the world have no conception of what genius is about and seem perfectly content in their ignorance. This is a very different assessment of modern society from the one that lay behind Goethe's earlier cult of original genius. There, the bulk of mankind were imagined as chafing under the constraints of an artificial civilization, waiting only for the clarion call of genius to inspire them to cast off the yoke and seize their natural birthright, the exhilarating liberty of unfettered spontaneity. Now we have a genius driven to the verge of insanity and maybe beyond (the ending of the play is deliberately unclear on this point) because he inhabits a self-possessed and contented world which is indifferent to his values, which patronizingly makes room for art as refined entertainment, but which has no sense of needing art as a purveyor of truth. This is a vision of an increasingly utilitarian world which neither courts nor fears genius, but treats it with chilling indifference, and as an antidote to that vision Goethe attempts in *Wilhelm Meisters Lehrjahre* to set up the achievements of artistic genius as paradigms for all practical activity, to make the hero's final espousal of an active life not an abandonment, but the fullest culmination of his original artistic ambitions.

There can be little doubt that Goethe aspired to achieve a synthesis of the imaginative and the practical in his own life and to set it against the current of history, and that he was impelled in this ambition by his perception of the course on which Western culture was set. Here Goethe's interest in artistic genius is all of a piece with his activities as scientist and as a historian of scientific discovery, above all in his *Theory of Colours*. He was both fascinated and repelled by the distinctively modern science that had emerged in the followers of Galileo and Newton, and he longed to share in the investigative advance of that science while diverting it from what he saw as its increasingly inhumane trajectory. Goethe was fascinated by the power of the new science to explain and unify, its capacity to meet Leibniz's criterion of goodness by encompassing a maximum of variety within a minimal set of laws. But the objectification of nature through Newton's particular combination of induction and deduction was a price Goethe was not prepared to pay. He was repelled by the abstraction involved in the formulation of a testable hypothesis, and by what he considered the distortion of ordinary sense experience through experimental conditions that were expressly designed to exclude the subjectivity of the observer. Goethe was no Blake:[8] he had a genuine hunger for scientific insight and explanation and spoke with admiration of the 'genius' of Galileo and Newton. But he longed for a science that would combine explanatory power with sensuous awareness, avoiding a divergence between the nature investigated by science and the nature perceived in everyday experience. The '*Urphänomen*' was Goethe's attempt at fusing scientific understanding with spontaneous perception. It was not so much a genetic notion as an attempt at an alternative mode of scientific explanation: the general laws of nature which the scientist sought were not to be abstractly formulated and experimentally tested but rather perceived and demonstrated in concrete phenomena in which the general regularities of nature were especially visible.[9] The '*Urphänomen*' as a model of scientific explanation clearly implies a notion of the scientist as genius, with special perceptive powers and a gift for conveying the intensity as well as the content of his perceptions. It also gives the scientist of Goethe's vision the same integrating function as the artist, the task of perceiving and fostering a humane wholeness against the perceived trend of history.

In his life and in his views, Goethe inescapably raises the difficult and important question of the relationship between the cult of genius and modernity, a question far too large to tackle here. On the one hand, the stress on originality and spontaneity seems the very stuff of individualism, and yet the claim that this spontaneity is rooted in natural order reveals an anxiety about the disintegration of cosmic, moral and social cohesion.[10] Goethe's views and achievements command respect in their own right: the difficult but essential task he poses twentieth-century readers is to enrich that respect with critical understanding. Both as commentator on genius and as genius personified, he claims to combat a complex cultural malady, offering a description of the syndrome, a diagnosis of its causes, a prescription for its cure. The description may seem with hindsight all the more plausible, but the diagnosis is less resistant to critical scrutiny, and after the destruction which ideologies of 'organic' wholeness have wrought in our century, no judicious apothecary would think of honouring the prescription without diluting it substantially.

All the same, one prominent ingredient in Goethe's views and Goethe's life is an unproblematic legacy. His last recorded reflections of any length, in a letter written a few days before his death, turn yet again to the subject of individuality, genius and tradition:

The sooner one realizes that there is such a thing as a craft, an art, which assists the orderly development of natural dispositions, the happier one is; no matter what is received from outside, it does no damage to innate individuality. [. . .] Imagine a talented musician composing an important score: consciousness and unconsciousness will interact like warp and weft, an image I am so fond of, uniting the human faculties [. . .] in free activity, joining the acquired with the innate, so that the result is a unity which astonishes the world.

(17 March 1832 to Wilhelm von Humboldt, XXI, 1042)

To the end, Goethe proclaims the power of genius to astonish, and to astonish by unity in diversity, by a dynamism which is contained by tradition but which also keeps tradition alive, by a self-expression and a self-discovery which are simultaneously a participation in a seamless fabric of human culture woven throughout history. He also asserts the power of art to make its creators and recipients happy. Astonishment and happiness, the two elements which here and on many other occasions in his life Goethe associates with genius, are a salutary embarrassment to us.[11] Intimidated by postmodernism, we think that being astonished by works of art, rather than by deconstructivist party-pieces, is ideologically suspect. And great art as bestower of happiness is at odds with the orthodoxy that, in modern literature at any rate, grimness is an index of truth. Goethe feared maybe more than any of his contemporaries for the future of mankind, and he frequently portrayed suffering, loss, misery and dejection, but the basic tenor of his life and art is emphatically not melancholic. As has been well observed,[12] there is no tradition of jovial genius in European culture. But there is one resplendent instance of it, and that instance is Goethe.

Notes

1 *The Spectator*, 160 (3 September 1711), ed. D. F. Bond (5 vols, Oxford, 1965).
2 Edward Young, *Conjectures on Original Composition* (London, 1759), p. 36.
3 See T. J. Reed, 'Theatre, Enlightenment and Nation. A German Problem', *Forum for Modern Language Studies*, XIV (1978), 143–64, and W. H. Bruford, *Theatre, Drama and Audience in Goethe's Germany* (London, 1950).
4 References to Goethe's writings are by volume and page number in the *Gedenkausgabe der Werke, Briefe und Gespräche*, ed. E. Beutler (24 vols, Zürich, 1948–64). All translations are my own.
5 When recreating in *Dichtung und Wahrheit* book 9 the first impact which Strasbourg cathedral had on him, Goethe noticeably goes out of his way to remedy this shortcoming, devoting two pages to an analysis of the articulation of the West Front (X 420–3).
6 See the splendid discussion of this poem in Jochen Schmidt, *Die Geschichte des Genie-Gedankens in der deutschen Literatur, Philosophie und Politik 1750–1945* (2 vols, Darmstadt, 1985), vol. 1, pp. 202–54.
7 This is reflected in the 'we' which Goethe repeatedly uses in *Dichtung und Wahrheit* when portraying the situation of writers in his youth, expressing with hindsight a solidarity with his fellow-countrymen precisely where we might have expected a claim to exceptional individuality. By this apparently trivial stylistic device, Goethe intimates that his nation's cultural backwardness and the peculiar energy of his youthful inspiration had common roots.
8 See Erich Heller, *The Disinherited Mind* (Cambridge, 1952).
9 See H. B. Nisbet, *Goethe and the Scientific Tradition* (London, 1972).
10 For an examination of these issues in connection with Goethe's Faust, see M. Beddow, *'Faust I': A Critical Guide* (London, 1986).
11 See T. J. Reed, 'Goethe and Happiness' in E. M. Wilkinson (ed.), *Goethe Revisited* (London, 1984).
12 By Professor Glenn Most in the course of the conference at which the original version of this chapter was given as a paper.

6
The Emptiness of Genius: Aspects of Romanticism

Drummond Bone

'Genius' raises with peculiar acuteness the ontology of word and idea. It has been almost a matter of historical necessity for some of the contributors to this volume to write of 'genius' independently of the word itself. In these cases the space has to be filled either with our contemporary concept of genius, or more convincingly perhaps with an historically extended concept, which must not only fill the absence of the word, but define the space which is read as empty. The peculiar difficulty is that the word 'genius' itself is often a kind of aporia. It refers to the 'what' which escapes the categories of comprehension and of speech. In eighteenth-century usage it is, in Jonathan Bate's phrase, an 'excuse' for the unfathomable exception, and it can still, in the late twentieth century, be a term used to displace or to suggest marginality. The actual occurrence of the word might thus be seen as the signal of the absence of a definable concept – to look for this concept, then, independently of the word, is a strange business indeed. The characterization of the word is often strewn with negatives. It is the categories from which it is in the act of escaping that tenuously define it. But once 'genius' has appeared, these categories become irrelevant. And *before* the word appears, either historically or simply in its absence, those categories which might be thought to suggest it could equally be seen as preventing its appearance. That is, if they are sufficient, the notion of genius is either unnecessary, or more likely inconceivable. It could be argued that the absence of the word genius is a positive quality in a lexical set where its existence might suggest that the set feels itself deficient in its powers of expression. But of course this way of thinking is predicated on a particular understanding of the word's function, and is itself historically and culturally determined. Nevertheless, it could at least be historicized critically by investigating particular usages of the word in the past. It is not quite so free-floating as an investigation of the area of reference of an absent word which must of necessity be determined by our own historical place and cultural identity, and which area of reference so determined would seem to be the indeterminable. It is with this somewhat ironic perspective on the project that I shall look at some examples of the use and context of the *word* in the Romantic period – the period which, it might be argued, is the most significant for our own experience of 'genius'. Within this period I shall allow myself a relative freedom from history – I am not concerned with the (certainly interesting) detail of development on a small time-scale.

Romantic usage of the term characteristically invokes the problem of the finite or secular absolute, and indeed can be seen as one of many attempts in the period to realize a secular absolute.[1] That is, the invocation in the religious sense attempted through the word 'genius' involves the writer in the impasse of the emptiness that lies beyond words. The attempt to reach beyond the partial and to express the total can only end in partial plenitude, or partial vacuum, and the two are agonizingly similar, since the will to the absolute dissolves the particularization which is difference. Beyond the differentiation of words lies the fullness *or*, indiscriminately, the emptiness of a noumenal absolute. Only because of and in the inevitable failure of the enterprise can one characterize its process. The idea of genius as a Promethean substitute for divinity, and the very involvement of the word philologically with 'spirit' or 'soul', involve us in contradictory movements towards both man and God, realization and essentialization, and the awkwardnesses of religious presence, secular absolute, and individual universality (in which expression the term 'individual' is no help to clarity either).

This can sometimes be seen to have alarming moral dangers. The dangers of Blake's 'Genius has no Error: it is Ignorance that is Error'[2] are clear – it assumes that there is an absolute conception of genius – the priest of which is of course the writer writing. But the conception is not articulated and therefore not challengeable, not reinterpretable. It is self-defining, and judgements based on it can only be, in short, the expression of the whim of its writer – it is unsupported opinion in the dress of an absolute, unless in an act of faith one is prepared to grant that it *is* a 'religious' absolute in the (necessary) mundane clothing of personal viewpoint.

The quiddity of the danger lies not on any one side of these two possibilities, but in their coexistence, for they map out a moral world in which there is no content to moral evaluation and choice, but only the flags of essential right and wrong. Even a disagreement is only a preliminary to a moral world, and must initially assume the same status of opinion or absolute, since it is not allowed any other ground on which to state its objection. The drive to see reality as being beyond the rules of man's limited perceptions leads with an inexorability which can be terrifying to the emptying of the particularity necessary for moral content, and a consequent vacuum which can only be filled by the outside–inside void–plenitude of personal universality. In Blake's formulation, genius is opposed not only to ignorance, but also implicitly to what is commonly called knowledge, for it is this which perceives genius to be in error. Knowledge's objection is, however, overruled by the redefinition of the error as the product of genius, and hence the redefinition of knowledge as ignorance. With this inversion of conceptual systems there can be no rational argument for it is rationality itself which is being subverted. Genius is beyond these 'normal' categories of judgement.

The problem is more disguised in Jean Paul Richter's rhetoric in the following two extracts, but perhaps, on rereading, the potential consequences are more alarmingly accepted:

Like every spirit, this world spirit of the genius animates all the members of a work, without inhabiting a single one. It can make the charm of form superfluous through its own higher charm; the genius of Goethe, for example, would still speak to us in his imperial prose as well as in his most careless poem. When a single sun is up, it can show time with a pin as well as with an obelisk. This is the spirit which never offers proofs, but only itself and its point of view; it then relies upon kindred spirits and looks down on those that are hostile. [. . .][3]

When the old men of prose, petrified and full of earth like men physically old, let us see poverty, the struggle of everyday existence or even its victories, we begin to feel as cramped and troubled at the sight as if we actually had to experience the adversity. One actually does experience the picture and its effect; their pain and even their joy lack a heaven. They trample down even the sublime in reality; [. . .] In the wound-fever of reality, let us avoid those who would inoculate a new fever into the old by painting our wounds with their prosaic poetry, who make true poems necessary as antidotes to their false ones. ·

When on the contrary, genius leads us over the battlefields of life, we survey them as freely as if glory or patriotism marched before us with flags fluttering behind; and next to genius poverty takes on an Arcadian form, as for a pair of lovers. Everywhere genius makes life free and death beautiful; on his sphere, as on the sea, we catch sight of the driving sails before the heavy ship. Like love and youth, he thus reconciles – indeed he weds – helpless life with ethereal sense, as at the edge of still water the real tree and its reflection seem to grow from a single root toward two heavens.[4]

The first paragraph piles up the non-particularity of its subject – genius is like 'every' spirit, it is a 'world' spirit independent of place, it animates 'all'; it does not however inhabit 'a single one' – the impression, in other words, is of it being everywhere and nowhere. It is not concerned with the forms that make perception possible, and it can do odd things to the adjectives which qualify prose and poetry. At this point a sleight of hand covers the contradictions involved in speaking of '*a single* sun', which involves the suggestion that a singularity could also be multiple, and hence underlines the universal quality of the genius primarily carried in the metaphor of the sun itself. For a genius scale too is irrelevant – 'pin' or 'obelisk' will do. The consequence is that, as in Blake's aphorism, genius is above proofs, only relying on its acolytes to despise unbelievers from the eminence of unreasoned acceptance. Clearly a more charitable reading would interpret Richter as meaning only that genius refrains from the pedantry of explanation, and that explanations are not nonexistent but on the contrary presented immediately as opposed to mediately (through reasoned logic). Similarly the first sentence stresses the integration of the organic as opposed to the atomic nature of the merely physical. But the perlocutionary effects of the rhetoric seem inescapable even by the rhetoric itself.

In the second paragraph quoted above Richter attempts to convey the idea of a failed art which does not render its subject 'meaningful', but leaves it as it were untouched. But in the third, which follows directly in the text, the result is that an art which does transform its material in the animating manner of the paragraph just discussed seems to dissolve moral content into a transfigured sublime. Here a battlefield is a glory, poverty is Arcadian, helplessness is etherealized, and in a memorable image which could be given a fine irony if we read it in the context of a Poe-like Cabbalism, up is down and down is up. Of course one should not reduce the struggle in this text either to non-sense nor, perhaps even more so, to some kind of mere political duplicity or moral hypocrisy. Richter is trying to use language to create a sense of something that language is reluctant to conceive – a secular absolute beyond the apparent limits of the categories of thought. That absolute he names genius. The passage works from the dreary and the temporal towards the gloriously spiritual and timeless. It uses the characteristic images of reflection and organic unity, and of bulk dematerialized. Genius becomes a word on the edge of the world and of comprehensibility pointing onwards into the necessarily silent. But the echo of that silence can be heard to have a sinister reverberation. And it seems irrelevant as we listen to it whether we conceive that silence as being the plenitude or the emptiness of 'genius'.

Connected with this a-morality of all or nothingness is a common notion of the period that genius, being a supra-personal quality, is a-personal, or indeed anti-personal. The most famous formulation is Keats's, though he rather slides away from the word 'genius' itself:

The best answer I can give you is in a clerklike manner to make some observations on two principle points, which seem to point like indices into the midst of the whole pro and con, about genius [. . .] [and Keats's own aims and achievements].

1st As to the poetical Character itself [. . .] it is not itself – it has no self – it is every thing and nothing – it has no character – it enjoys light and shade; it lives in gusto, be it foul or fair. [. . .] What shocks the virtuous philoso[p]her, delights the camelion Poet. It does no harm from its relish of the dark side of things any more than from its taste for the bright one; because they both end in speculation. A Poet is the most unpoetical of any thing in existence; because he has no Identity – [. . .] creatures of impulse have about them an unchangeable attribute – the poet has none, no identity[5]

This of course is an extreme statement of the case. The moral problem is accepted and dismissed, and virtue can be shocked if it likes. Keats is in fact apologising for changing his opinions – how can he be expected to be constant if he has no identity? The poet's access to the primary reality of all things wipes out his secondary reality of individuality – and again the ironic reading of 'nothing' is suppressed by the 'gusto' of the viewpoint. If energy is all, its direction is unimportant. The 'speculation' returns us to the idea of negative capability sketched by Keats the year before:

capable of being in uncertainties, Mysteries, doubts, without any irritable reaching after fact and reason. [. . .] with a great poet the sense of Beauty overcomes every other consideration, or rather obliterates all consideration.[6]

Or in other words the 'dark side' and the 'bright' side indiscriminately conduct the poet towards 'the sense of Beauty', and this sense itself overrides 'all consideration', and is connate with mystery and doubt. The reader has again no choice but to accept the analytic *a priori* assertion of the poet, and Beauty, as the boundary of conceivable good, marking the limits of normal judgement of what is 'foul' or 'fair'. Beyond this is only a leap of faith into the unresolvable. By the second half of the nineteenth century, Wagner's *Parsifal* embodies the notion that emptiness is purity, and the steps between Keats's position and this, and between this and twentieth-century developments in Germany are not too difficult to trace.[7] Keats is here symptomatic of the elision of the particular, and hence of the basis for reasoned judgement, in the search for the universal. Individual behaviour is irrelevant before the acknowledgement of the Poet – thus the secular absolute, indistinguishable from personal assertion. In the invocation of 'genius' we have the last articulation of any sort of distinction, and properly 'genius' does not denote the presence of an attribute or identity, but the *absence* of attribute and identity. It belongs rather to silence (or emptiness) and faith (or doubt) than to language and understanding. The logical conclusion to this is, of course, that the true natural genius may well *be* silent. This is an idea common to such diverse spirits as Wordsworth and Byron. Coleridge has some fun at Wordsworth's expense when he discusses this notion in *Biographia Literaria* chapter XXII. The passage he takes exception to is in the *Excursion* I:

> These favor'd beings,
> All but a scattered few, live out their time
> Husbanding that which they possess within,
> And go to the grave unthought of.

Coleridge comments: 'To use a colloquial phrase, such sentiments, in such language do one's heart good; though I for my part, have not the fullest faith in the *truth* of the observation. On the contrary I believe the instances to be exceedingly rare.'[8]

Ignoring this peculiar but characteristic extreme let us return for a moment to Richter:

> *The belief in* an instinctive, single faculty of genius could only arise and endure through a confusion of philosophical or poetic genius with the artistic instinct of the virtuoso. [. . .] Our age presents me with every possible challenge to battle with sinners against the holy ghost. Shakespeare, Schiller, et al. distribute all the individual faculties among their individual characters, and they must be within a single page witty, discerning, understanding, rational, fiery, learned, everything just so that those faculties can shine like jewels, not like a candle-end lighting up poverty. Only the one-sided talent gives a single tone like a piano string struck by a hammer. Genius is like a string of an aeolian harp; one and the same string resounds in manifold tones in the manifold breezes. In genius all faculties are in bloom at once, and imagination is not the flower, but the flower-goddess, who arranges the flower calyxes with their mingling pollens for new hybrids, as if she were the faculty of faculties.[9]

Aside from the fact that Richter's knowledge of the physics of sound makes nonsense of his metaphor if we look too closely – or closely at all! – the drift is recognizable: the universality of genius transcends any limitation of singularity. It has to be *all*. The figure of genius as the holy ghost is appropriate, but could open up unintended irony once more, for there is indeed a chimerical quality to the chameleon genius, and the all-pervasiveness of the German '*Geist*' is, if anything, more nebulous than the English 'ghost', if for somewhat different reasons. Nevertheless Richter escapes some of the uneasiness of Keats's rhetoric by, for one thing, insisting on the multiplicity of qualities, rather than on the fact that such universal multiplicity subverts the notion of quality itself. Moreover his imagery invites the reader to hold on to the ideas of 'singleness' ('within a single page') and unity ('one and the same string') at the same time as these ideas are being exploded by the idea of universality. And in the section omitted above 'understanding' is seen as crucial to genius – it is not blind instinct. But what *kind* of understanding, one might ask, though rhetorically his point is made. On the other hand Keats faces, perhaps rather naively, the logical negative inherent in his manner of thinking. Richter is careful one might say to ensure that the echo from the other side of the word genius is the echo of a full and not an empty beyond. But one might still check slightly at the imagery of poverty transformed into jewelery – this transformation has again somewhat the ease of reductivity. Keats's barrier against the potential horror of what he is saying lies in his shift away form the word 'genius', and his substitution of the word 'poet'. This works two ways – first by keeping in mind the hard autobiographical context of the letter – and indeed my extract already distorts by omission the specific historical reality of his remarks – and secondly *through* this by giving an implicit specificity to the activity of genius. Genius has here both personal history and, by implication, the attributes of a particular craft. Of course – in English as in Richter's German – the word 'poet' can be a virtual synonym for 'genius', but that is to miss the point. It is *not* the same word, and it is in nuance marginally more specific. Here it becomes more so both in the move from 'genius' to poet, and in the colouring it takes from Keats's occupation.

Related thoughts on the a-personality of genius can be found in Coleridge too, though maybe more judiciously expressed. Early on in *Biographia Literaria* we find him characterizing genius as having its sensibility

excited by any other cause more powerfully than by its own personal interests; for this plain reason the man of genius lives most in the ideal world, in which the present is still constituted by the future or the past; and because his feelings have been habitually associated with thoughts and images, to the number, clearness, and vivacity of which the sensation of *self* is always in inverse proportion.[10]

Here is a fine example of what one might call genius as abstraction – from both personal identity and the temporal and physical world. Presented as it is here, it of course argues that genius is 'selfless' in the morally good manner – indeed Coleridge uses it to argue against the cliché that genius is ill tempered through personal tetchiness. However, the very abstraction of the case for abstraction makes it peculiarly susceptible to the kind of inversion we have been examining, in which selflessness becomes identifiable with god-hood.

In his discussion of poetic genius in *Biographia Literaria* XV, using *Venus and Adonis* as an example of the product of genius, Coleridge characterizes Shakespeare first as '*myriad minded*'. Later he picks up the same thread:

A second promise of genius is the choice of subjects very remote from the private interests and circumstances of the writer himself. At least I have found, that where the subject is taken immediately from the author's personal sensations and experiences, the excellence of a particular poem is but an equivocal mark, and often a fallacious pledge, of genuine poetic power.[11]

This in isolation does not in truth go much further than the observation that autobiographical immediacy may temporarily make up for poetic skill, but that it is unlikely to sustain an artist throughout a career – though the shadow of a-personality might be felt to be hovering close by. The idea is then developed, in a manner very reminiscent of Keats on the differences between Milton and Shakespeare, with perhaps more resonant undertones:

It is throughout as if a superior spirit more intuitive, more intimately conscious, even than the characters themselves, not only of outward look and act, but of the flux and reflux of the mind in all its subtlest thoughts and feelings, were placing the whole before our view; himself meanwhile unparticipating in the passions. [. . .] I should have conjectured from these poems, that even then the great instinct, which impelled the poet to the drama, was secretly working in him, prompting him by a series and never broken chain of imagery [. . .] to provide a substitute for that visual language, that constant intervention and running comment by tone, look and gesture, which in his dramatic works he was entitled to expect from his players. His 'Venus and Adonis' seem at once the characters themselves, and the whole representation of those characters by the most consummate actors. You seem to be told nothing, but to see everything and hear everything. Hence it is [. . .] above all from the alienation, and, if I may hazard such an expression, the utter *aloofness* of the poet's own feelings, from those of which he is at once the painter and the analyst; that though the very subject cannot but detract from the pleasure of a delicate mind, yet never was poem less dangerous on a moral account.[12]

There is no question here of denying the poet an identity – he has his 'own feelings' – but yet the suppression of this identity is a hallmark of his genius. The use of the terms 'unparticipating', 'aloofness' and notably 'alienation' in this positive context are likely to be difficult for the modern reader, and clearly one must maintain some awareness of the shift in their implications. But they may nevertheless be symptomatic of a tendency in the argument, particularly in conjunction with the provision of a moral excuse. The sense is clearly that we are provided with a higher perspective on what Coleridge calls the 'animal impulse' of the text – but the effect is to identify us with this position of genius so to speak 'above the law'. Had the poet sullied his hands with the material of his text, the moral effect *might* have been dangerous. But genius, and the readers of genius, are untouched by the subject matter. The projection of the characters beyond the individuality of the writer into almost the three dimensions of the stage again shows the ability of the writer to suppress his own identity. In short, part of the paragraph's rhetorical force is its constant suggestion that genius is 'elsewhere' – withdrawn above, behind or beyond the phenomenal world, yet the very guarantor of that phenomenal world's completeness: 'You seem to be told nothing, but to see and hear everything.' Genius is transparent, present and absent at the same time. There are other aspects to this chapter of the *Biographia* to which I shall return shortly, but for the moment let us simply note that even this discussion relatively firmly grounded in a particular example is not wholly free from suggestions that genius is a movement of abstraction.

It might be thought that realizations of 'genius' as Promethean would be a clear counterpoint to realizations of 'genius' as abstract secular absolute. Such images characteristically have a sense of energies turned inward – the kind of movement typified by Nietzsche in *The Joyful Science*: 'How high a river rises when it is dammed. How high would man rise did he not flow out into a God!'[13]

In our period Byron's Prometheus can provide a paradigm, though he does not use the word genius:

> [Man's] [. . .] sad unallied existence:
> To which his Spirit may oppose
> Itself – an equal to all woes,
> And a firm will, and a deep sense,
> Which even in torture can descry
> Its own concentered recompense.[14]

Edward Young had long ago used the phrase 'mind concentered' to describe genius,[15] and Shelley, possibly under Byron's influence (either from here or from *Childe Harold* III[16]) since it is of Byron that he is effectively writing, also associates concentering and genius:

[Maddalo] is a person of the most consummate genius [. . .] but [. . .] his ambition preys upon itself. [. . .] I say that Maddalo is proud, because I can find no other word to express the concentered and impatient feelings which consume him.[17]

But such images are at a theoretical level also caught in the game of absolutes. The totally inward-turned has as little to do with the particularities of existence as has the totally diffuse. The self-consuming genius vanishes into an inner space quite as much as the self-dissolving genius is absorbed in an outer one. However, and it is a 'however' of crucial importance, in so far as individuality represented is never totally 'concentered' – to use the obvious metaphor of a black hole something is inevitably emerging across the event horizon, otherwise there would be no representation – such images of genius do provide a dialectic counter to genius as a-personality. It is a dialectic which collapses if either side is taken to 'degree zero', and it is a dialectic which history was indeed to collapse, arguably with disastrously real consequences. But in Romantic texts it still has at least some force. It is one more example of the archetypal Romantic paradox of the central importance of the individual who is constantly seeking a resolution – in an overarching other – to the tension of his isolated individuality. The post-Romantic association of genius with uniqueness or at a lower level eccentricity constantly hovers over its opposite – that genius is the dissolution of the merely personal into the universal, and that in a merely personal world the universal will inevitably appear as the *reductio ad absurdum* of personality. The genius of individuality may thus be an ironic representation in a fallen world of the genius of universality in the pure world beyond.

Some kind of balance point might be thought to exist in descriptions of the genius as the bringer of unity to multiplicity. Here the force of the individual's mind acts, as if it were the force of a universal mind, to unify the diversity of the mundane world. Particularlity is in a sense reduced, but it is also felt to be strengthened by its integration under the force of the genius's particular mind. We can return to *Biographia* XV for examples:

But the sense of musical delight, with the power of producing it, is a gift of imagination; and this together with the power of reducing multitude into unity of effect, and modifying a series of thoughts by some one predominant thought or feeling, may be cultivated and improved, but can never be learned.[18]

Or more explicitly:

It has been before observed that images, however beautiful, though faithfully copied from nature, and as accurately represented in words, do not themselves characterize the poet. They become proofs of original genius only as far as they are modified by a predominant passion; or by associated thoughts or images awakened by that passion; or when they have the effect of reducing multitude to unity, or succession to an instant; or lastly, when a human and intellectual life is transferred to them from the poet's own spirit,
  'Which shoots its being through earth, sea, and air.'[19]

The underlying image of the first extract is obviously that of harmony – the genius resolves discord. His power to do this is instinctive, and this may lead us some way down the road to impersonality, but not very far. Much stronger here is the feeling of the genius's personal 'style' of thought and feeling. In the second extract the phrase 'original genius' strongly suggests the new personality as well as the transforming power. The image of time reduced to an instant, on the other hand, brings out the transcendent implications of reducing 'multitude to unity', which might be missed in that phrase which could itself easily be read in simply materialist terms as description of formal effect. The final sentence quoted begins by warming the heart in wholly human terms, in which the existence of the genius as a recognizable individual being for once seems paramount – but it ends with the diffusion of that human being through three of the universal elements. The effect of this may indeed be to personalize these elements, to bring them into the sphere of a single humanity, and the pace of the passage up to the quotation which punctuates it does tend to suggest a mounting energy of insistence on the singleness of genius which is then released in fulfillment rather than loss by the image of the quotation. Whatever, there is in this kind of image a suggestion that genius is filled with the things of the world, or that the world is filled by the things of humanity – in the sense of individual beings – and less of a feeling that genius as inner or outer absolute could also be an infinity of nothing.

A much less precarious counter to the genius of emptiness, but not one much used, can be found in the idea of the cheerful genius, as in Chapter II of Coleridge's *Biographia*:

The men of the greatest genius, as far as we can judge from their own works or from the accounts of their contemporaries, appear to have been of calm and tranquil temper in all that related to themselves. In the inward assurance of permanent fame, they seem to have been either indifferent or resigned, with regard to immediate reputation. Through all the works of Chaucer there reigns a chearfulness, a manly hilarity, which makes it almost impossible to doubt a correspondent habit of feeling in the author himself. Shakespeare's evenness and sweetness of temper were almost proverbial in his own age.[20]

Such descriptions present genius as in balance with its worldly surroundings, neither consuming the world into itself, nor dissipating that self throughout the world. Eternity does peep round the door in the phrase 'permanent fame' however. Nevertheless they are also firmly based in an idea of individual personality which resists erosion by the quality of genius which is *one* of its characteristics. If one may twist a Wordsworthian phrase, they are images of relationship before they are images of love. They are, however, not all that common in the period, it has to be said, and later in the same chapter Coleridge awkwardly undercuts the effectiveness of his view here while trying to defend it:

Yet even in instances of this kind [the moody and irritable genius], a close examination will often detect, that the irritability, which has been attributed to the author's *genius* as its cause, did really originate in an ill conformation of body, obtuse pain, or constitutional defect of pleasureable sensation. What is charged to the *author*, belongs to the *man*.[21]

It is entirely reasonable from Coleridge's point of view here to distinguish the quality of genius from the holder's other qualities – so long, that is, as genius remains a personal and not a noumenous quality. But in leaving genius somehow untouched by so fundamental a human deficiency as 'defect of pleasureable sensation' he sells the pass. Genius has once more escaped the particularly human. This idea of the cheerful genius must also be distinguished from the idea of the *calm* genius, an image which rarely includes the sense of worldly balance I have been discussing. When Richter writes that 'Only the foolish youth can believe that the fire of genius burns like that of emotion. [. . .] The true genius is calm from within; not the upheaving wave but the smooth deep mirrors the world,'[22] we have not left the still depths of the beyond – on the contrary, the image detaches us from the worldly and lets us loose on the dimensionless.

Perhaps the best defence offered against the temptations of nihilistic genius can be found in those passages where particularity and judgement – the two are intimately connected – are admitted to the Romantic pantheon. My example is an extreme case, and perhaps sounds of the eighteenth century rather than of the second decade of the nineteenth. Coleridge is writing to Lady Beaumont:

> The sum total of all intellectual excellence is good sense and method. When these have passed into the instinctive readiness of habit, when the wheel revolves so rapidly that we cannot see it revolve at all, then we call the combination Genius. But in all modes alike, and in all professions, the two sole component parts even of *Genius*, are GOOD SENSE and METHOD.[23]

'Habit' is here substituted for 'instinct', allowed only to be *like* instinct, and genius does not escape the mundane fact of artifice – genius itself has 'component parts'. Even if it appears to exist outside of time ('we cannot see it revolve at all') it is, in fact, a product of method and discrimination ('Good Sense') within it. This is a decisively secular account of genius, and stands in sharp contrast to much of the above. Genius has a content, and that content itself must have content, since it is a matter of choice and order. In fact it is so radically different from absolute genius that one might think it could not serve as an argument against it, for, as I noted above, absolute conceptions do not admit of other than absolute responses. More intriguing is the integration of ideas of order and method into Romantic discourse more characteristically concerned with the will to transcendence.

I shall not rehearse yet again the paradoxes involved in the concept of organic form as conceived by the British Romantics. But Coleridge's most famous formulation includes his stated refusal to oppose 'genius to rules':

No! [. . .] The spirit of poetry, like all other living powers, must of necessity circumscribe itself by rules, were it only to unite power with beauty. It must embody in order to reveal itself; but a living body is of necessity an organized one – and what is organization but the connection of parts to a whole, so that each part is at once end and means.[24]

The difficulty we have been discussing is here made the enabling fact of genius. Genius is that which has *both* specific content and is also beyond any one particular. Here the paradox is accepted as just that – it does not sheer off into the assimilation of one movement of the paradox by the other. Genius is of place and time – it is 'circumscribed' by particular judgements – it is embodied. Each part of genius – it is once more an artefact – is allowed to be an end in itself. Yet genius and its particular form, the spirit of poetry, are antecedent to their embodiment: they are 'a whole' to which parts are 'connected' as well as actually forming that whole, and they have the disembodiment of 'power'. As he writes elsewhere, 'decided genius' consists in 'just that proportion, that union and interpenetration of the universal and particular'.[25] In his note he continues:

No work of genius dare want its appropriate form; neither indeed is there any danger of this. As it must not, so neither can it, be lawless! For it is even this that constitutes genius – the power of acting creatively under the laws of its own origination.

Of course this is slippery stuff, but the intention, in the context of seeing Shakespeare as not in the crude sense *merely* instinctive, is undeniable – genius cannot be empty of the stuff of judgement. Even if, more than slightly awkwardly, it might be thought to be its own judge and jury, the ground is totally different from that cut from under us by ideas of genius as the limiting case for judgement. It is subject to form and to rules and to laws. It must have shape and organization. Indeed it is the very type of organization. Genius is here constantly being held back from the brink of the unspeakable, the a-personal, and the a-moral. Coleridge insists on its genuine secularity in the face of the will to the absolute. The tension is considerable, and nowhere more obvious than in his concluding sentence:

Shakespeare, himself a nature humanized, a genial understanding directing self-consciously a power and an implicit wisdom deeper than consciousness.

The infinite depth of nature is a particular man; genius is also understanding; it is subject to direction, and that direction is not impersonally instinctive, but chosen self-consciously. Genius may be a word given to an echo from a beyond that is fullness or emptiness, but it had better perhaps be given the specific note of an action in the real, and therefore moral, world. Our inheritance from Romanticism is an ambiguous gift.

Notes

1 This aspect of Romanticism has been much discussed over the years. See for example H. G. Schenk, *The Mind of the European Romantics: An Essay in Cultural History* (London, 1966); M. H. Abrams, *Natural Supernaturalism* (New York, 1971); and for a recent dissenting view, Marilyn Butler, 'Nymphs and Nympholepsy: The Visionary Woman and the Romantic Poet', in *Studien zur Englischen Romantik*, I (1985), 11–31.

2 Annotation to p. 111 of his copy of Sir Joshua Reynolds's *Discourses*. It would be possible to cite Blake on the other side, as one of the Romantics most aware of the dangers of emptying meaning into universality. Also from the *Discourses*' annotation we have: 'To Generalize is to be an Idiot. To particularize is the Alone Distinction of Merit'; or 'Distinct General Form Cannot Exist. Distinctness is Particular, Not General.' These are notes to p. xcviii and p. 74 respectively; all are in the form given in Geoffrey Keynes (ed.), *Blake: Complete Writings*, rev. edn (London, 1966).

3 All translations from Jean Paul Richter are from Kathleen Wheeler (ed.), *German Aesthetic and Literary Criticism: The Romantic Ironists and Goethe* (Cambridge, 1984) – hereafter Wheeler. Where it is a question of close reading I have included the German in the note locating the quotation. The edition quoted is the revised *Vorschule der Aesthetik* (Stuttgart and Tübingen, 1813) – hereafter 1813. It should be noted that Wheeler's bibliographical information on p. 162 needs clarification – the revised text is (more humbly?) the *Vorschule*, and not *Vorlesungen*, as she arguably implies. The paragraph quoted here is from Wheeler p. 172. Significant to the close reading might be: '*Dieser Weltgeist des Genius beseelet, wie jeder Geist, alle Glieder eines werks, ohne eine einzelnes zu bewohnen.* [. . .] *So-bald nur eine Sonne dasteht, so ziegt sie mit einen Stiftchen so gut die Zeit als mite einem Obeliskus. Dies ist der Geist, der nie Bewiese gibt, nur sich und seine Anschauung und dann vertrauet auf den verwandten, und herunter sieht auf den feindselig geschaffnen.*' 1813, pp. 85–6.

4 Wheeler, pp. 173–4. Significant to the close reading might be: '*Wenn hingegen der Genius uns über die Schlachtfelder des Lebens führt: so sehen wir so frei hinüber, als wenn der Ruhm oder die Vaterlandsliebe vorausginge mit den zurückflatternden Fahnen; und neben ihn gewinnt die Dürstigkeit wie vor einen Paar Liebenden eine arkadische Gestalt. Ueberall macht er das Leben frei und den Tod schön.* [. . .] *Auf diese Weise versohnet, ja vermählt er – wie die Liebe und die Jugend – das unbehülfliche Leben mit dem ätherischen Sinn, so wie am Ufer eines stillen Wassers der aussere und der abgespiegelte Baum aus Einer Wurzel nach zwei himmeln zu wachsen scheinen.*' 1813, pp. 91–2.

5 Letter to Richard Woodhouse, 27 October, 1818. Keats is picking up the same question of the '*genus irritabile*' which exercises Coleridge in the quotation on p. 123 below.

6 Letter to George and Thomas Keats, 21 December, 1817.

7 This possible history is suggested by the likes of George L. Mosse, *The Crisis of German Ideology: Intellectual Origins of the Third Reich* (New York, 1964), and receives its classic fictional treatment in Thomas Mann's *Doktor Faustus* (1947).

8 From *Biographia Literaria*, ed. J. Shawcross, rev. edn (London, 1969), II.105 – hereafter *Biographia*. One might compare, for the same commonplace as Wordsworth's, Byron, *Prophecy of Dante*, Canto IV, the opening lines: 'Many are poets who have never penn'd / Their inspiration.' From *Lord Byron: The Complete Poetical Works*, ed. J. J. McGann (Oxford, 1980), IV.234 – hereafter McGann.

9 Wheeler, p. 167. There is no italicization in the 1813 text. Mentioned in the close reading: '*Unsere Zeit schenkt mir jeden Krieg mit dieser Sünde gegen den heilige Geist. Wie vertheilen nicht Shakespeare, Schiller u. a. alle einzelne Kräfte an einzelne Charactere, und wie müssen sie nicht oft auf Einer Seite wissig, scharfsinnig, verständig, vernunstend, feurig, gelehrt, und ales sehn, noch dazu bloss, damit der Glanz dieser Kräfte nur wie Juwelen spiele, nicht wie Licht-Endchen der Nothdurst erhelle? – Nur das einsseitige Talent gibt wie eine Klaviersaite unter dem hammerschlage Einen Ton; aber das Genie gleicht einer Windharfen-Saite; eine und dieselbe spielet sich selber zu mannichfachem Tönen vor dem mannichfachem Unwehen. In Genius stehen alle Kräfte auf einmal in Blüte.*' 1813. pp. 65–6.

10 *Biographia*, chapter II, I.30.

11 *Biographia*, II.14–15.

12 *Biographia*, II.15–16.

13 Nietzsche, *Die frohliche Wissenschaft*, I. My translation.

14 *Prometheus*, 11.52–7. McGann, IV.32–33.

15 Edward Young, *Conjectures on Original Composition* (London, 1759).

16 *Childe Harold*, III.89.6 – 'All is concentered in a life intense.' McGann, II.109.

17 Preface to *Julian and Maddalo*. Text from *Shelley: Selected Poetry and Prose*, ed. K. N. Cameron (New York, 1965), p. 154.

18 *Biographia*, II.14.

19 *Biographia*, II.16.

20 *Biographia*, I.21.

21 *Biographia*, I.24.

22 Wheeler, p. 168.

23 Letter of June, 1814. Text from *Biographia*, II.268.

24 From B. M. Egerton MS 2800, f24, as printed by T. M. Raysor (ed.), *Coleridge's Shakespearean Criticism* (London, 1930), p. 223. The quotations following n. 25 are from the same lecture note.

25 Coleridge, *The Friend* (1818), II.4.

7
Nietzsche on Genius

Michael Tanner

'Genius' is not a crucial term in Nietzsche's vocabulary, which is initially surprising, for two reasons: first, his preoccupation with art and artists at every stage of his career might well lead one to expect that he would use the term, and the concept, by which great artists had been designated at least as much in Germany as in other European countries during the century preceding him. Secondly, his obsession with greatness in all its forms means that he has recourse to a fairly extensive set of terms to characterize its manifestations, and again one might expect that 'genius' would therefore occur fairly frequently. That it doesn't is, I believe, the result of two main factors, one of them to a large degree biographical, the other an elaborately conceptual matter – though, as usual with Nietzsche, they are closely related, and indeed often intertwined.

The biographical element in his relative neglect of the term is, not surprisingly, his relationship with Richard Wagner. Whatever else one might say about Wagner, it is not possible, even for someone so addicted to hyperbolic iconoclasm as Nietzsche, to deny him the title of genius – he is as paradigmatic a representative of it as Michelangelo or Beethoven. And Wagner was the only genius that Nietzsche knew or even met, indeed the only great man of any kind. The experience of prolonged and intimate contact with Wagner, followed by disillusionment and disapproval, therefore put Nietzsche in a most embarrassing position, though that wouldn't have been the way he put it; Nietzsche the man was very prone to embarrassment, but Nietzsche the writer would never have admitted to so humble and humiliating a feeling, and only uses the word when he wishes to demean the cause of such a feeling, as when he refers to Wagner's 'embarrassing tragic grunts'.[1] What his psychology led him to do was, characteristically, to transform their friendship into bitter enmity, though in fact that was not how either of them ever felt about it. Wagner's reaction to Nietzsche's apostasy was unusual in that instead of accusing him straightforwardly of treachery and unworthiness, he was pained and concerned – one of the bizarre minor episodes in their relationship was Wagner's correspondence with Nietzsche's doctor, in which he attributed Nietzsche's excessively excited state of mind to overindulgence in masturbation.[2] Though enmity was a word that Nietzsche often used in describing his feelings about Wagner, he preferred to see himself as Wagner's antipode, an expression which allowed for a wealth of metaphoric associations, including those of magnetic attraction and repulsion. It isn't possible to go into the complexities of the matter here, but clearly they disabled Nietzsche from using 'genius' in an uninhibitedly favourable way, quite apart from the other qualms which he felt about the phenomenon, and which I'll be investigating later.

There remains the question as to why Nietzsche didn't use the term more frequently, and with greater charge, in the one work in which he had no doubts or anxieties about Wagner's greatness, his first book, *The Birth of Tragedy*. For that marvellous though highly questionable work is concerned among other things with the conditions which make the phenomenon of tragedy possible, and the investigation would seem bound to involve a consideration of the nature of those few artists who have, in Nietzsche's view, completely expressed the tragic view of life: Aeschylus, Sophocles – and Wagner. But in fact there is very little about any of them, just as there is strangely little about their specific works, most of which indeed are hardly mentioned. That is not an oversight on Nietzsche's part. For him the tragic artist is little more than the spokesman for a society which is strong enough to confront and accept the tragic nature of existence, and Nietzsche's overriding concern is here, as it was always to be, with the philosophy of culture. At the stage of his life when he wrote *The Birth of Tragedy* Nietzsche was still a disciple, in many respects, of Schopenhauer, and that meant that the individual had only a phenomenal existence, not a genuine metaphysical being. What is true for the tragic hero, who is no more than a kind of focus of passion and affliction, is just as true of his creator. Thus Nietzsche writes: 'The Dionysian musician is, without any images, himself pure primordial pain and its primordial re-echoing.'[3] And in the next paragraph, writing about Archilochus, admittedly not a tragedian but as a lyrist at least half-way towards being one, Nietzsche continues in the same vein:

For, as a matter of fact, Archilochus, the passionately inflamed, loving and hating man, is but a vision of the genius, who by this time is no longer merely Archilochus, but a world-genius expressing his primordial pain symbolically in the symbol of the man Archilochus – while the subjectively willing and desiring man, Archilochus, can never at any time be a poet.[4]

This is not Nietzsche at his clearest, but nonetheless the point he is making in Wagnerian prose is that in the act of creating music, or by extension tragedy, the Dionysian artist becomes impersonal in a sense more radical and literal than any envisaged by T. S. Eliot in his celebrated formulations in 'Tradition and the Individual Talent'. As such, he becomes indistinguishable from the 'world-genius', a notably unspecific concept that Nietzsche invokes with merciful infrequency, making it a little clearer in the 'Attempt at a Self-Criticism' that he wrote for the third edition, which he brought out in 1886:

Indeed, the whole book knows only an artistic meaning and crypto-meaning behind all events – a 'god,' if you please, but certainly only an entirely reckless and amoral artist-god who wants to experience, whether he is building or destroying, in the good and in the bad, his own joy and glory – one who, creating worlds, frees himself from the *distress* of fullness and *overfullness* and from the *affliction* of the contradictions expressed in his soul.[5]

Though there is an element of wishful reading-back into this passage of what he ought to have said, it still captures to a considerable extent the force of the first edition, and does as much as can be hoped to explain why there is so little in the book about the psychology of the tragic artist: he doesn't have one, for he doesn't, in so far as he is a genuine artist, possess individuality. His genius consists in the realization that the *principium individuationis* is an illusion, and in his conveying of that fact in his inspired and inspiring works, which make his spectators and auditors temporarily realize it too. But only up to a point. If we fully grasped and felt the truth that the tragic-Dionysiac artist presents us with, we would die. As it is, only the tragic hero does that: he dies in order that we may live – Tristan in Act III of Wagner's music-drama being the latter-day archetype. Tragic genius consists in the creation of figures who suffer and perish, while, as Nietzsche was to write much later, and with quite different intent, 'We possess *art* lest we *perish of the truth*.'[6] (It is wholly and strikingly characteristic of Nietzsche that he uses very similar formulas at different stages to mean drastically different things.)

So, strangely enough, in the one work in which Nietzsche has no worries about the beneficent effects of art, those who create it are deliberately and rightly (given the peculiar dialectic of *The Birth of Tragedy*) under-characterized, while their enemies, the men who were responsible for the death, or suicide, of tragedy, are given a very full and brilliant portrayal. Whatever one's view of Nietzsche's account of Euripides and Socrates, the two great destructive anti-geniuses, he has certainly given a stunning description of a certain kind of mind: 'While in all productive men it is instinct that is the creative-affirmative force, and consciousness acts critically and dissuasively, in Socrates it is instinct that becomes the critic, and consciousness that becomes the creator.'[7] That is as close as he gets in his first book to an account of the relationship between the elements in the creative man's mind.

There is no further illumination on the topic of genius to be found in the four *Untimely Meditations* which Nietzsche wrote in the succeeding four years, though two of them, 'Schopenhauer as Educator' and 'Richard Wagner in Bayreuth', are ostensibly concerned to celebrate his two greatest cultural heroes. The latter was written as part of Nietzsche's propaganda effort for the first Bayreuth Festival, which took place in 1876, and whilst he was writing it he was already having grave doubts about Wagner's personality and work, which he confided to his notebooks. The published monograph shows the strain, and is in every way his least interesting and most unsatisfactory piece of work. Significantly it is in his next book, *Human, All Too Human*, the first volume of which was published in 1878, that he has most to say about the nature of genius, and it is of a highly equivocal kind. Section 4 of the book, called 'From the soul of artists and writers', shows scepticism operating on several fronts. In the first place, there seems to Nietzsche to be a great deal that is dubious about the artist as such. Secondly, he is worried that even when an artist is genuinely great, his effects on his successors may be harmful, in fact are bound to be. Paragraph 158 runs:

Fate of greatness. Every great phenomenon is followed by degeneration, particularly in the realm of art. The model of the great man stimulates vainer natures to imitate him outwardly or to surpass him; in addition, all great talents have the fateful quality of stifling many weaker forces and seeds, and seem to devastate the nature around them. The most fortunate instance in the development of an art is when several geniuses reciprocally keep each other in check; in this kind of struggle, weaker and gentler natures are generally also allowed light and air.[8]

This can hardly be seen as other than a prediction – and an extraordinarily accurate one, as it turned out – of Wagner's influence on subsequent composers. Wagner's name is nowhere mentioned in *Human, All Too Human*, but its absence is all the more significant because he was so much in the forefront of Nietzsche's mind, and in the most painful way – he knew that he had broken with Wagner, but he also knew that Wagner didn't know. The result is a circling round the subject, in which 'artist' almost always means one particular artist, and one gets a sense that he can't win. The passage just quoted meditates gloomily on the effects of Wagner's prodigious success. But the immediately preceding passage had dwelt on the sorrows of the artist who is unappreciated, and the kind of postures that such a figure is thrown into as a consequence of his neglect. 'One feels his sorrows excessively, because the sound of his lament is louder, his tongue more eloquent. And *sometimes* his sorrows really are very great, but only because his ambition, his envy, are so great.'[9] And just in case the sufferings of the artist are 'transpersonal, in sympathy with [. . .] all existence', we have still to ask 'What measure, what scale is there for their authenticity? Is it not almost imperative to be distrustful of anyone who *speaks* about having feelings of this kind?'[10] (as Wagner and for that matter Schopenhauer often had spoken). The net closes a few sections later, in number 164, entitled 'Danger and benefit of worshipping the genius', which runs in part:

it is at least questionable whether, when it takes root in him, superstition about the genius, about his privileges and special capabilities, is advantageous to the genius himself. At any rate, it is a dangerous sign when a man is overtaken by awe of himself, be it the famous awe of Caesar, or (as in this case) awe of the genius, when the aroma of a sacrifice, which by rights is offered only to a god, penetrates the genius's brain, so that he begins to take himself for something superhuman. The eventual results are a feeling of irresponsibility, of exceptional rights, the belief that he blesses merely through his company, and mad rage at the attempt to compare him to others, or, indeed, to judge him lower and reveal what is questionable in his work.[11]

Such a detailed description of Wagner's well-known ways of behaving was not lost on its object, though Wagner was baffled as to the motivation for Nietzsche's attack. What must strike anyone who is in the least acquainted with Nietzsche's general views on greatness, and on the necessity for the great man to be able to behave differently from the rest of mankind, is that he is here indulging in an attack on genius which is only distinguished by its eloquence from the kind of line that mediocrities regularly take when confronted with the exceptional and the superior. This is one of the points at which Nietzsche's hostility to Wagner's domination over him and his growing suspicion of art and artists in general merge to a degree which makes disentanglement impossible.

As we read on in *Human, All Too Human* perplexity deepens. For Nietzsche soon moves on to a defence of the genius against the forces which militate against his flourishing. He contrasts what 'a warm heart' might desire, namely the greatest happiness of the greatest number, and what someone who hungers after greatness as a vindication of humanity must see is necessary. It is one of the most fruitful confusions in Nietzsche's work, for he is confronting an issue which those who passionately espouse one side or the other of this argument customarily avoid. In paragraph 235, he writes 'The highest intelligence and the warmest heart cannot coexist in one person, and a wise man who passes judgment on life also places himself above kindness, considering it only as something to be evaluated along with everything else in the sum of life.'[12] These are not the terms in which his later philosophy will be worked out, for in that he seeks a more decisive resolution of the issue than he can hope to achieve so long as he uses 'the warmest heart' and 'the highest intelligence', both expressions which register a favourable valuation. Those who claim – and they are almost all of Nietzsche's commentators – that he failed to work out the political implications of his views on the *übermensch*, etc., must have forgotten that at this comparatively early and transitional stage in his progress he had put in the clearest and most succinct terms precisely the problem that he is accused of ignoring. 'Perhaps' he writes in the preceding paragraph, 'the engendering of genius is reserved to only a limited period of humanity.'[13] That sounds like a piece of bad news, even if it is hypothetical – not Nietzsche's usual mode. And that he views the prospect with dismay seems to be borne out by a further speculation in the same paragraph: 'Perhaps mankind, in the middle of its path, the middle period of its existence, is nearer to its actual goal than it will be at the end.' But as this astonishing piece of tentative speculation reaches its climax Nietzsche again shows how aware he is of the pros and cons:

The energies that condition art, for example, could very well die out; pleasure in lying, in vagueness, in symbolism, in intoxication, in ecstasy, could come into disrepute. Indeed, once life is structured in a perfect state, then the present will no longer offer any theme for poetry whatsoever, and only backward people would still demand poetic unreality. They would then look back longingly to the times of the imperfect state, the half-barbaric society, to *our* times.[14]

This passage induces the same sense of unease in its readers that its author must have felt. Do we want to see the end of genius and its productions? Surely not. But the price of genius is that 'life retains its violent character', which we probably, as we become more and more civilized, don't want it to. However, since the preconditions of art include 'pleasure in lying, in vagueness, in symbolism, in intoxication', perhaps its elimination wouldn't be so bad. Nonetheless, it would certainly occasion nostalgia on the part of those who no longer needed it, but wished that they did. As the dilemmas multiply Nietzsche provides one further twist to the argument, in paragraph 241, entitled 'Genius of culture':

If one were to dream up a genius of culture, what would be his nature? He uses lies, power, the most inconsiderate self-interest so confidently as his tools that he could only be called an evil, demonic creature; but his goals, which shine through here and there, are great and good. He is a centaur, half animal, half human, and even has angel's wings at his head.[15]

Once again, the reference to Wagner is too plain to be missed, and it was no doubt such passges that occasioned offence at Wahnfried when

Wagner and Cosima perused with dismay the signed copy of the book which Nietzsche had sent them. It isn't surprising that Wagner failed to register that Nietzsche was arguing that without such monstrous characteristics as he took Nietzsche to be attributing to him, he would have failed to produce his works. After all, subsequent generations have delighted in what Wagner produced and lamented that such a monster should have been their author. They too have failed to grasp Nietzsche's point. So have apologists for Wagner's character, whether or not they are right to defend him against the torrents of moralizing recrimination that most comfortably placed biographers have directed at, for example, Wagner's habit of borrowing huge sums. For Nietzsche is claiming that without the 'flaws' of genius, there would be no production. Over and over again in his later works he insists on the preposterousness of expecting the exceptional (which alone is valuable) to proceed from someone who leads a model bourgeois existence. But the crucial difference between those later pleas for privilege and the ambivalence of his attitude towards it in *Human, All Too Human* is that in the later works he is talking about beings of whom there has so far been no instance, while here he is concerned with someone whom he had known at first hand, whose weaknesses, excesses and vagaries he had observed with every bit as prim an eye as any member of the 'herd' whom he is later to excoriate.

It is only to be expected, then, that Nietzsche's attitude towards 'genius' should be so agonizing for him that in his later writings the term rarely appears, and when it does it is used in a much less specific, more lyrical way, as when he talks of 'the genius of the heart'[16] in *Beyond Good and Evil*. For his anguish was that he himself was a refutation of the claim that 'the highest intelligence and the warmest heart cannot coexist in the same person.' What he should have said was that if they do coexist, the person who is thus afflicted will either have to abjure one or other of them, or find himself in a state of incessant desperation. In all his later writings Nietzsche presents himself as a person without a warm heart, so they preserve the consistency of manifesting the highest intelligence. Only occasionally do any signs of regret show, as in the unpublished note which constitutes paragraph 981 of *The Will to Power*:

Not to make men 'better,' *not* to preach morality to them in any form, as if 'morality in itself,' or any ideal kind of man, were given; but to *create conditions* that *require stronger men* who for their part need, and consequently will *have*, a morality (more clearly: a physical-spiritual discipline) *that makes them strong!*

Not to allow oneself to be misled by blue eyes or heaving bosoms: *greatness of soul has nothing romantic about it*. And unfortunately nothing at all amiable.[17]

By the time he wrote that, in 1887, Nietzsche was solely concerned with the conditions under which mankind as we know it, or them, can be surpassed. He has effected, in some respects, a drastic simplification of his position. Although when, a decade earlier, he was considering the genius in a way that would have struck his predecessors in the investigation of that phenomenon – for instance Herder, Kant, Goethe and Schopenhauer – as extreme and unnecessarily paradoxical, he was dealing with it, as they had done, in relation to the culture from which genius arose and which it fertilized. Such a consideration, even when it was as idiosyncratic as that of Nietzsche, presupposed a reasonably settled account of culture and the values which constituted it and which it maintained. It is probably futile to speculate on whether his hostile analysis in *Human, All Too Human* would never have occurred if the genius with whom he had been acquainted had been a less extravagant member of the species than Wagner. As Erich Heller has written, Wagner's art 'is merely an extreme, and extremely successful, expression of propensities almost always present in the artistic constitution'.[18] To the degree that that is true, it could be said that the relationship with Wagner merely accelerated a thought-process which Nietzsche would have gone through in any case. Nietzsche's suspicions about art and artists, for example that 'When it comes to recognizing truths, the artist has a weaker morality than the thinker; on no account does he want his brilliant, profound interpretations of life to be taken from him, and he defends himself against sober, plain methods and results'[19] he is, after all, and as he recognized, restating the traditional Platonic doubts on the subject. Wagner brought these doubts to a rapid head, since the creator of *Tristan* moving on a mere twenty years later to *Parsifal* must clearly give one pause – but pause of a traditional kind. For Nietzsche, of course, the problem was exacerbated beyond endurance because of the specific nature of *Parsifal*, and to the extent that his worries about artistic sincerity and integrity were compounded by his being confronted with an ostensibly Christian work (and Nietzsche didn't bother to look beyond the surface of *Parsifal*) he found himself confronted, as so often, with several devastating problems at the same time.

As Nietzsche saw things, Wagner had capitulated on two fronts simultaneously. Having been a fighter all his life, he now had become a conformist both in his public and his private life. In public, he became a supporter of the Reich, an admirer of Bismarck and an anti-semitic reactionary, while in private he transformed himself in the most unlikely way into a Christian paterfamilias. How far that account is from being the whole truth is something that Nietzsche, having distanced himself from Wagner, couldn't have known. But he could have guessed how much more than that there was to it if he had not needed, as he always did, to establish the starkest antitheses.

It is at this point that the complex conceptual issue that I mentioned in the first paragraph of this essay comes into play. Nietzsche is distinguished among philosophers by his concern with the drives behind various central manifestations of the human spirit. While other philosophers have been, and still are, concerned with the nature of truth, for example, Nietzsche was much more interested in the will to truth. 'Suppose we want truth: *why not rather* untruth? and uncertainty? even ignorance?'[20] he asks at the beginning of *Beyond Good and Evil*. He is never content with taking the manifestations of human drives at their face value, and the result is the psychologization of the most unlikely phenomena. Of course in the case of art it is much more natural to us to enquire into its relationship to its origins than in the case of what we like to think are much more impersonal matters. Even so, there are good reasons for not enquiring into the source and origins of what we prize most. But for Nietzsche those reasons are only good insofar as they shield us from the unpalatable truth. At the same time as he is calling for an investigation into our will to truth he is himself carrying it into the most dangerous areas. And none is more dangerous than the relationship of the artist to his art. It isn't that Nietzsche was so naive that he could only bear a beautiful work of art to proceed from a beautiful soul. He knew that, if anything, the reverse is more likely to be the case. But he wasn't prepared to be content with that knowledge. For, for him, a state of radical discrepancy between the inner and the outer, wherever it manifested itself, was a source of alarm. And it was the growing awareness that artists are, in certain crucial ways, paradigmatic of the rupture between inner and outer, while the works of the greatest of them proclaim the supreme value of wholeness, which led him to his suspicion of the whole phenomenon of art, even though he could never bring himself to stop loving a great deal of it.

What made the situation still more acute for him was that he never ceased to take art as the archetype of worthwhile human activity, and precisely because of the kind of wholeness which works of art themselves can possess. So he solved the problem of the gulf between art and artist, the almost necessary 'insincerity' of art, by advocating, first tentatively, and then with ever greater insistence, and finally stridency, that we ourselves should become works of art. In a wonderful extended aphorism in *Daybreak*, the book which succeeded *Human, All Too Human*, he considers how prone we are to go on our knees before genius, and how necessary it is to begin an assessment of the strength which genius manifests. He continues:

But for such an assessment there are still far too few eyes, indeed the assessment of the genius is still usually regarded as a sacrilege. And so perhaps the most beautiful still appears only in the dark, and sinks, scarcely born, into eternal night, – I mean the spectacle of that strength which employs genius *not for works* but for *itself as a work*; that is, for its own constraint, for the purification of its imagination, for the imposition of order and choice upon the influx of tasks and impressions.

The great human being is still, in precisely the greatest thing that demands reverence, invisible like a too distant star: his *victory over strength* remains without eyes to see it and consequently without song and singer. The order of rank of greatness for all past mankind has not yet been determined.[21]

In spite of the great lyrical force of this passage, it prompts some urgent questions. The idea that the true genius is to be found not in the man who produces publicly available artefacts – not necessarily works of art, but they do spring first to mind – but in the man who, by his very victory over his own strength is all too likely to be overlooked, surely results in our never being able to ascertain 'the order of the rank of greatness' not only for 'all past mankind' but for anyone who is truly great. Of course that might be the case, but if it is, then the concept of greatness itself must in time lapse, and so much of Nietzsche's thought depends on it that it seems that he must find a way in which the true genius, who is himself a work of art but would never stoop to the ultimate spiritual vulgarity of proclaiming himself as such, will still register on the consciousness of mankind for what he is. As his work proceeds, Nietzsche sets the stakes both for greatness, and for its appreciation, higher and higher. It is perhaps not too much to claim that this aphorism, which I have never seen a commentator refer to, is the turning point for Nietzsche's thought. It certainly can help us to see how Nietzsche's later characterizations of greatness become more repulsive, or more vague, or more obscure.

More repulsive, when, for instance he gives Cesare Borgia as an example of greatness. Some commentators have been so appalled by this that they have gone so far as to insist that Nietzsche doesn't mean what he obviously does. That is especially true of Walter Kaufmann, although he translated the passage in which Nietzsche writes, 'Even now one believes one must disapprove of a Cesare Borgia; that is simply laughable [. . .] If one reflects with some consistency, and moreover with a deepened insight into what a "great man" is, no doubt remains that the church sends all "great men" to hell – it fights *against* all "greatness of man." '[22] In taking Cesare Borgia as an example of greatness, still more of naturalness against the perversions of herd morality, Nietzsche was clearly indicating that one way of being great is to simply ignore the moral code of one's society – though in Renaissance Italy Cesare Borgia's behaviour didn't stand out as it does for us. 'Let us not doubt' he writes in *Twilight of the Idols* 'that we moderns, with our thickly padded humanity, which at all costs wants to avoid bumping into a stone, would have provided Cesare Borgia's contemporaries with a comedy at which they could have laughed themselves to death.'[23] However, Nietzsche is under no allusions that we can recapture the perspective of Borgia's contemporaries. He provides the shocking example in order to awaken us in the most decisive way to alternative perspectives, and to show how far the process of egalitarianism has gone; it is his point, wholly missed by Kaufmann *et hoc genus omne* that the sheer idea of Cesare Borgia possessing greatness merely appals us.

More vague and obscure when instead of instancing particular cases of greatness he evokes for us the idea of the *übermensch*. It is one of the most common criticisms of Nietzsche that he seriously underdescribes his ideals, so that we are left wondering what an *übermensch* would be like if we met one, and whether Nietzsche himself had any but the vaguest notions on the subject. The famous formulations of 'The Socrates who practises music' and 'Caesar with the heart of Christ' are notable because they are unresolved oxymorons: it is the whole point of Nietzsche's characterization of Socrates in *The Birth of Tragedy* that he does not, because he could not, practise music; and Caesar could never have carried out all those successful campaigns if he *had* had the heart of Christ. In producing such exciting-sounding but ultimately unhelpful formulations Nietzsche was perhaps trying to do what cannot be done – to give an account of a work of art which has not yet been created so that we will recognize it when it is. 'There has never yet been an *übermensch*' says Zarathustra, and since when he arrives he will be such a drastic departure from anything that has gone before we shouldn't hope, at the same time as we can't help hoping, that we shall know him when we see him, any more than Christians can restrain themselves from speculating on what heaven will be like, though they know that the effort is vain, if not blasphemous. And even if we lower our sights somewhat, as Nietzsche seems to have done (the *übermensch* is rarely mentioned after *Thus Spoke Zarathustra*), we are still left largely in the dark. For if we hold onto the thing that Nietzsche consistently tells us to, that is to the concept of ourselves as 'artists of life' or as works of art, the problems of working out what it would be for a person to make his life, or himself, into an artwork are dauntingly large. One of the most obvious difficulties with the idea is that whereas an artist can go on revising his work until it satisfies him, and then present it as a completed whole to the world, we can do nothing to change our pasts; the most that we can hope to do is to work on ourselves until we become much more satisfactory (but by what criteria?) than we have previously been, or in Nietzsche's terminology, until we have 'become what we are'. But that isn't enough for Nietzsche. We must make our *whole* lives into works of art, so that the analogy is not only the extremely demanding one of achieving a character or self that 'has style', but the apparently impossible one of giving style to what we have already done and been, to 'redeem the past' while not being in any kind of bondage to it.

Given this degree of exigence, it is not surprising that recent commentators on Nietzsche, for instance Alexander Nehamas in his *Nietzsche: Life as Literature*, have had recourse to Proust, who gave his existence meaning and style by literally turning it into a work of art, and, according to Nehamas, a perfect one (nothing less would do). But even if we grant the success of Proust's enterprise, it can no more serve as a model for the rest of us than any other unique achievement. It is, in fact, a dangerous, though obviously very tempting example to take, precisely because Proust spent the latter part of his life making literary sense of the first part. But that is hardly a recommendable course for the rest of us, and one can even imagine some caustic remarks that Nietzsche might have made on someone who insulates himself from existence in order to cope with what it had once been. In other words, Proust's career and creation fit Nietzsche's formula all too well. What about the rest of us? Nietzsche insists that we should be both spontaneous and also recognize that nothing that we do is new, since everything recurs eternally; that we should be creative and yet love our fate, which presumably preordains what we are; that we should, like so many metaphysically minded Piafs, regret nothing and yet always be striving to overcome ourselves, since up till now we have all been so much less than we might have been. Paradox is piled on thick – but we can still sympathize with both parts of each of Nietzsche's commands, because once the idea of turning ourselves into works of art has been mooted it is so alluring that, in a post-Christian age, it seems to offer us our best hope. And aren't these paradoxical demands only the reflection of what, in any case, we find achieved in great works of art? In them inevitability is conjoined with seeming spontaneity, in our responses to the ones we love best we know perfectly well what is coming but wait for it with agitated anticipation. Nietzsche felt those things as strongly as anyone ever has, so it was no accident that what he loved most in art he wanted taken over into life, especially since he refused to acknowledge their separation.

On the other hand, and finally, those works he loved so much were the creations of genius, a concept which in his 'sceptical' books, from *Human, All Too Human* to *The Gay Science*, he had deconstructed, and not only because of his disillusionment with one contemporary case of it. If the term is rarely used in his later works it is because he wanted to cleanse life-become-art of the impurities which he thought he had discovered in all art which wasn't life, and which were partly the result of the gap between them. Whether or not he succeeded it is still too early to say – we are only at the beginning of the process of understanding him.

Notes

1 *Nietzsche contra Wagner*, in *The Portable Nietzsche*, trans. Walter Kaufmann (New York, 1954), p. 674.
2 See Martin Gregor-Dellin, *Richard Wagner, Sein Leben, Sein Werk, Sein Jahrhundert* (Munchen, 1980), pp. 749–54, where he claims that Nietzsche's discovery of the correspondence between Wagner and Dr Eiser was the 'fatal wound', and the real cause of the break between them. His argument is not convincing.
3 *The Birth of Tragedy*, trans. Walter Kaufmann (New York, 1967), p. 50.
4 Ibid., p. 50.
5 Ibid., p. 22.
6 *The Will to Power*, trans. Walter Kaufmann and R. J. Hollingdale (London, 1968), p. 435.
7 *The Birth of Tragedy*, p. 88.
8 *Human, All Too Human*, trans. Marion Faber, with Stephen Lehmann (Lincoln and London, 1984), p. 108.
9 Ibid., p. 108.
10 Ibid., p. 108.
11 Ibid., p. 113.
12 Ibid., p. 145.
13 Ibid., p. 144.
14 Ibid., p. 144.
15 Ibid., pp. 148–9.
16 See *Beyond Good and Evil*, trans. Walter Kaufmann (New York, 1966), pp. 233–4.
17 *The Will to Power*, p. 513.
18 Erich Heller, *Thomas Mann, The Ironic German* (Cambridge, 1981), p. 135.
19 *Human, All Too Human*, p. 103.
20 *Beyond Good and Evil*, p. 9.
21 *Daybreak*, trans. R. J. Hollingdale (Cambridge, 1982), pp. 220–1.
22 *The Will to Power*, pp. 466–7.
23 *Twilight of the Idols*, in *The Portable Nietzsche*, p. 539.

8
Deconstructing Genius:
Paul de Man and the Critique of
Romantic Ideology

Christopher Norris

In his essay 'Sign and Symbol in Hegel's *Aesthetics*', Paul de Man addresses what he takes to be the crucial and unresolved problem inhabiting all versions of high-Romantic or Symbolist aesthetics.[1] This problem has to do with the relationship between art and philosophy, and the fact (as de Man argues) that Hegel's compulsion to *theorize* the nature of art leads to a series of discrepancies or blindspots in his argument which undermine his own explicit claims. I want to look closely at this essay, which, together with another of de Man's late productions, 'Phenomenality and Materiality in Kant',[2] presents a detailed working out of de Man's arguments on the topic of Romantic ideology, a topic that focused all his major concerns, from the early essays collected in *Blindness And Insight* (1971) to the posthumous volume *The Resistance To Theory* (1986). In Kant and Hegel, de Man reads a series of persistent contradictions, aporias or antinomies which characterize the discourse of Romanticism and continue to vex modern thought in its attempts to come to terms with that problematic heritage.

What is at issue here is the high valuation of artistic creativity vested in privileged poetic tropes, especially metaphor and symbol. This valuation goes along with the Romantic belief in art as the manifestation of genius, of creative powers that lie beyond the reach of mere craft, learning or applied technique. Metaphor and symbol supposedly transcend the order of quotidian language and perception. They give access to a realm of intuitive or visionary insight where thought overcomes its enslavement to the laws of time, contingency and change. The true mark of genius is the power to create such moments out of time, moments when the mind can contemplate nature and its own 'inner' workings with a sense of achieved harmony, a sense that such distinctions have fallen away in the act of unified perception. And this power has been associated, at least since Aristotle, with metaphor above all other tropes, since metaphor is the means by which language renews its creative resources and breaks with routine, stereotyped habits of thought. For a long line of critics and theorists – including the present-day mainstream interpreters of Romanticism – metaphor becomes the very touchstone of aesthetic value, that which distinguishes the language of poetry from other, straightforwardly referential or cognitive uses.

In Hegel's *Aesthetics* it is symbol, rather than metaphor, that occupies this privileged position.[3] For Hegel, the symbolic is the highest form of art, the most advanced stage that aesthetic consciousness can reach in its striving for a realm of unified knowledge and perception beyond the antinomies of alienated spirit. 'Nowhere else does the structure, the history, and the judgment of art seem to come as close to being systematically carried out, and nowhere else does this systematic synthesis rest so exclusively on one definite category [. . .] called the aesthetic' (SS, 762). Art holds out the utopian promise of a knowledge that would reconcile the hitherto disparate orders of sensuous intuition and conceptual understanding. It does so by restoring a sense of physical or concrete immediacy to those elements of meaning, structure or form that would otherwise belong on the side of abstract intellection. The symbol represents this unifying power at its highest stage of development, since here (as Hegel argues) we witness the capacity of art to transcend or reconcile all those antinomies that plague the discourse of conceptual reason.

It is in terms of this saving imaginative vision that other Romantic theorists – Coleridge among them – will put forward their claims for poetry as a source of secular salvation. For Coleridge, poetic genius partakes of an essentially 'organic' creativity, a condition of restored natural grace where mind is at one with the external world and rejoices in the exercise of its own spontaneous powers. It is here – in the moment of supposedly transcending all commonplace limits of thought and perception – that the symbol (or a certain beguiling idea of the symbol) asserts its paramount claims. For Coleridge, such moments are characterized 'by the translucence of the special in the individual, or of the general in the special, or of the universal in the general; above all by the translucence of the eternal through and in the temporal'.[4] And this can only come about through the grace of genius, manifest chiefly in privileged tropes like metaphor and symbol, tropes that reveal a creative power which is also a kind of second nature, a token of the 'one life, within us and abroad' envisioned by poets like Wordsworth and Coleridge. Thus in Hegel's *Aesthetics*, as de Man writes, 'the symbol is the mediation between the mind and the physical world of which art manifestly partakes, be it as stone, as color, as sound, or as language' (SS, 763).

This follows from Hegel's all-embracing dialectic, his conception of the movement of Mind (or Spirit) as a world-historical progress through successive phases of increasing self-consciousness and interiorized reflective grasp. The beginning of this journey is the state of primitive sense-certainty where the mind has not yet learned to distinguish subject and object – or noumenal and phenomenal realms – and therefore exists in a kind of rich but confused harmony with nature. (This idea finds a parallel in Freud's account of the infant as passing through a phase of 'polymorphous', undifferentiated instinct and desire, and in Lacan's development of the Freudian thesis in terms of a pre-symbolic 'imaginary' stage where desires are as yet unbounded by the Oedipal law that sets limits to the self and prohibits such forms of anarchic self-gratification.[5]) As consciousness evolves, so it comes to recognize the difference between itself and the objects of its knowledge and desire, the ontological gulf that opens up as soon as reflection starts out on its arduous course of discovery. This recognition is both necessary and painful. It is the only way forward for consciousness in its overcoming of naive sense-certainty and its progress toward a reflective, philosophical grasp of its own prehistory. But this advance goes along with a deepening sense of the mind's estrangement from nature, its confinement to a realm of ideas, concepts and representations which enjoy nothing of that primitive, spontaneous being-in-the-world.

This ambivalence in Hegel is of course reproduced in numerous texts of Romantic poetry, criticism and philosophy. It is the basis of Schiller's widely influential distinction between 'naive' and 'sentimental' art, the one existing in a state of undisturbed (because largely pre-reflective) proximity to nature, the other able to evoke that state only from a distance of self-consciousness, nostalgia and ironic hindsight. There is the same underlying pattern to be found in those poems of Wordsworth and Coleridge that look back regretfully to a period in childhood when the visionary sense of communion with nature was as yet untouched by the dislocating, alien effects of self-consciousness and adult knowledge. But this sentiment of loss goes along with the faith that such communion *can* be restored, if only momentarily, by acts of creative imagining that overcome the ontological and temporal void fixed between subject and object, mind and nature. In fact it has been argued – notably by M. H. Abrams – that this is precisely the organizing principle and characteristic form of the 'greater romantic lyric'.[6] It involves, according to Abrams, a three-stage dialectical movement of thought, from recollection of an erstwhile innocence and grace, through despair at the mind's present sense of having lost the strengths and consolations of nature, to a newly found mood of tranquillity and hope based on a wise acceptance of this same predicament. As with Schiller, the mind takes comfort in a knowledge that all is not lost, that the pleasures of reflective or 'sentimental' thought may compensate for whatever is relinquished in the way of spontaneous, natural instinct. And it is chiefly through the agencies of metaphor and symbol that poetry achieves this restorative vision. Thus it comes about, according to Abrams, that 'nature is made thought and thought nature, both by their sustained interaction and by their seamless metaphorical continuity'.[7]

Such a reading finds copious evidence to support its case in the canonical texts of English Romanticism, including the Odes of Wordsworth and Keats and the Coleridge 'Conversation Poems'. And it also acquires a more generalized sense of philosophical conviction from the echoes of Hegelian dialectic that accompany its major claims. For Hegel likewise, art promises to restore that happy reciprocal relation between mind and nature, subject and object, which was once a matter of spontaneous 'natural' grasp. But it does so at a higher dialectical stage of the progress toward reflective self-knowledge, a standpoint from which that earlier condition can only appear as naive and deluded. Hence the pre-eminence of the symbol in Hegel's aesthetic discourse. For 'symbolic art' is that which not only reconciles mind and nature (like metaphor in the passage from Abrams above), but also incorporates a power of inward or phenomenological reflection on its own nature, history and genesis. In de Man's words:

the commanding metaphor that organizes this entire system is that of interiorization, the understanding of aesthetic beauty as the external manifestation of an ideal content which is itself an interiorized experience, the recollected emotion of a bygone perception.

(SS, 771)

It is for this reason, de Man conjectures, that Hegel's *Aesthetics* has found so many echoes among critics (like Abrams) in the mainstream Romantic line of descent. The allusion to Wordsworth ('emotion recollected in tranquillity') is an index of this strong elective tie. What Hegel provides is the basis (or, as de Man would have it, the *putative* basis) for a working faith that poetry can indeed make good its ultimate promise: that language can recapture those moments of inward communing with nature when mind overcomes the melancholy knowledge of its own self-estranged or belated predicament. 'Hegel is indeed, from the relatively early *Phenomenology* to the late *Aesthetics*, prominently the theoretician of internalization, of *Erinnerung*' (SS, 771). His entire philosophy is built upon this root conviction: that mind can only aspire to true knowledge through a thinking-back into the history of cultures, life-forms, ideas and representations that mark the various stages of its progress to date.

Erinnerung – or the power of active, living memory – is both the key to this triumphal progress and the means by which reflection may at last overcome the conflicts and antinomies of philosophic reason still present in thinkers like Kant.

Hence the importance of aesthetics for Hegel, and – more specifically – of the symbol as a means of fulfilling (or appearing to fulfil) this high promise. '*Erinnerung*, recollection as the inner gathering and preserving of experience, brings history and beauty together in the coherence of the system' (SS 771). It is this Hegelian movement of 'interiorization' – this inward turn toward living memory as a source of redemptive insight – that has shaped the reading of English Romanticism offered by interpreters like Abrams. And this reading claims warrant as a faithful account of what these poets manifestly wrote, thought and intended. That is to say, it can point to numerous passages in their work where imagination is indeed credited with a power of overcoming the limits of quotidian knowledge and perception: where language (most often the language of metaphor and symbol) seems to take on an 'organic' or quasi-natural power of creativity, and where the poet celebrates a power of living recollection that transcends all mere contingencies of time and change. So much is a matter of plain self-evidence as long as one takes the word for the deed, assuming – like Abrams – that there *must* be a power vested in metaphor and symbol that enables this passage to rise from the level of declarative statement to the level of achieved effect. And this assumption is indeed a staple of Romantic criticism, as de Man shows in his essay 'The Rhetoric of Temporality', where he gathers a number of representative statements from various present-day commentators. Thus Earl Wasserman takes it as read (so to speak) that Coleridge is genuinely able to reconcile 'the phenomenal world of understanding with the noumenal world of reason'.[8] And Abrams likewise states it as a matter of demonstrable truth that 'the best Romantic meditations on a landscape, following Coleridge's example, all manifest a transaction between subject and object in which the thought incorporates and makes explicit what was already implicit in the outer scene.'[9] Once again, the measure of true Romantic genius is its power to reconcile antinomies, to create (through metaphor and symbol) an autonomous realm of unified thought and perception.

For these critics, the assertion of an 'organic' relationship between mind, nature and language is not to be regarded merely as a topos, a recurrent theme or preoccupying metaphor. On the contrary, they press as far as possible toward *literalizing* the metaphor, taking it in earnest as a sign that poetry can indeed transform the very nature and condition of language. Such is the suasive force of this aesthetic ideology that critics are led to invest in its claims to the point of forgetting that it is, after all, a species of analogy or fiction, and not in any sense a truth about the workings of language. De Man finds a classic illustration of the point in W. K. Wimsatt's well-known essay 'The Structure of Romantic Nature Imagery'. Wimsatt argues that there *did* indeed occur a marked shift in the currency of poetic language at around the turn of the eighteenth century. He sets out to analyse the effects and the extent of this change by comparing two sonnets, one by Coleridge and one by Coleridge's early mentor, the poet Bowles. What chiefly differentiates these two productions is, according to Wimsatt, the greater specificity of surface detail in the Coleridge poem, its 'more faithful observation of the outside object', and – paradoxically – its achievement of a more authentic 'inwardness', a sense that it communicates 'experiences of memory and of reverie that stem from deeper regions of subjectivity than in the earlier writer' (cited *BI*, p. 194).[10] Again, Wimsatt is not content to regard this difference as simply a matter of Coleridge's having achieved a more effective, condensed or metaphorically striking treatment of his theme. In fact he is not overly impressed by this performance, but thinks it is a useful pointer to much greater things. Thus 'the meaning might be such as we have seen in Coleridge's sonnet, but it might more characteristically be more profound, concerning the spirit or soul of things – "the one life within us and abroad". And that meaning especially was summoned out of the very surface of nature' (*BI*, p. 194).[11]

This statement is remarkable partly for the fact that Wimsatt was a chief theorist and spokesman for the American New Criticism. That is to say, his sympathies were far removed from the kind of neo-Romantic position that Abrams and Wasserman clearly represent. For the New Critics – as for Eliot before them – Romanticism figured as a source of manifold tempting errors and delusions. In particular, it tended to blur the distinction between poetry and subjective experience, the line that Eliot insisted should be drawn between 'the man who suffers' and 'the mind which creates'. This classicist demand for impersonality in art was translated by the New Critics into a series of prescriptions for the practice of responsible reading. Hence the various 'fallacies' – biographical, intentionalist and so forth – which Wimsatt and his colleagues regarded as a species of well-nigh heretical confusion. Indeed, one of Wimsatt's last essays was a polemical piece taking on what he saw as the threat to this position from critics like J. Hillis Miller, those who were engaged at the time in a form of applied phenomenology (or 'criticism of consciousness') aimed at breaking down the ontological distinction between author, work and reader-response.[12] Such excursions struck Wimsatt as exhibiting a wilful disregard for the standards of disciplined, objective response established by New Critical method. So it is surprising to find him, in the essay on Coleridge, equating the highest achievements of Romantic poetry with its power to efface ontological differences, to reconcile mind and nature, subject and object, experience in its 'noumenal' and 'phenomenal' aspects.

But in a sense this bears out de Man's contention: that the Hegelian assumptions of post-Romantic criticism cut across the widest divergences of method and principle. In his early essay, 'Form And Intent in the American New Criticism', de Man shows how the anti-intentionalist case rests on a misunderstanding of its own main premise, how poetic 'intentionality' doesn't involve '[the] transfer of a psychic or mental content that exists in the mind of the poet to the mind of a reader', but rather 'the activity of a subject regardless of its empirical concerns, except as far as they relate to the intentionality of the structure' (BI, p. 25). In short, the New Critics were right to reject any simplistic appeal to authorial intentions, but wrong to suppose that their methods were or could be 'objective' in the sense of breaking altogether with intentionalist premises and assumptions. De Man goes on to show how New Criticism mistook the nature of its own privileged metaphors, notably (again) that of the poem as a kind of 'organic' entity. 'Because such patient and delicate attention was paid to the reading of forms, [these] critics pragmatically entered into the hermeneutic circle of interpretation, mistaking it for the organic circularity of natural processes' (BI, p. 29). New Criticism can therefore be seen – despite its more dogmatic disavowals – as belonging very much to the post-Romantic or Hegelian history of thought.

Wimsatt himself gives a hint of this when he describes the poem as a 'concrete universal', an autonomous structure of inwrought meaning which compels a due respect for its objective mode of existence.[13] But the phrase of course derives from Hegel, and carries along with it a range of suggestions that complicate Wimsatt's programmatic message. These include the antinomies of mind and nature, subject and object, the inwardness of reflective self-knowledge and the various forms of phenomenal or naturalized perception that mark the stages of Hegelian dialectic. As de Man writes, 'these categories are susceptible to infinite refinement, and their interplay can undergo numberless combinations, transformations, negations, and expansions' (SS, 771). In Wimsatt's usage, the term 'concrete universal' seems designed to keep these suggestions at bay, to insist on the objective character of poetic meaning, and hence its existence in a realm apart from the vagaries of idealist or speculative thought. But this attempted sublimation of the term's prehistory cannot disguise its Hegelian provenance and its involvement with all those co-implicated themes and metaphors that make up the heritage of Romantic–Symbolist aesthetics. In de Man's words (from the late essay on Hegel):

The dialectics of internalization make up a rhetorical model powerful enough to overcome national and other empirical differences between the various European traditions. Attempts, for instance, to mediate between Hegel and English Romantics such as Wordsworth, Coleridge and Keats often turn around the distinctive topoi of internalization [. . .] In all these instances, Hegel can be invoked as the philosophical counterpart of what occurs with greater delicacy in the figural inventions of the poets.

(SS, 771)

We can now perhaps appreciate the far-reaching character of de Man's proposed revision to the standard history of modern (post-Romantic) critical thought. He is suggesting that this history has been programmed or determined in every last detail by the system of 'commanding metaphors' that Hegel most consistently expounds. This system comprehends not only the poetics of Romanticism but all those schools and movements in the wake of Romanticism which supposedly rejected its claims.

Thus when Eliot (and the New Critics after him) set out to rewrite the canonical Tradition of English poetry, they did so by means of an historical myth which expressly devalued the Romantics but implicitly invoked a whole series of arch-Romantic values and assumptions. If there did indeed occur, as Eliot thought, a 'dissociation of sensibility', a cultural malaise that set in some time toward the mid-seventeenth century, then the only possible standard by which this decline could be measured is that of the 'organic' or unified sensibility, a condition of reconciled thought and sensibility conceived very much in Hegelian terms.[14] And this is exactly the kind of language that Eliot uses when writing about Shakespeare, Donne and other such exemplars of English poetry at its finest. Thus Eliot's avowed antipathy to Romanticism goes along with a covert adherence to its whole working system of evaluative terms and categories. As with Hegel, so with Eliot's potent mythology: the aesthetic becomes a privileged ground on which poetry (or a certain idea of poetry) lays down the terms for historical understanding. And the same applies (so de Man argues) to other, more recent varieties of critical thought. Thus Hans-Georg Gadamer speaks for the enterprise of modern hermeneutics when he affirms the superiority of symbol over allegory, since the language of symbolism opens the way to a deeper, more intimate communion of minds between text and interpreter.[15] And again this involves a very marked preference for that period of Romantic speculative thought when such organicist metaphors attained their greatest prominence. For Gadamer, in short, 'the valorization of symbol at the expense of allegory' coincides with 'the growth of an aesthetics that refuses to distinguish between experience and the representation of this experience'. Furthermore, it is the 'poetic language of genius' that transcends such prosaic distinctions and 'can thus transform all individual experience into general truth' (*BI*, p. 188). There is thus a very direct line of descent from the poetics of Romanticism to the methods and principles of modern hermeneutic philosophy.

De Man typically asserts the need for a watchful, resistant practice of reading in a language that carries strongly marked ethical overtones. 'The aesthetic is, by definition, a seductive notion that appeals to the pleasure principle, a eudaimonic judgment that can displace and conceal values of truth and falsehood likely to be more resilient to desire than values of pleasure and pain' (*RT*, p. 64). Thus when de Man speaks of the 'resistance to theory' – as in the title of a late essay and the posthumous collection of which that essay forms a part – his use of the phrase is distinctly double-edged. On the one hand it denotes the overt *hostility* to literary theory among critics who regard it as an alien, subversive discourse, or at best a mere distraction from the common pursuit of true judgement which is all that criticism can hope to achieve. This response is familiar enough, from F. R. Leavis's famous refusal to 'philosophize' when challenged by René Wellek in the mid 1930s,[16] to the various attacks on deconstruction, post-structuralism and other such recent theoretical trends. It reflects the deep attachment to commonsense-intuitive values and assumptions which has characterized the discourse of literary criticism from Arnold to Leavis and beyond. To this extent, the 'resistance to theory' is a matter of largely institutional forces and pressures, a resistance that comes, so to speak, from outside and defines itself in straightforwardly adversary terms. But there is also, according to de Man, a resistance internal to theory itself, a point at which that enterprise comes up against problems resulting from its own methodological commitments. It is here precisely that de Man locates the source of those persistent errors, confusions and misreadings that critics are prone to when their judgement is in the grip of some powerful *a priori* theory. The effect is to generate a kind of prematurely synthesizing method, an approach that takes for granted the ultimate compatibility of linguistic, historical and aesthetic values.

Hence the seductive power of any theory that promises to reconcile these disjunct dimensions, to provide an all-embracing hermeneutic model that would overcome every such resistance. Close reading is to this extent the active antithesis of 'theory' in its more doctrinaire or reductive form. That is to say, it forces the critic to recognize those problematic elements of meaning, structure and style which hold out against a reading intent upon reducing them to consistency with its own fixed ideas. This is one reason why de Man often praises the American New Critics, despite what he sees as their unfortunate tendency to raise certain privileged rhetorical tropes (paradox, irony, etc.) into a species of premature aesthetic ontology. For there was always, he argues, a strong countervailing impulse in their work, a devotion to the business of close reading and detailed textual explication which put up a resistance to such preconceived aesthetic absolutes. We might recall that de Man became acquainted with New Critical practice soon after his arrival in America, at a time (the early 1950s) when it was set to bring about the most far-reaching changes in the way that literature was taught and understood. Its emphasis on close reading and its apparent unconcern with larger, 'philosophical' issues would no doubt have struck him all the more forcibly for the fact that up to then he had been very much influenced by thinkers like Heidegger, Sartre and Blanchot, for whom such issues were inseparable from the interests of literary criticism.

For de Man, therefore, the resistance in question has a negative and a positive aspect. On the one hand 'theory' is the willingness to question received ideologies of language, literature and historical method which otherwise succeed in imposing their values in the form of self-evident, commonsense knowledge. To this extent theory is a liberating force, an active critique of those aesthetic beliefs and preconceptions that characterize the discourse of modern (post-Romantic) thought. The 'resistance' to it would then be an index of the strength, depth and tenacity of purpose mustered on the side of that aesthetic ideology. But there is also, as we have seen, a sense in which the phrase turns back upon itself and implies that such resistance may be a matter of reading *against* theory as well as theorizing the blindspots in other, naive or self-deluded readings. This is much more what preoccupies de Man in his late essays on Jauss, Riffaterre and those other proponents of literary theory in a form that aspires to methodological completeness and rigour.[17] In these critics, 'the resistance to theory [. . .] is a resistance to language itself or to the possibility that language contains factors or functions that cannot be reduced to intuition' (*RT*, pp. 12–13). What prevails in their reading is always the desire that texts should make sense according to some model of historical, aesthetic or hermeneutic grasp that overcomes any obstacles in its way. In such cases the 'resistance to theory' is itself a very strong theoretical *parti pris*, but one that protects its own methodological assumptions by not exposing them to textual problems and resistances that might jeopardize its whole project.

So theory is a strictly impossible venture in so far as it aims – as most theories do – to achieve a sense of having thoroughly mastered the relevant problems and issues. To de Man, such illusions are precisely what criticism has to give up as it comes to recognize those deviant linguistic structures, or elements of rhetorical 'undecidability', that work to undermine any form of self-assured hermeneutic understanding. 'Nothing can overcome the resistance to theory since theory *is* itself this resistance' (*RT*, p. 19). Theory, that is to say, in the form of an applied rhetoric that would mark exactly those points of divergence between what a text says – the stubborn materiality of the words on the page – and what the various critics have made it say for theoretical and ideological reasons of their own. Rhetorical readings of this kind are, de Man suggests,

> the most elastic theoretical and dialectical model to end all models and they can rightly claim to contain within their own defective selves all the other defective models of reading-avoidance [. . .] They are theory and not theory at the same time, the universal theory of the impossibility of theory. To the extent however that they are theory [. . .] rhetorical readings, like the other kinds, still avoid and resist the reading they advocate.
>
> (*RT*, p. 19)

This extraordinary passage brings out all the tensions and paradoxes that run through de Man's late essays. It presents a number of provocative theses in a language of straightforwardly constative or truth-telling force which scarcely seems to brook any kind of dissenting response. Yet in each case this authoritative stance is directly undercut by what the passage goes on to suggest: namely, that there is no vantage-point from which *any* kind of theory, de Man's included, could possibly claim to control or comprehend the workings of figural language.

The fact that this conclusion is arrived at nonetheless through a series of assertive propositions – sentences that claim to state the truth about language, or rather the lesson that no such truth can finally, properly be stated – is a difficulty that de Man never seeks to deny. It is addressed most directly in one of the essays on Nietzsche from *Allegories of Reading*, where he begins by contrasting two dimensions of language, the 'constative' and 'performative', and ends by effectively collapsing that distinction or revealing its undecidability in any given case. Nietzsche goes as far as possible toward showing up the inherently rhetorical nature of all those concepts, categories and truth-claims that 'philosophy' accepts at face value.[18] Like de Man, he suspects that we are imposed upon by language to the point of forgetting how our notions took rise from certain long-since naturalized tropes or figures of thought. And one major target of Nietzsche's sceptical critique is precisely that phenomenalist set of assumptions which maintains the primacy of physical perception (or some analogue thereof) at every level of thought and language.

For Nietzsche, this amounts to no more than a species of persistent rhetorical illusion, brought about by the trope of *metalepsis* (or reversal), the figure that substitutes cause for effect through a covert exchange of priorities. Thus in Nietzsche's words (from a passage entitled 'Phenomenalism of the Inner World'):

pain is projected in a part of the body without having its origin there; [conversely] the perceptions which one naively considers as determined by the outside world are much rather determined from the inside; [. . .] the fragment of outside world of which we are conscious is a correlative of the effect that has reached us from outside and is then projected, *a posteriori*, as its 'cause'.

(cited in *AR*, p. 109)

De Man is careful to state that he is not so much concerned with Nietzsche's specific 'thesis' at this point as with 'the general manner in which his argument is conducted'. That is to say, the relevance of this passage for de Man's purposes has nothing to do with any claims it may make as to the causes of pain, the nature of perception or human experience in general. What he wishes to examine is the structure of an argument that approaches the limits of intelligible discourse by attributing every last concept and category to the workings of language or rhetoric. Thus de Man is not obliged to go along with some of Nietzsche's more immoderate or downright nonsensical claims, like the wholesale dismissal of causal explanations as a species of rhetorical imposture. (That others have not been so circumspect in their reading, whether of Nietzsche or de Man, is of course a quite different story.) Rather, he is concerned to isolate the source of that *particular* phenomenalist error that dominates the thinking of aesthetic philosophers from Hegel to the present. And Nietzsche provides a most effective means to this end when he shows that, in some cases at least, rhetoric assists in the effacement or forgetting of its own operations by allowing us to think of language in naively phenomenalist terms.

This has all taken us a long way around from that original question as to the bearing of deconstructionist theory on the Romantic ideology of genius. But the connection is not, after all, so remote if de Man's arguments hold good and it can indeed be shown that the whole development of modern critical thinking derives from a certain endemic confusion of language (or the signifying structures of language) with the order of phenomenal cognition. For then it would appear – as de Man implicitly argues – that 'genius' is very much an idea resulting from the will to find *proof* of exactly that ideal convergence between mind and nature, language and whatever belongs to the world of sensuous experience. It is in Kant that these issues first achieve the status of primordial questions that philosophy needs to address before it can claim the least warrant to pronounce on matters of epistemic, ethical or aesthetic judgement. For de Man, Kant's thinking is a reference-point by which to assess the various errors, misreadings and ideological mystifications that have subsequently overtaken the history of critical and philosophic thought. I shall therefore now turn to Kantian aesthetics by way of drawing out some further implications of de Man's late essays.

For Kant, genius is 'a talent for producing that for which no definite *rule* can be given'.[19] The productions of genius have this as their characterizing mark: that no amount of learning, acquired skill or imitative talent can possibly suffice for their creation. Aesthetic perception is therefore distinguished from *theoretical* understanding – from the kind of knowledge that mainly preoccupies Kant in his first *Critique* – by its not conforming to the cardinal rule that every intuition be brought under an adequate or corresponding concept. It is precisely this incommensurable nature of artistic genius that sets it apart from science, theory and the labours of enlightened (epistemological) critique. Thus 'the concept of beautiful art does not permit the judgment upon the beauty of a product to be derived from any rule which has a *concept* as its determining ground, and therefore has as its basis a concept of the way in which the product is possible' (*KS*, p. 418). This is why Kant rejects any form of phenomenalist aesthetic that would treat art as possessing the power to reconcile concepts with sensuous intuitions. Such thinking fails to register what is distinctive in the nature of aesthetic experience: namely, the capacity of genius to create new forms, ideas and images that exceed all the bounds of theoretical (or rule-governed) understanding. The author of such works 'does not himself know how he has come by his Ideas', and certainly lacks the kind of knowledge that would allow him 'to devise the like at pleasure or in accordance with a plan' (*KS*, p. 419). Whence the basic difference between art and all other forms of cognitive activity: that in art there is no question of intellectual *progress*, of collective advance through a shared application of the truths discovered by previous thinkers.

Kant's great example here is Newton, a figure whose intellect indeed took him voyaging into strange seas of thought, but whose findings, once established, opened up the trade-routes of received, communal knowledge. Such scientific truth-claims are warranted precisely by their power of bringing intuitions under concepts, or showing that determinate rules can be given for the understanding of natural phenomena. Thus 'Newton could make all his steps, from the first elements of geometry to his own great and profound discoveries, intuitively plain and definite as regards their consequence, not only to himself but to everyone else' (*KS*, p. 420). But this is not the case with those whose genius lies in the production of beautiful artworks. Theirs is a strictly *incommunicable* gift which cannot be taught, reduced to precepts, or in any way simply handed on. Such genius

produces individual creations for which the mould (so to speak) is broken
with each new endeavour and allows of no progressive building on
previous achievements. Or more exactly, if artists can indeed learn from
their great precursors, the lesson is more by way of general inspiration
than anything pertaining to form, style or technique. For genius,
according to Kant, is 'imparted to every artist immediately by the hand of
nature; and so it dies with him, until nature endows another in the same
way, so that he only needs an example in order to put in operation in a
similar fashion the talent of which he is conscious' (*KS*, p. 420). So art
exists at the furthest possible remove from that spirit of enlightened,
cooperative enterprise that for Kant belongs to both science and
philosophy in its aspect of rational critique. Art may be said to 'stand still'
in the sense that its productions exhibit no signs of advancing toward an
enlightened consensus on the 'rules' of judgement or taste.

This is why Kant rejects the idea that beauty resides in the object of
aesthetic contemplation. If this were the case, then there could be no clear
distinction between theoretical knowledge (that which applies concepts to
the realm of sensible intuitions) and aesthetic understanding (that which
allows us a privileged grasp of our own appreciative faculties at work).
Kant is very firm about this need to resist any form of phenomenalist
reduction. Aesthetic judgement contributes nothing to our knowledge of
the objects that solicit its regard. Of course those objects must possess
certain attributes, qualities that mark them out in the first place as
capable of arousing such response. Otherwise art would be an empty
concept and aesthetics would lack any claim to exist as a self-respecting
discipline of thought. But we are equally mistaken, Kant argues, if we
assimilate whatever is distinctive in the act of aesthetic judgement to those
properties supposedly inherent in the object itself. For beauty is not
determined by any concepts (or rules) that would find adequate
exemplification in the features – or objective characteristics – of this or
that artwork. It should rather be sought in the manner of our responding
to such features, or the way that our various faculties are engaged in the
act of aesthetic understanding. And this is where the experience of art
differs essentially from other forms of cognitive experience. 'In order to
decide whether anything is beautiful or not, we refer the representation,
not by the Understanding to the Object for cognition but, by the
Imagination (perhaps in conjunction with the Understanding) to the
subject, and its feeling of pleasure or pain' (*KS*, p. 375). Such is the inward
or transcendental turn in Kantian aesthetics, the movement away from all
forms of phenomenalist reduction. In the act of responding sympathetically
to a beautiful object, the mind is thrown back (so to speak) upon its own
resources, required to seek a sense of purposive relationship or harmony
not between sensuous intuitions and concepts of understanding (as in

all forms of theoretical knowledge), but rather between those various faculties whose interplay thus defines the nature of aesthetic experience.

But of course Kant is at pains not to suggest that this 'subjective' character of aesthetic judgement amounts to a species of relativism in matters of artistic taste. To pronounce a work beautiful is always to claim a validity for one's judgement that cannot be compared with the expression of mere personal *preference* in this or that regard. Thus one may (indeed must) be content to differ with other people on the question of what makes a good wine, a satisfying meal or a pleasant way of spending one's time. Such opinions are specific to the judging individual and can lay no claim to universal validity. It would be folly, Kant says, to 'reprove as incorrect' another person's sentiments in the hope of persuading them to see reason and admit one's own superior taste. But this principle – '*de gustibus, non est disputandum*' – cannot apply in the realm of aesthetic judgement, any more than with issues of ethical reason. Here it is a question of requiring assent to one's evaluative statements, or putting them forward as considered judgements with a claim to universal validity. So the reflective individual learns to distinguish between matters of idiosyncratic taste and matters of absolute or principled judgement. 'Many things may have for him charm and pleasantness; no one troubles himself at that; but if he gives out anything as beautiful, he supposes in others the same satisfaction – he judges not merely for himself, but for everyone, and speaks of beauty as if it were a property of things' (*KS*, p. 384). So the argument here goes by way of analogy, deriving the universal character of aesthetic judgements from our need to treat them *as if* they related to qualities somehow objectively present in the work or natural phenomenon concerned.[20] But what is really at issue in such judgements is the utterer's fitness to pronounce them with authority owing to his or her possession of the requisite taste or appreciative powers. And this means that there is, after all, a realm of properly subjective judgements whose nature is nonetheless universal (or prescriptive) in so far as they effectively demand our assent and brook no denial on grounds of mere personal taste.

Kant attaches the highest importance to this legislative aspect of aesthetic judgement. Thus it cannot be a matter, as Hume had argued, of the social interests that are best served by our reaching some measure of agreement on questions of good taste and beauty. For this could be no more than an *empirical* fact about our present social arrangements, and so a source of value only as related to our short-term motives and interests. To see the limits of such thinking, Kant argues, 'we have only to look to what may have a reference, although only indirectly, to the judgment of taste *a priori*' (*KS*, p. 381). For even if reflection does find traces of self-interest or social motivation, still we are compelled by the very nature of such judgements to accord them a validity beyond anything accountable on those terms alone. At this stage, according to Kant,

taste would discover a transition of our judging faculty from sense-enjoyment to moral feeling; and so not only would we be the better guided in employing taste purposively, but there would be thus presented a link in the chain of human faculties *a priori*, on which all legislation must depend.

(*KS*, pp. 381–2)

So there exists an analogy between aesthetic judgement and practical reason (or ethics), as well as that other which Kant perceives between aesthetics and the order of phenomenal cognition. Both are in the nature of 'as if' arguments, designed to give universal import to aesthetic values while *not* confusing them either with purely theoretical knowledge, on the one hand, or with ethical judgement on the other. Thus Kant insists that art take its place as a 'link in the chain' of human faculties, an indispensable link, to be sure, but one whose role in the total system – the Kantian 'architectonic' – needs defining with considerable care and circumspection. Otherwise aesthetics will overstep the limit of its own legitimate domain, with untoward results not only for itself but for the whole enterprise of enlightened critique.

We can best understand what de Man has to say about Kant, Hegel and the subsequent discourse of 'aesthetic ideology' if we read his work against this background of contesting truth-claims and legislative faculties. It will then become clear that he, like Kant, is concerned to set limits to the play of seductive metaphors and analogies that characterize aesthetic understanding, that he sees a real danger in the various moves to extend or annul those limits, to apply aesthetic notions *directly* to other domains of knowledge, and that this is what leads him to treat such attempts with an unrelenting suspicion. I have already tried to show how this argument takes shape in de Man's readings of Hegel and Romantic criticism. It fastens on those moments of critical 'blindness' where thought falls prey to the phenomenalist delusion, the idea that language – especially the language of metaphor and symbol – can become in some way consubstantial with the world of natural objects and processes, and so transcend the ontological gulf between words (or concepts) and sensuous intuitions.

The best-known example is the chapter on Proust (*AR*, pp. 57–78) where de Man takes a single, exemplary episode – the young Marcel reflecting on the solitary pleasures of reading and their superiority over other, more extravert or outdoor kinds of enjoyment – and shows how the passage in fact turns on the systematic privilege attaching to metaphor, as opposed to pedestrian or routine tropes like metonymy.[21] Metaphor is on the side of inwardness, imagination, contemplative withdrawal and all that belongs to the realm of pure, self-delighting creative reverie.

Metonymy, by contrast, is a literalistic trope that works on the basis of external or real-world relationsips, those (like contiguity) which allow no room for exploring the freedoms of a rich imaginative life. Thus the passage presents a veritable 'allegory of reading', one where every detail reinforces the idea that it is somehow *better* for Marcel to be sitting indoors with a book – thus allowing his mind the full scope of its self-sufficient inward resources – rather than leaving his room and suffering all the nuisances, perils and distractions of the outside world. As de Man reads this passage,

> two apparently incompatible chains of connotations have thus been set up: one, engendered by the idea of 'inside' space and governed by 'imagination', possesses the qualities of coolness, tranquillity, darkness as well as totality, whereas the other, linked to the 'outside' and dependent on the 'senses', is marked by the opposite qualities of warmth, activity, light, and fragmenation.
>
> (*AR*, p. 60)

Metaphor connotes 'totality' along with its other positive values because, unlike metonymy, it implies that special power of creative imagination to evoke a whole world of unified thought and feeling untouched by the crass contingencies of everyday life. What is more, it suggests a yet higher stage in the totalizing process, a moment of consummate or hypostatic union when the very difference between inward and outward realms would at last fall away, and imagination reign supreme through the gift of metaphorical insight. Thus Marcel 'finds access to the "total spectacle of Summer", including the attractions of direct physical action, and [. . .] possesses it much more effectively than if he had been actually present in an outside world that he then could only have known by bits and pieces' (*AR*, p. 60). What the passage from Proust therefore seeks to convey is a sense of radically transformative vision whose enabling trope is metaphor and whose claim is nothing less than to have overcome all the bad antinomies of rational (prosaic) thought.

But there are, according to de Man, rhetorical forces at work in this passage which effectively resist and subvert that claim. For the metaphors that carry the main weight of implication also turn out, on a closer reading, to depend on a certain tropological sleight of hand, a covert series of 'exchanges and substitutions' whose structure is undeniably *metonymic* in the last analysis. De Man makes this point in a few remarkable pages whose sheer complexity of detailed textual exegesis defies any attempt at paraphrase. But the upshot is to show (1) that the inner realm of Marcel's imagining has to borrow its descriptive terms at every point from the 'contingent', 'fragmentary' world of natural experience; (2) that this amounts to a virtual undoing of metaphoric truth-claims through the effects of a generalized metonymy; and (3) that any reading which accepts those claims at face value will be blind to what is *really* going on in the

Proustian text, and thus complicit with the force of 'seduction' exerted by its leading metaphors and analogies. 'A rhetorical reading of the passage reveals that the figural praxis and the metafigural theory do not converge and that the assertion of the mastery of metaphor over metonymy owes its persuasive power to the use of metonymic structures' (*AR*, p. 15). In which case – as de Man goes on to argue – we shall have to recognize some large obstacles in the way of any critical reading, aesthetic philosophy or theory of language that thinks to negotiate or short-cut the passage from linguistic signs to the order of perceptions and natural experience.

This may come down to an ultimate choice between 'aesthetically responsive' and 'rhetorically aware' readings, those which go along with the metaphoric drift for its yield of imaginative pleasure, and those which hold out against such easy satisfactions for the sake of a better, less deluded understanding. De Man makes some pretence of even-handedness in this. He declares that the two kinds of reading are 'equally compelling', and denies that it is possible to read at all without in some measure submitting one's judgement to the suasive operations of metaphor. But the terms in which de Man presents this choice – on the one hand 'seduction', naive enjoyment, a relaxed and pleasurable complicity with the text, on the other an ethos of undeceived rigour, a determination not to be thus beguiled or seduced – can leave no doubt as to which is for him the right option. 'The relationship between the literal and the figural senses of a metaphor is always,' he writes, 'metonymic, though motivated by a constitutive tendency to pretend the opposite' (*AR*, p. 71). This tendency is a product of the same deep-laid aesthetic ideology that de Man finds at work in the texts of critics and philosophers after Kant. It is 'constitutive' in the sense that it is *not* a mere mistake or local aberration that could always be corrected in the wisdom of critical hindsight. Rather it is a kind of permanent temptation to which thought is subject whenever it approaches the complex terrain of language, ideology and aesthetic understanding. That the error persists through such a range of texts – poems, novels, works of philosophy, critical theory and so forth – should be evidence enough that its sources go deep into our 'natural', received or commonsense grasp of these matters.

This is why de Man makes a point of insisting that his chapter on Proust has nothing in common with the usual literary-critical forms of thematic or interpretative discourse. Since it does, after all, single out an episode in which *reading* – the reading of imaginative literature – figures as a central theme, one might be forgiven for assuming that this was what sparked de Man's interest in the passage, and that therefore his chapter is an ingenious example of thematic commentary in the modern reflexive or self-conscious mode. Not so, de Man urges, 'for we cannot *a priori* be certain to gain access to whatever Proust may have to say about reading by way of such a reading of a scene of reading' (*AR*, p. 57). That is to say, the exemplary value of the episode lies not so much in its thematization of issues that happen to engage de Man's interest, but in the fact that it raises these issues at a level of generalized import beyond any such local concern. 'The question is precisely whether a literary text is *about* that which it describes, represents, or states' (*AR*, p. 57). And for de Man that question must clearly be answered in the negative. The problems encountered in reading a fictional text like *Du Côté de chez Swann* cannot be distinguished in any rigorous or clear-cut way from those presented by Hegel's *Aesthetics* or other such works of philosophy and theory. In each case there is the choice between simply accepting what the text has to say – reading along with its persuasive drift – and deconstructing the figural devices by which such effects are achieved. Thus the real dividing line is that which separates readings that are somehow imposed upon by forms of rhetorical mystification from readings that possess the rhetorical means to resist such unwitting collusion.

The idea of genius is closely bound up with that complex of 'metaphysical' themes and motifs that de Man contrasts with the labours of enlightened or demystifying thought. Genius, like the Sublime, is a category that transcends all categorization; that 'gives the rule just as nature does' but cannot itself be reduced to any rule; whose hallmarks are, on the one hand, its power to tease philosophy almost out of thought, and on the other its kinship with the highest ('supersensible') faculties of human reason. To theorize the nature of genius is an impossible undertaking from the start, although this has not prevented Kant and subsequent aesthetic philosophers from making the attempt. We can now return to de Man's essay on Hegel, where he finds early signs of that persistent misreading of Kant that has characterized the discourse of aesthetic ideology down to this day. De Man singles out two propositions in Hegel which between them – as he argues – exemplify the impossible predicament of theory *vis-à-vis* the Romantic ideology of art. One is Hegel's statement that 'the Beautiful is the sensory manifestation of the Idea', a claim that clearly represents, for de Man, a considerable slackening of philosophic rigour when compared with Kant's more complex, circuitous and endlessly self-qualifying treatment of cognate themes. The other is his dictum that 'Art is for us a thing of the past,' by which Hegel means that philosophy (or Reason in its all-embracing reflective and historical mode) has usurped the privileged role once occupied by the highest forms of aesthetic experience. De Man's point is that these two propositions should be taken together and read as symptomatic of the errors and confusions that overtake aesthetic theory after Kant. What makes art a 'thing of the past' for Hegel is not, as he would have us think, its belonging to an earlier, relatively undeveloped stage in the history of culture and thought. Rather, it results from the impossible demand that Hegel himself places upon art, his retreat into a form of aesthetic ideology which seeks to bypass the antinomies of critical reason. It is Hegel's great project in this work 'to bring together, under the aegis of the aesthetic, a historical causality with a linguistic structure, an experiential and empirical event in time with a given, non-phenomenal fact of language' (SS, 763). Such would be the nature of the symbol – the highest manifestation of artistic genius – if Hegel could indeed make good his claims. But on a closer reading it is language itself that turns out to frustate this project, language that undoes the *a priori* valuation of symbol over other, more pedestrian tropes like allegory.

De Man's closing paragraph in the Hegel essay can stand as a summary statement of how deconstruction – on his understanding of that term – relates to the Romantic ideology of genius as manifest in the discourse on symbol and metaphor. 'We would have to conclude,' he writes,

> that Hegel's philosophy which, like his *Aesthetics*, is a philosophy of history (and of aesthetics) as well as a history of philosophy (and of aesthetics) – and the Hegelian corpus indeed contains texts that bear these two symmetrical titles – is in fact an allegory of the disjunction between philosophy and history, or, in our more restricted concern, between literature and aesthetics, or, more narrowly still, between literary experience and literary theory.
>
> (SS, 775)

It is this conviction that gives de Man's writing its singular austerity and rigour, its refusal to countenance what he regards as the easy satisfactions of naive, uncritical reading. Adorno is another of those modern theorists whom de Man cites as responding very warily to the totalizing claims of Hegel's *Aesthetics*. And if one wanted to find a parallel for de Man's hermeneutics of suspicion, his thoroughgoing principled mistrust of all aesthetic ideologies, then Adorno provides the most striking instance.[22] Deconstruction is indeed a form of negative dialectics, an activity that carries on the project of immanent or self-reflective critique developed by Hegel out of Kant, but which turns this project against its own desire for such premature end-points as Symbol or Absolute Reason. That de Man pursues these problems by way of their textual or rhetorical manifestation – rather than taking the 'philosophic' path of self-assuredly conceptual exegesis – should by now not blind us to the truly philosophical character of his work.

The kinship with Adorno comes out most clearly on those rare occasions in his later writing when de Man allows himself to generalize briefly on what deconstruction 'is' or 'does'. One such occasion is the passage on Rousseau from *Allegories of Reading* where he offers the following programmatic statement:

Since a deconstruction always has for its target to reveal the existence of hidden articulations and fragmentations within assumedly monadic totalities, nature turns out to be a self-deconstructive term [. . .] Far from denoting a homogeneous mode of being, 'nature' connotes a process of deconstruction redoubled by its own fallacious retotalization.

(*AR*, p. 249)

In a sense, this passage recapitulates everything that we have seen so far of de Man's engagement with aesthetic ideology, his critique of prematurely 'totalizing' truth-claims, and his will to deconstruct the powers of rhetorical mystification vested in privileged tropes like metaphor and symbol. For it is always through the appeal to *nature* – nature as the ultimate source and analogue for human creativity or genius – that aesthetic ideology most strongly asserts its hold. For Kant, we may recall, genius 'does not describe or indicate scientifically how it brings about its products, but it gives the rule just as nature does' (*KS*, p. 418). And again: 'Nature by the medium of genius does not prescribe rules to Science, but to Art; and to it only in so far as it is to be beautiful Art' (*KS*, p. 419). The legacy of these and other such statements can be read everywhere in the Romantic discourse on art, imagination, genius and the reconciling power of aesthetic experience. In particular, they generate that single most persistent and seductive of Romantic tropes: the organicist idea of art as a kind of second nature, a 'heterocosm' where all bad antinomies fall away and imagination achieves a perfect union of subject and object, inward and outward worlds.

What is disguised in this idealizing movement of thought, so de Man argues, is the autocratic power and potential violence by which imagination may seem to secure its claims. These possibilities are spelled out most clearly when de Man turns to Schiller and the idea of 'aesthetic education' as a kind of utopian promise, a passage beyond the various conflicts – the symptoms of 'dissociated' thought and sensibility – that currently prevail. For de Man, this promise is more in the nature of a subdued threat, a vision of the faculties as existing *apparently* in a state of harmonious freedom and grace, but *in fact* as constrained by an imperative power of 'aesthetic formalization'. His remarks about Schiller appear in the course of an essay on Kleist's remarkable text '*Uber das Marionettentheater*' ('On the Puppet Theatre').[23] His point in juxtaposing the two authors is to bring out the essential kinship between Schiller's ideal of aesthetic education and Kleist's disturbing allegory of human perfection (bodily and spiritual) as a kind of mechanical, puppet-like capacity to transcend all forms of disabling self-consciousness or inward division. For Kleist as for Schiller, this perfection is imaged in terms of an ideal *choreography*, a dance in which (as Schiller writes) 'everything fits so skilfully, yet so spontaneously, that everyone seems to be following his own lead, without ever getting in anyone's way.'[24] And the corresponding stage of aesthetic education is the point at which we glimpse 'a wisdom that lies somehow beyond cognition and self-knowledge, yet can only be reached by ways of the process it is said to overcome' (*RR*, p. 265). Thus dance takes on all the attributes of that transcendent, synthesizing power of imaginative vision that Hegel and his followers ascribe to language in its highest creative forms.

De Man sees good reason – on political grounds chiefly – to mistrust this apparently benign promise of an end to our present, self-divided condition. What emerges from the intertextual reading of Schiller and Kleist is 'the trap of an aesthetic education which inevitably confuses dismemberment of language by the power of the letter with the gracefulness of a dance' (*RR*, p. 290). So seductive is the promise of aesthetic formalization that it can easily overcome that other, more critical mode of reading which allows for the resistance that language puts up to any forced or premature merging of the faculties. 'The "state" that is being advocated [in Schiller's *Letters On Aesthetic Education*] is not just a state of mind or of soul, but a principle of political value and authority that has its own claims on the shape and the limits of our freedom' (*RR*, p. 264). As with his reading of Proust, de Man is here concerned to detect that movement of conceptual overreaching where aesthetics – or a certain prevalent form of aesthetic ideology – seeks to legislate in realms beyond its proper epistemological grasp. These are the realms of ethics and politics, the domain of practical reason where Kant found room for *analogies* drawn from aesthetic understanding, but always and only on terms laid down by a rigorous critique of their powers and limits. What distinguishes Kantian aesthetics from the subsequent misreading of Kant by Schiller and others is the blurring of these properly critical lines of demarcation between art, epistemology, history and ethics. And the fact that such errors may have worldly consequences beyond the specialized sphere of textual hermeneutics is exemplified plainly enough by the aftermath of German idealist metaphysics. 'The point,' de Man says, 'is not that the dance fails and that Schiller's idyllic description of a graceful but confined freedom is aberrant. Aesthetic education by no means fails; it succeeds all too well, to the point of hiding the violence that makes it possible' (*RR*, p. 289).

To deconstruct the ideology of genius is to see just how such notions have carried across into other, potentially more dangerous spheres. It reveals the charge conserved in the word's very etymology, that is to say, its relation to the *genius loci*, the tutelary spirit of homegrounds and origins, a figure that translates readily enough into forms of nationalist mystique. And indeed there were those, like Herder, who found no difficulty in revising Kant's doctrines so as to give them a romantic-nationalist appeal totally at odds with their enlightenment character. In 'The Rhetoric of Temporality', de Man refers to Herder's debate with Hamann – a debate on hermeneutics and the origin of language – as one that brought out the main points at issue between symbolic and allegorical modes of understanding. In Herder, the desire to assimilate language to a mystified ontology of nationalist spirit goes along with the swerve from a Kantian rigour of epistemological critique. And this attitude encounters in Hamann 'a resistance that reveals the complexity of the intellectual climate in which the debate between symbol and allegory will take place' (*BI*, p. 189). The ideology of genius is very much a part of this Romantic drive to naturalize art and language in terms of their authentic national provenance and destiny. Kant himself might appear to invite such a reading when he remarks that the notion of genius probably derived from 'that peculiar guiding and guardian spirit given to a man at his birth, from whose suggestion these original Ideas proceed' (*KS*, p. 419). But this passage is untypical and goes clean against the most basic precepts of Kantian critical reason. That the aesthetic can exert such a mystifying hold upon the 'faculties' of enlightened thought is a theme that continually preoccupied de Man in the writings of his last decade. And we are mistaken, he warns, if we treat these as marginal or ultra-specialized problems, of interest only to a handful of philosophers or literary theorists. For 'the political power of the aesthetic, the measure of its impact on reality, necessarily travels by way of its didactic manifestations' (*RR*, p. 273). It is hardly surprising, in the light of these claims, that de Man's work continues to generate such widespread hostility and resistance.

Notes

The following works are referred to by initials only with page numbers in the text:

AR = Paul de Man, *Allegories of Reading: figural language in Rousseau, Nietzsche, Rilke, and Proust* (New Haven, 1979).
BI = de Man, *Blindness and Insight: Essays in the Rhetoric of Contemporary Criticism*, 2nd edn, revised & expanded (London, 1983).
KS = *Kant: Selections*, ed. Theodore M. Greene (New York, 1957).
PMK = de Man, 'Phenomenality and Materiality in Kant', in Gary Shapiro and Alan Sica (eds), *Hermeneutics: Questions and Prospects* (Amherst, 1984), pp. 121–44.
RR = de Man, *The Rhetoric of Romanticism* (New York, 1984).
RT = de Man, *The Resistance To Theory* (Minneapolis, 1986).

SS = de Man, 'Sign and Symbol in Hegel's *Aesthetics*', *Critical Inquiry*, VIII (1982), 761–75.

1 See details under SS, above. De Man takes up some connected lines of argument in his essay 'Hegel on the Sublime', in Mark Krupnick (ed.), *Displacement: Derrida and After* (Bloomington, Ind., 1983), pp. 139–53.

2 Details under PMK, above. For a discussion of related topics in Kant, see de Man, 'The Epistemology of Metaphor', *Critical Inquiry*, V (1978), 13–30.

3 See G. W. F. Hegel, *Aesthetics*, trans. T. W. Knox (Oxford, 1975).

4 S. T. Coleridge, *The Statesman's Manual* (New York, 1875), p. 438. Cited by de Man, *BI*, p. 192.

5 See Jacques Lacan, *Ecrits: A Selection*, trans. A. Sheridan-Smith (London, 1977).

6 M. H. Abrams, 'Structure and Style in the Greater Romantic Lyric', in F. W. Hillis and H. Bloom (eds), *From Sensibility To Romanticism* (New York, 1965), pp. 530–59.

7 Ibid., p. 551.

8 Earl Wasserman, 'The English Romantics: the Grounds of Knowledge', *Essays in Romanticism*, IV (1964). Cited in *BI*, p. 194.

9 Abrams, 'Structure and Style', p. 536.

10 See W. K. Wimsatt, 'The Structure of Romantic Nature Imagery', in *The Verbal Icon: Studies in the Meaning of Poetry* (Lexington, Ky., 1954).

11 Ibid., p. 110.

12 W. K. Wimsatt, 'Battering The Object: the Ontological Approach', in M. Bradbury and D. Palmer (eds), *Contemporary Criticism* (London, 1970).

13 See Wimsatt, *The Verbal Icon*.

14 T. S. Eliot, 'The Metaphysical Poets', in *Selected Essays* (London, 1964), pp. 241–50.

15 Hans-Georg Gadamer, *Truth and Method*, trans. G. Barden and J. Cumming (New York, 1975).

16 F. R. Leavis, 'Literary Criticism and Philosophy' (reply to René Wellek) *Scrutiny*, VI (1937), 59–70.

17 See for instance de Man, 'Hypogram and Inscription' (on Riffaterre's poetics), in *RT*, pp. 27–53.

18 At this point de Man refers principally to the following texts of Nietzsche: *On The Genealogy of Morals*, trans. Walter Kaufmann (New York, 1967); *The Will To Power*, trans. Kaufmann and R. J. Hollingdale (New York, 1967); also his early lectures on rhetoric, translated by Philippe Lacoue-Labarthe & Jean-Luc Nancy in *Poetique*, V (1971).

19 *Kant: Selections*, ed. Theodore M. Greene (details under *KS* above). I have cited this text as a readily available source for comparative reading in the three *Critiques*. See also principally the *Critique of Judgment*, trans. J. H. Bernard (New York, 1951).

20 On the role of metaphor, fictions and analogies in Kant, see also J. Hillis Miller, *The Ethics of Reading* (New York, 1986).

21 Marcel Proust, *Du Côté de chez Swann* (Paris, 1954). De Man gives his own translation of the passages from pp. 82–8.

22 See especially T. W. Adorno, *Negative Dialectics*, trans. E. B. Ashton (London, 1973) and the essays collected in *Prisms*, trans. Samuel and Shierry Weber (London, 1967).

23 Paul de Man, 'Aesthetic Formalization in Kleist', in *RR*, pp. 263–90. De Man provides his own translation of passages from Kleist's 'Essay on the Puppet Theatre'. There is a version by Eugene Jolas in *Partisan Review*, XIV (1947), 67–72.

24 Friedrich Schiller, *On the Aesthetic Education of Man, in a series of letters*, trans. E. M. Wilkinson and L. A. Willoughby (Oxford, 1967), p. 300. Cited by de Man, *RR*, p. 263.

9
What is Musical Genius?

Wilfrid Mellers

The foundation of the kingdom of God is pure Yes, as powers of the separable world. And the foundation of the wrath of God is pure No, whence lies have their origin [. . .] In this question regarding God's love and anger two kinds of fire are to be understood. First, a love-fire, where there is light only; and this is called God's love or the perceptible unity. And secondly a wrath-fire derivable from the receivability of the emanated will, through which the fire of love becomes manifest. This wrath-fire is the principle of the eternal Nature, and the centre of its inwardness is called an eternal darkness and pain. And yet the two fires form but a single principle.

Jacob Boehme, *Quaestiones Theosophicae* (1624)

In discussing genius it is in the nature of the slippery subject that one cannot expect to know what one is talking about. The Latin root of the word is *genere*, to generate, beget, create, and the fabled Genie of the Lamp, were one able to summon him, spread light by 'inexplicably' fulfilling, in a blinding flash, one's dearest dream, wildest wish, most hazardous hope. The generative act is magic, for creation, the source of life, is the ultimate mystery. The ancient Greeks mythologized this in the legend of Orpheus, probably once a real man – a shamanistic priest of Thrace – who as poet, composer, singer and lyre-player acquired mythical status, challenging the gods, and even death itself.

Two opposite yet complementary potentialities coexist in the myth: man may become a 'vehicle' through which or whom the divine spirit may become incarnate, or man may himself aspire to the condition of godhead, since an artist is *ipso facto* a maker and god-like creator. The ancient Greeks, though aware of the perils, on the whole came down in favour of the second alternative, establishing the basis of European humanism. Christian Europe, however, drew back from such presumption, appalled. That astonishing and formidable woman the Abbess Hildegard of Bingen –

born in 1098 at Rheinhessen and by the mid-twelfth century internationally celebrated as naturalist, poet, playwright and composer as well as saint and visionary – had talents and skills that seem to us evidence of genius because we cannot rationally account for them; she herself, however, took no credit for them, remarking that she was 'a feather on the breath of God'.[1] Similarly, in the next century, Alonso X, King of Leon and Castille, brilliantly endowed as poet, composer, and probably astronomer and mathematician, in composing and/or collating his *cantigas* – hymns to the Virgin Mary poised between God and the World, man and woman, spirit and flesh – had himself portrayed, in the beautifully illuminated manuscripts, as an Orpheus metamorphosed into the biblical psalm-singing harp-twanging King David; as such he was not a human aspirant to Godhead but a creature who sought the Eternal Return to his creator. In the later Middle Ages and early Renaissance, incipiently polyphonic composers of the Church hardly regarded themselves as individualized creators, let alone as geniuses. They rather dealt in acts of revelation, exploring and delineating the 'laws' of the cosmos, as did the astronomers and mathematicians in whose skills musicians were as often as not trained.

With the Renaissance, Europe veered again to the Greek ideal; indeed the Renaissance was a rebirth precisely because its values owed as much to classical antiquity as to Christianity. Climacterically, in 1607, Monteverdi's Orfeo, in his sublime '*Possente spirto*' arioso, woos and wins of humanism. Through his genius as poet, singer and lyre-player, Monteverdi's Ordeo, in his sublime '*Possente spirto*' arioso, woos and wins over the powers of darkness by employing all the sensual artifices of which Renaissance man was capable, rioting in vocal arabesques of fantastic virtuosity, doubled or echoed by voluptuous violins and cackling cornetti, reinforced by a luxuriance of continuo instruments, including, of course, lyre-simulating lutes and harps. Yet Orfeo's triumph over death when, through his music's seductions, dead Eurydice is reprieved, is only apparent: a tribute to man's heroic courage which cannot cancel the fact that man differs from God in being fallible and mortal. A happy ending can be achieved only in wish-fulfillment, when the sun god Apollo effects an act of transubstantiation for patriarchal Orfeo, who from on high looks *down* and *back* on Eurydice, now twice-dead, if pretty as a picture, which is of its nature an illusion.

Monterverdi probably thought of his Orfeo as a genius in the same sense as was his Greek prototype, but he also knew that Eurydice was called the Wise One because she eschewed her husband's would-be-divine arrogance. His Orfeo, Monteverdi commented in a famous letter of 1616, moved people so much 'simply' because he was a man, his Ariadne because she was a woman.[2] But we may doubt whether he identified himself with the beings he created, for he still regarded himself as an *instrument* whereby creation might become manifest. Only later, in the age of the High Baroque, were man's pride and presumption potent or foolhardy enough to dispense with metaphysics and the promise of celestial bliss. Dryden's ceremonial odes to St Cecilia, patron saint of music, and Handel's settings of them – not to mention baroque opera and oratorio in general – equate the power of genius with material, and even sexual, consummation; if we can believe enough in what we are physically in command of, that may suffice. At that time only Bach was an exception to this, as to much else, for as a theological, even mystical, as well as humanistic composer, he reinstated the Christian version of the Orpheus story, equating the power of genius with the dayspring from on high that may, should we know how to let it, visit us. But Bach was anachronistic as well as, in a superficial sense, archaistic. As humanism evolved from confidently self-enclosed autocracy into what we now call democracy, power became less a matter of (possibly divine) inspiration, more a consequence of intellectual enlightenment for basically common men – for Toms, Dicks and Harrys, even for Janes and Joans. In 1762 Gluck's version of the Orpheus story pays another tribute to human fortitude, now deprived of metaphysical sanctions. At this date a happy ending may be envisaged; since both Orfeo and Eurydice have been unafraid in face of the irremediable fact of death – and have attempted to resolve inner conflict in techniques that veer towards democratic sonata form – she can be brought back to *this* world. Her marriage is identified with the foundation of an enlightened New Order in society. That that utopia is also really a cheat – since even Kings and Queens, Presidents and First Ladies, must grow old and die – may be momentarily ignored, since the general weal outweighs personal destiny.

Though genius may not have much scope in the Enlightenment's higher education, it *may* prove deeply relevant to a life founded on democratic principle, as the two supreme 'geniuses' in European history testify. In 1791 Mozart's Masonic opera *The Magic Flute* reanimates Gluckian Enlightenment with metaphysical dimensions, as did Masonic creeds *in potentia*. Mozart's *Magic Flute*, like Gluck's *Orfeo*, deals with a trial and a test, but what is now being tested is not merely the human capacity to endure and to imagine a physical consummation and socially sanctioned morality, but also the ability of the individual soul – mind, heart – to recover the wholeness on which private (and ultimately public) fulfillment depends. Significantly, woman is for Mozart essential to this redemptive process, as she was not for Monteverdi.

Everybody thought, and still thinks, of Mozart as a *wunderkind*, the quintessence of genius whose talents must be superhuman because in his art everything seems to happen 'even in the twinkling of an eye'. The

familiar story of the child Mozart writing out a note-perfect score of the
Allegri *Miserere* after one hearing may be no more than a, to us
miraculous, feat of aural memory. Yet can it be *merely* a matter of mind-
and-ear-boggling intellectualization? Must it not have been also an
experience as sensuously instantaneous as the blaze of a single note on a
trumpet (at which the child Mozart fainted), the fragrance of a rose, or the
silky caress of the paw of a cat? When in his own day Mozart was
compared to an angel it was hardly because he was concerned with
supernatural grace – he certainly didn't know himself to be so concerned –
but rather because his humanity is totally 'realized' in the sounds he
created or evoked. The supreme technical perfection of a piece like the E
flat Divertimento for String Trio K563 resembles that of the mathematical
problem-solving or chess-playing child genius in its instantaneity, but
differs from it in that its moments outside time embrace the heights and
depths of human joy and suffering. His wholeness is his and our
humanity, freed of mutability and imperfection. It is not fortuitous that
Mozart teeters between 'Classicism' and 'Romanticism'. His musically
prodigious intellect functions as intuitively as does Rousseau's Wise Child
and Noble Savage. Imagination and Intellect, Innocence and Experience,
are interdependent, as Mozart's contemporary Blake said they were.

This is why the trite adage that genius is 10 per cent inspiration and 90
per cent perspiration contains a smidgen of truth. Mozart may have
envisaged – rather than 'placed together' – compositions in a flash,
meticulous to the minutest detail; even so the labour, even agony, within
his psyche that made this possible was formidable: as he confessed in
reference to the series of string quartets he dedicated to Haydn.[3] The same
is more palpably true of Beethoven, whose autograph scores, in contrast to
Mozart's apparently virgin efforts or non-efforts, betray evidence of inner
torment in savage, paper-lacerating erasures, furious deletions, frenzied
overwritings.

Goethe, the supreme poet of the time as Beethoven was its supreme
composer, saw the 'laws' of Nature and of the human psyche as closely
related, if not identical. Such a 'morphological' view of human growth and
of artistic creation, whereby both function in organic curves like a spiral,
or flower like a plant, would seem to be manifest in Beethoven's methods
of work, on the evidence of his Sketchbooks and recorded comments. 'My
realm is in the air,' he wrote to Count Brunswick in 1814, 'as often as the
wind whirls, so do the sounds whirl and so, too, does it whirl in my soul.'
Musical ideas may be snatched from the air, in the woods, in the silence of
the night; giving him no respite, they are sounds that, becoming musical
tones, 'roar and rage until at last they stand before me in the form of
notes'.[4] Considering a passage such as the coda to the first movement of
the last Piano Sonata opus 111 we may say that, although Beethoven

could not have achieved that magical metamorphosis of tempest into music except through the struggle within his psyche, yet what is born in the music is something other and greater than the creating mind. It is Hegel's 'absolute knowledge of the Absolute in its absoluteness', independent of anything that happened to Beethoven, though audibly manifest only through him. Not Beethoven's personal crisis but what Hopkins, in his noble sonnet to Henry Purcell, called 'meaning motion', here fans Beethoven's 'wits with wonder and awe'. In the few bars of this coda, musical motion is 'freedom in prospect, necessity in retrospect', to use the terminology of Zuckerkandl in his great book *Sound and Symbol*.[5]

Musicality, according to Zuckerkandl, is not an individual gift but one of man's basic attributes. In music man does not give expression to something (his feelings), nor does he build autonomous structures: *he invents himself*. In music, the law by which man knows himself to be alive is realized in its purest form. Of course some lives are 'better than' others in that more self is invented. No man ever had more self than Beethoven or manifested more 'thought' in the process of inventing it. However valid or invalid Zuckerkandl's account may be in general reference to music's nature, it is precisely apposite to the Beethovenian 'genius'; and although the composer did not theorize about his musical thought and had no need to, he made several pronouncements that lend this credence.

The most remarkable is a long conversation transcribed in 1810 by Bettina Brentano, a romantic young lady who, being a lion-hunter with a highly coloured imagination, is usually deemed an unreliable authority. This quotation none the less *sounds* authentic and, as Thayer points out, was certainly pieced together from notes she had made at the time. According to Bettina, Beethoven said:

music grants us presentiments, inspiration of celestial sciences, and that part of it which the mind grasps through the senses is the embodiment of mental cognition. Although the mind lives on it, as we live on air, it is a different thing to be able to grasp it intellectually. Yet the more the soul takes nourishment from music, the more prepared does the mind grow for a happy understanding with it. Yet few ever attain this stage; for just as thousands marry for love and love is never manifest in these thousands, though they all practise the art of love, so thousands have intercourse with music and never see it manifested [. . .] All true invention is a moral progress. To submit to these inscrutable laws, and by means of these laws to tame and guide one's mind so that the manifestations of art may pour out: this is the isolating principle of art. To be dissolved in its manifestations, this is our dedication to the divine which calmly exercises its power over the raging of the untamed elements and so lends to the imagination its highest effectiveness. So art always represents the divine, and the relationship of men towards art is religion: what we obtain through art comes from God, is divine inspiration which appoints an aim for human faculties, *which aim we can attain*. [My italics].[6]

Beethoven's account thus fuses the contradictory poles of Orphic genius, which descends from on high, but may be incarnate *only* in human form. Still more remarkable, he goes on to admit that:

we do not know what it is that grants us knowledge. The grain of seed, tightly sealed as it is, needs the damp, electric warm soil in order to sprout, to think, to express itself. Music is the electric soil in which the spirit lives, thinks and invents. Philosophy is a striking of music's electric spirit; its indigence, which desires to found everything on a single principle, is relieved by music. Although the spirit has no power over that which it creates through music, it is yet joyful in the act of creation. Thus every genuine product of art is independent, more powerful than the artist himself, and returns to the divine when achieved, connected with men only in as much as it bears witness to the divine of which they are the medium. Music relates the spirit to harmony. An isolated thought yet feels related to all things that are of the mind; likewise every thought in music is intimately, indivisibly related to the whole of harmony, which is Oneness. All that is electrical stimulates the mind to flowing, surging creation. I am electrical by nature.[7]

In this extraordinary passage Beethoven ventures beyond the process of Hegelian dialectic, beyond the Goethean conception of 'morphological' form; extending the metaphor into the field of electricity, he anticipates very recent theories about the nature of the human mind. There is something awe-inspiring in the fact that Beethoven, employing a key-word of his time then imperfectly understood, should prophetically hint at speculative truths of which we are just becoming aware. His sublimation was born of 'the pain of consciousness', and affinities between Hegel's definition of Spirit, Zuckerkandl's account of the process of musical creation, and the dialectic of musical 'thought' in Beethoven's works (especially his late ones) cannot be accidental.

Beethoven threw off the yokes of both Classical decorum and Christian discipline to achieve a synthesis of intellect and imagination perhaps even more astounding than Mozart's – as well as a Blakean Marriage of Heaven and Hell, of Lamb and Tyger. There is a sense in which he may count as the most 'modern' composer there is, since his 'forms' – at least from the opus 59 Quartets onwards – override process and progress existing in time to embrace *alternative futures*,[8] as well as the classically ironic 'recognition of other modes of experience that may be possible'. Beethoven's own 'explanation' of his simultaneous vision of alternative futures was that he created in the state he called *raptus*, wherein he was an instrument of the Holy Spirit, but not its passive recipient, since he was at once ravished and ravisher. It is interesting that Einstein, a scientist as great in his field as was Beethoven in music, has maintained that the mystical is the sower of all true art and science. 'To know that what is impenetrable to us really exists, manifesting itself as the highest wisdom and most radiant beauty, which our dull faculties can comprehend only in their most primitive forms – this knowledge, this feeling, is the centre of true religiousness.'[9] In the light of this, Beethoven's statement that he wrote out the last three Piano Sonatas without pause, in between work on the movements of the *Missa Solemnis*, is not nonsensical, though in one sense it took him a lifetime to create the Sonatas.

Similarly, he toiled for four years on the *Mass*, yet its grandeur of scale and elaboration of structure – involving what we are apt to call 'incredibly' complex interrelationships of motif, theme, rhythm and harmony – surely argue for a compositional principle beyond rational understanding. There is some evidence that such may be the case, for Schindler tells us that, towards the end of August 1819,

> I arrived at the Master's house in Mödling, accompanied by the musician Johann Horzalka [. . .] It was four o'clock in the afternoon. As soon as we entered we were told that during the same morning both of Beethoven's maidservants had run away and that at some time after midnight there had been a scene which disturbed all the inmates of the house, because, tired of waiting for their master, both the maidservants had fallen asleep and the meal prepared for him had become inedible. In his drawing room, behind a locked door, we heard the Master singing, howling and stamping over the fugue for the *Credo* [. . .] After listening to this almost gruesome sound for some time, we were just about to leave when the door opened and Beethoven stood before us, a wild look on his face, which was almost terrifying. He looked as if he had just emerged victorious from a life and death struggle with the entire host of contrapuntists, his constant antagonists.[10]

About the mortal combat there can be no question, though contrapuntists were not Beethoven's unworthy adversaries. The fight was rather between Yahveh and Moses, 'waylaid by night'; between Jacob and the God with whom he 'wrestled until the break of day'; between Blake's (and Beethoven's) Jesus as the Human Imagination and Lucifer as fallen angel and *mysterium horrendum*, the savage beast in whose belly the soul may – according to St John of the Cross, must – be buried. The distraught Beethoven, emerging from closeted conflict into the light of day, seems the personification of Goethe's Daimonic Man, one of those beings from whom 'a tremendous energy seems to emanate, and who exercise an incredible power over all creatures, indeed over the elements. And who can say how far such an influence may extend?' To the young Goethe this power seemed to manifest itself only in contradictions: it was neither human nor divine, neither angelic nor devilish; it was 'like chance, for it pointed to no consequence; like providence, for it indicated connection and unity. All that hems us in seemed penetrable to it; it seemed to dispose at will of the fundamental elements of our being, contracting time and expanding space.'[11]

Such power is shamanistic, as was the original Orpheus, and embraces the basic meaning of the Greek word *daimon*, which was corrupted into demon when medieval Christianity, distrustful of sensual possession, tended to reduce daimons to near-comic emanations of our lower natures, armed with prongs with which to torment our fallen selves, threatening our divine potentiality. In the same spirit the seventeenth-century creators of the humanist ritual of the masque admitted an antimasque of satyrs only in order that the inchoate elements of our being could be laughed away as irrelevant to our presumptive earthly paradise. But Beethoven, like Goethe and Rilke, came to see that if his devils were to leave him, his angels might leave him as well, to recognize that if daimonic possession is a madness, it may also be the sublimest sanity, since only in embracing the destructive along with the constructive principle may we hope to attain the Whole. According to Aristotle, happiness is *eudaimonism*, being 'blessed with a good genius'. Eros is a daimon and Nature, like Blake's Tyger, is herself dynamic and daimonic. To deny the daimon makes us accomplices – as Rollo May has put it – 'on the side of the destructive principle',[12] and leads to atrocities such as those perpetrated in the death camps of Hitler and Stalin and in the racial persecutions of the immediate present, by our ostensibly enlightened century.

Goethe himself said of the daimonic Beethoven that 'it should be a matter of indifference whether he speaks from feeling or from knowledge, for here the gods are at work, scattering seed for future revelations, and our only wish should be that they may thrive and develop undisturbed [. . .] His genius lights his way, and often illuminates him as with lightning, while we sit in the dark and scarcely guess from which direction the day will break upon us.'[13] Oddly enough Goethe, who had been himself a daimon and who admitted in 1812, after the meeting at Teplitz, that he had never met a man with more formidable inner force than Beethoven, was in old age as scared of Beethoven as he would presumably have been of his own Faust. He considered the Fifth Symphony a work subversive enough to threaten civilization, and would have been unable to see that, but for the wrath of God incarnate in the ferocity of the *Missa Solemnis*'s *Gloria*, the celestial serenity of its *Benedictus*, when the Holy Ghost gently floats from on high in the guise of a solo violin, would have been unattainable. For the venerable Goethe, Beethoven's reprimand to those negligent servants who slept, instead of feeding him, while he was locked in mortal combat, would have been a blasphemy, the more so because Beethoven's question, 'Could you not watch with me one hour?', involved a lie, since the one hour was actually five or six! Yet if, with Blake, we equate Christ with the human imagination, Beethoven's question was not blasphemous at all. No artist demonstrates more potently than Beethoven how the word 'experience' derives from the Latin *ex periculo*, from or out of peril. In the Hammerklavier Sonata and the closely related *Missa Solemnis* he had experienced Calvary and had cried 'My God, my God, why hast thou forsaken me?' Beethoven's apprehension of God was identical with his apprehension of the creative act; as Robert Duncan has put it:

Jehovah [. . .] declares himself a God of Jealousy, Vengeance and Wrath. Reason falters, but our mythic, our deepest poetic sense, recognises and greets as truth the proclamation that the Son brings, that just this wrathful Father is the First Person of Love. As Chaos, the Yawning Abyss, is First Person of Form. And the Poet, too, like the Son, in this myth of Love or Form, must go deep into the reality of his own Nature, into the Fathering Chaos or Wrath, to suffer his own Nature. In this mystery of art, the Son's cry to the Father might be too the cry of the artist to the form he obeys.[14]

In this sense the Beethovenian artist *becomes* God in receiving the Holy Spirit, an identification of the two opposed yet complementary aspects of Orphism which has been neatly encapsulated by William H. Gass, who writes:

when the *real* inspirational storm strikes it strikes not John Jerk but a genius; it is as prepared for as a Blitzkrieg; and it is the consummation of a lifetime of commitment and calculation. If we think it odd that the gods should always choose a voice so full and gloriously throated, we should remember that it is their choice of such a golden throat, each time, that makes them gods.[15]

Not surprisingly, therefore, Beethoven's art, life and death are singularly of a piece. Anselm Huttenbrenner's much-quoted account of the moment of death reads like a parable of Beethoven's creative life: a snow-clad scene, the death rattle in the composer's throat, a deafening clap of thunder, a bolt of lightning which illuminated the death-chamber 'with a harsh light'. At this unexpected natural phenomenon Beethoven 'raised his right hand and, his fist clenched, looked upwards for several seconds with a very grave, threatening countenance, as though to say "I defy you, powers of evil".' Then his heart ceased, in an infinite quietude.[16] These abnormal weather conditions have been confirmed by meteorological investigation, so perhaps Goethe was on the mark in suggesting that supremely daimonic genius may have 'an incredible power over all creatures, indeed over the elements'. Zuckerkandl's view that man in his music 'invents himself' proves to be true of Beethoven in a startlingly literal as well as philosophical sense. 'The closest analogy to the functioning of a musical composition is the functioning of a human life [. . .] A man's death might be compared to the moment when a melody ceases to "grow" and enters actual existence.' If we think of Beethoven's life-work as one evolving composition, which it is, we can hardly deny that his last minutes on earth and his death in a snow-besprent world, accompanied by Promethean thunder and Goethe's 'lightning stroke', re-enact his music's story, from the earliest years until the last.

There is a passage in Grillparzer's noble funeral oration that epitomizes our awareness of Beethoven as an instrument of cosmic forces, of the Energy which is God:

He was an artist, and who can bear comparison with him? As Behemoth rushes, tempestuous, over the oceans, so he flew over the frontiers of his art. From the cooing of doves to the rolling of thunder, from the most subtle interweaving of the self-determined media of his art to the awe-inspiring point where the consciously formed merges in the lawless violence of the striving forces of Nature, all these he exhausted, all these he took in his stride. Whoever comes after him will not be able to continue, he will have to begin again, for his predecessor ended only where art itself must end.[17]

And it is true that there is no real successor to Beethoven's third-period music. His slightly younger contemporary Schubert was, of course, with Mozart, music's most 'instinctive' genius, apocryphally scribbling inspired songs on the backs of café menus while still little more than a boy. His life was even briefer than Mozart's; yet when he created the indeed miraculous masterpieces of his last few years he had no need of Mozart's or Beethoven's intellectuality, because his last three Piano Sonatas and the sublime String Quintet in C have discovered the only intellectual formulation appropriate to their imaginative necessities. That their technical expertise, if more 'Romantic' than, is as consummate as, that of Mozart and Beethoven, is the core of Schubert's genius.

In the Romantic age proper, genius becomes 'near allied to madness' in a more clinical sense. The type-case is Schumann, whose genius consists of his ability to 'project' his dreams and nightmares into rigidly disciplined auralization, which nonetheless did not forfend his becoming certifiably lunatic. Chopin controlled nervous hypersensitivity in the classical restraint he imposed on his yearning melodies, undulating dance rhythms, and sensuously volatile textures. For Liszt, the manifestation of genius was a form of play-acting, associated with his legendary prowess as a piano virtuoso. To be self-consciously a genius is perhaps a contradiction in terms, certainly Liszt's symphonic poem on the Orpheus story – not one of his better works – romanticizes and sentimentalizes the myth, presenting Orpheus as a hero in cinematic narrative, prophetic of Hollywood, with the strings emulating a celestial choir at the end. Not surprisingly, Liszt's genius is most evident when he is most overtly autobiographical, presenting his inner life with outgoing theatrical panache but with total conviction – as in the great one-movement Piano Sonata.

Interestingly enough, this work was in many ways anticipatory of the mature compositional techniques of the arch-Romantic egotist, Wagner, who regarded himself, to a degree justifiably, as Beethoven's successor, and cultivated the daemonic view of life, only to end with a great renunciation and with the twilight, rather than apotheosis, of the gods. We accept Wagner as a bardic genius whose technique richly fulfils his imaginative intentions. We probably accept Bruckner as a bard whose talent was not quite equal to his genius – though for some that makes his music only the more poignant. Yet on the whole it would be true to say that 'apocalyptic' musical genius ended, as it began, with Beethoven, and that the gradual encroachment on Europe of nineteenth-century industrialism proved inimical to bards and visionaries, as Blake had said it would. Offenbach, in the commercially dedicated Second Empire, pushed Orpheus over the brink and into the abyss, leaving him '*aux enfers*', happy as a sandboy to be there. 'Serious' artists in the Waste Land of the twentieth century have mostly rebelled against their age's material values, but have done so in anger or despair, only occasionally in visionary *ecstasis*.

It may not be fortuitous that Britain, most rapidly industrialized of European nations, entered the musical doldrums during the nineteenth century, when our few indigenous composers laboured under the German yoke. Certainly when our music rose phoenix-like at the very end of the century it was a phenomenon attributable to the 'genius' of two composers, both profoundly English though German-trained. Elgar, brought up in the heart of rural Worcestershire, came to relish Britain's material might and imperial majesty, writing jingoistic music in the form of pompous and circumstantial marches that, like Kipling's comparable verses, still send shivers down even reluctant spines. Had he not believed, or thought he believed, in Edwardian opulence, affluence and munificence he could hardly have achieved, in his 'serious' music, a technical sophistication rivalling that of Richard Strauss, whom Busoni called 'an industrialist even in his music'. Yet what makes Elgar a great, not merely a socially efficacious, composer is that beneath the gloss and the panoply of power lurks Shelley's visionary 'spirit of delight' which, though it comes but 'rarely', illuminates Elgar's major works, notably the two magnificent Symphonies, the Violin Concerto and the explicitly elegiac Cello Concerto. The Second Symphony, for all its prideful grandeur, ends with a dying fall – on the eve of the Great War that put paid, in both spiritual and material terms, to that Land of Hope and Glory. Elgar's genius validates his social pretension in a way the more impressive because his materialistic world, viewed superficially, seemed not to warrant it.

Delius, Elgar's complement and polar opposite, was born not in the English countryside but in industrial Bradford, and abominated the materialism of his age as violently as Elgar appeared to relish it. Having an affluent business man for tolerant if not deeply empathetic father, Delius was able to escape to Scandanavian mountains, up which he climbed wide eyed, to Parisian Montmartre, where he hobnobbed with conventionally unconventional poets, painters and prostitutes, and to sultry Florida, where he listened to the locals crooning at the close of day. Whereas Elgar had metamorphosed the central Teutonic (Brahmsian) tradition into English terms, Delius forged his aggressively private idiom out of the chromaticism of German Wagner, the only composer whom, in his Nietzschean self-dedication, he could tolerate. Yet *his* nirvana, his release from self-consciousness, he found in the impersonal forces of Nature, of wind, sea and sky. His two greatest, and certainly most representative, works are *A Song of the High Hills*, which is destitute of human population, apart from the composer, and *Sea Drift*, which is about a small boy's first apprehension – against the eternal murmuration of *la mer* which is also *la mère* – of the fact of mortality, the boy being, of course, both the poet, Walt Whitman, and the composer, Delius himself. The technical manifestation of the Delian experience – whereby long, undulating lines, precipitated out of surging chromatic harmony, themselves aspire to the pentatonic innocence of folk song (most magically in the wordless choral episode in *Song of the High Hills*) – is so aboriginal that one has to call on the word genius to categorize though not explain it. At his best, Delius is both a visionary and an ecstatic; at his worst he is grossly self-indulgent. This indicates how rare, and precarious, the bardic type of genius has become.

A later duo of English composers, Britten and Tippett, do not so much accord with as create the evolving pattern of our music from the thirties through the fifties; they are geniuses because they 'make it new' instead of adapting themselves to given circumstances as, according to Kierkegaard, does even the finest talent. Though Britten and Tippett complement one another, they are not opposites, like Elgar and Delius. Indeed, their relationship is strikingly similar to that between Mozart and Beethoven. Britten, though without Mozart's Shakespearean range of experience, has his *wunderkind* innocence that proves to be wisdom. His 'instantaneous' technique, whereby all is audible 'in a flash', *is* his essential theme, as is revealed in the literary and dramatic burden of his vocal and dramatic works no less than in the heart of his musical technique, wherein a Boy is Born, renewing the worn heart (mind, nerves, senses) in a midsummer night's dream that is all we can know of truth. Tippett too is concerned with rebirth and renewal but, far from being instantaneous, is a striver like Beethoven, whose *search* for technical fulfillment is his (often painful) search for the undivided Whole. Tippett does not always, or perhaps often, achieve it, but when he does – most notably in his miracle-making masque-opera *The Midsummer Marriage* – he sings psalms of praise from the brink, if not quite within, Beethoven's hard-won paradise, even in the winter of our discontent and from the hell of our wasted land. If Britten is the Wise Child, Tippett is the seer, the bard who seemed to have been rendered obsolete.

Stravinsky, certainly the most representative and probably the greatest composer of the twentieth century, is not conspicuously bardic, for he is self-consciously unselfconscious even in reinvoking the primitive springs of our being in fertility rite and sacrificial murder. Indeed his genius consists not in bardic aspiration but precisely in those seismographic qualities which at one time were said to discredit him. His 'newness' lay in the fact that, a cosmopolitan twice deracinated, he became a mouthpiece for us all, 'shoring' the battered fragments of Europe's past against our ruin, steering us into the 'pluralistic' universe we now inhabit. (Significantly, the rigid formalism of Stravinsky's late serial works has much in common, philosophically as well as technically, with *pre-*Renaissance polyphony.)

In his middle years, Stravinsky composed a series of works gravitating around the Orpheus story, beginning in 1928 with *Apollon Musagètes*, and ending in 1948, at the close of his neo-Classic period, with *Orpheus*, a direct balletic dramatization of the myth. In the wake of two world wars to destroy, not save, civilization, Stravinsky reinstates the primitive savagery of the tale, allowing the Terrible Mothers to rend Orpheus to pieces in revenge on his patriarchal pride. That dire event recurs when in 1986 the British composer Harrison Birtwistle produced a mammoth opera, *The Masks of Orpheus*, reinterpreting the story in terms appropriate to our post-electronic age. Again one has to fall back on the word genius in failing to account for so profound and multifaceted an exploration of Orpheus's present destiny in relation to the future of civilization, if it has one.

For Birtwistle also makes it new, and opera, after *The Masks of Orpheus*, will never be the same, nor will we who experienced it. The world has come a long way, for better and worse, since post-Renaissance Francis Bacon wrote in his *Advancement of Learning*:

Which merit was lively set forth by the Antients in the feigned relation of Orpheus Theatre; where all birds and beasts assembled, and forgetting their several appetites, some of prey, some of game, some of quarrel, stood all sociably together listening unto the airs and accord of the Harp; the sound whereof no sooner ceased, or was drowned by some louder noise, but every beast returned to his own nature: wherein is aptly described the nature and condition of men; who are full of savage and unreclaimed desires, of profit, of lust, of revenge, which as long as they give ear to precepts, to laws, to religion, sweetly touched with the eloquence and persuasion of books, of sermons, of harangues, so long is society and peace maintained.[18]

Bacon here is once more a prophet of that 'modern' world which suspected that Blake (who disapproved of dark satanic mills) was lunatic, and in fact incarcerated vision-seeing Kit Smart and guileless John Clare, and which today would probably regard Beethoven as ripe for psychiatric treatment, thereby cancelling his need or ability to compose. Birtwistle erases the Baconian blueprint; the *Advancement of Learning* ('books, sermons, harangues') has little bearing on the fearsome and fearful, the wondrous and wonderful world his masque and masks evoke. He begins his opera with the metaphor of an egg, and prophesies new births, *ab ovo*. He does not tell us what 'new beast' may be shambling towards Bethelehem to be born, and what is to come is still (very) unsure. But an artist is not concerned with Baconian solutions, only with the need, in circumstances however unpropitious, to *generate, beget and create*. The bardic genius is not, of course, the only type, but if, as one suspects, only he – by calling, in Blake's terms, on the 'lapsed soul' to reanimate the 'starry floor' of Reason, the 'dewy grass' of sense impressions, and the 'wat'ry shore' of material reality – may 'fallen, fallen light renew', we can have no doubt that our need for him is desperate. In our time, in Britain, not only Britten, Tippett and Birtwistle have made this manifest, but also the Beatles, one of whom – the dead one (of course?) – was a genius and another a man of exceptional talent, while as a foursome they formed a regenerative tribe of the sixties young.

Their bard was called The Fool on the Hill.[19]

Notes

1 From the Abbess Hildegard's *Scivas*, translated by Christopher Page and quoted on the sleeve to the Gothic Voices recording of *Sequences and Hymns of the Abbess Hildegard* (Hyperion A66039).
2 Letter to Alessandro Striggio, 9th December 1616 in D. Arnold and N. Fortune, (eds) *The Monteverdi Companion*, (London, 1968), p. 42.
3 Letter to Haydn, 1st September 1785, quoted in S. Morgenstern, *Composers on Music* (London, 1958).
4 M. Hamburger, *Beethoven: Letters, Journals and Conversations*, 2nd paperback edn (London, 1984) pp. 124, 195.
5 Victor Zuckerkandl, *Sound and Symbol* (2 vols, Princeton, 1956–73).
6 Hamburger, *Beethoven*, p. 89.
7 Ibid., pp. 89–90.
8 On 'alternative futures' in Beethoven's music see David B. Greene, *Temporal Processes in Beethoven's Music*, (New York, 1982).
9 Quoted by Phillip Frank in *Einstein, His Life and Times* (London, 1948).
10 Hamburger, *Beethoven*, pp. 174–5.
11 *Dichtung und Wahrheit*, part IV, book 20 = *Gedenkausgabe der Werke, Briefe und Gespräche*, ed. E. Beutler (24 vols, Zurich, 1948–64), vol. X, pp. 842, 839–40.

12 Rollo May, *Love and Will* (New York, 1969) p. 131. See also pp. 121–77.

13 Hamburger, *Beethoven*, pp. 90–1.

14 Robert Duncan, *The Truth and the Life of Myth* (New York, 1968), p. 24.

15 William H. Gass, *The Habitations of the World* (New York, 1985).

16 See H. C. Robbins Landon, *Beethoven, a Documentary Study* (London, 1970), p. 392.

17 Hamburger, *Beethoven*, pp. 269–70.

18 Francis Bacon, *The Advancement of Learning*, quoted by Hardin Craig in *The Enchanted Glass* (Oxford, 1952), p. 113.

19 My recent book, *The Masks of Orpheus* (Manchester, 1987), published after the writing of this essay, deals in greater detail with the Orphic aspects of the theme.

10
Genius in Mathematics

Clive Kilmister

The concept of genius in the sense of an inexplicable creativity and insight is rarely used by mathematicians in their assessment of each other. It is otherwise with that section of the general public who take an interest in mathematical doings. I shall argue here that the difference arises because the prime interest of mathematicians in each other's work is in its correctness. Nevertheless the general public is right in using the concept in assessing past mathematics. Only when hindsight enables one to assess the unfolding developments that resulted from a given piece of work can it be said that 'there was the hand of genius', just as in the other arts.

Mathematics is one aspect of our wide creative culture with a history of two and a half millenia. Over the last 500 years it has acquired the additional characteristic of being the 'language of science', thus playing a critical role in our mastery of the physical world. Inside the subject this dual character is enshrined, at least in England and other countries playing Test Cricket, in the division between pure and applied mathematics. Since it suggests two kinds of mathematics, rather than two aspects of a single subject albeit carried out frequently by two different communities, this convenient division is basically misleading. None the less, I shall discuss the two aspects in turn.

It is commonly felt that mathematics has a character of exactness. Once a problem has been clearly and correctly formulated, it has a unique solution. This will lead some to question my description of mathematics as creative. Such a misunderstanding only arises with the Romantics and ignores such examples as the Parthenon, J. S. Bach and the Palladian villa, which all show that exactness is not an enemy of creativity. But in any case it is an inappropriate quibble here, for the real mathematical creativity arises in making the clear and correct formulation of the problem, and this process is rarely exact.

The busy activity of mathematics is evidenced by the large number of workers in it, the continually increasing number of journals in which their work appears and the difficulty faced by a young person in reaching the stage where his own creativity can operate. Yet this is a very isolated subject and this isolation is a social phenomenon which arises from a long-standing bias in our educational system. The smugness of the response heard at a hundred parties, that 'I never could add up,' contrasted with the stigma which would be attached to 'I was never able to learn to read', is evidence enough of the isolation. It was not always so. It is said that Plato's Academy had the injunction: *ΑΓΕΩΜΕΤΡΗΤΟΣ ΜΗ ΕΙΣΙΤΩ* ('Let none unskilled in geometry enter') over the door. In the visual creativity of the Italian Renaissance it is sometimes hard to draw a distinction between the mathematicians, architects and painters. Piero della Francesca, who would now certainly be claimed as a painter, thrills by a wonderful combination of mathematical relations in his strange *Flagellation*.

But the present isolation means that I must begin by trying to answer the question 'What is mathematics?' This question has at least three layers of meaning. The first layer, which arises from the isolation, requires me simply to inform non-mathematical readers about the actual activity of mathematicians. The second requires the delimitation of the activity, so as to be able to say: 'This we call mathematics, that is not.' This second layer of meaning of the question is of no great importance to my argument because there is general agreement about the main core of the subject and this will do for my discussion. So I shall ignore it except to mention that it is a question which is becoming harder and harder to answer as the activities of some composers and some painters become nearer and nearer to mathematics. We can look forward to a continuum of activities stretching from there, through the main branches of mathematics as now understood, and fading away into the complexities of modern computing. The third layer of meaning, which is a preoccupation of the present century, starts with some sort of agreement about the second, and asks about the nature of this activity and the justification for it. Inside the subject this is often referred to as 'Philosophy of Mathematics' but this is somewhat misleading, and Foundational Studies would be more exact. This third aspect of the question, which is, surprisingly, ignored by most working mathematicians, is important for my argument, as it is here that the area of creativity is delineated.

I begin by trying to give a picture of the professional activity of mathematicians. Here two concepts are essential, those of *proof*, and *abstraction*. Historically we know that mathematics began with geometry and the notion of proof is made clear, if not quite captured, in Euclid's *Elements*, the most successful textbook ever, for it was still in use over 2000 years after it was written. Geometry itself, it was said, had evolved from the rules of thumb used by the Egyptians to restore the agreed boundaries of fields after the Nile subsided each year. But although they knew and used the fact that a triangle of sides 3, 4 and 5 units had a right angle opposite the longest side, the notion of proving this from other, supposedly simpler assumptions was foreign to them. It is unimportant whether there is any truth in the Greek tradition that Pythagoras, on discovering the proof of the general relation between the three sides of a right-angled triangle, sacrificed an ox, or a herd of oxen. The importance lies in the tradition and the high value that it attributes to proof, and proof has continued till the present day to be the unique essential constituent of any piece of mathematics. It is not at all uncommon for a new proof to be given of results that are already proved, and the value attached to such new proofs, because they illuminate the connections of the result to other parts of the subject, shows that, for mathematicians, it is not mathematical facts that are important but mathematical proofs. The facts have no importance of their own and they can acquire such importance only to the extent that they form possible constituents of some new later proof of another result.

Two further remarks need to be made about proof. It is here that mathematicians use the concept of beauty to describe a subjectively perceived superiority of one proof over another, and one might search here for an aspect of creativity. I believe it would be fruitless to do so for two reasons. One is because it is as hard to pin down the concept of beauty in mathematics as it is anywhere else. Sometimes it refers to an element of surprise, when the proof proceeds up to a certain point in a way which would be expected and then, when it seems there is still a long path to tread, a totally unexpected consideration is brought to bear which serves at once to complete the proof. Sometimes beauty is seen in the way in which the various considerations used in the proof come from a very wide field, so that the result follows by appreciating a hitherto unsuspected connection between widely different parts of the subject. There are other features which may be described as beauty, which relate to the extent to which the proof increases our understanding of the result, but all such notions of beauty have a subjective character. Moreover, to concentrate too much on this is to downgrade the one essential property of proofs, that of correctness. Until a few years ago, one of the famous open questions in mathematics was the four-colour conjecture. This stated that the problem of colouring a map, like that of England divided into counties, so that each county had one colour and no two counties with a common boundary had the same colour, could be solved with four colours only. Progress towards a proof of this over a century had reached a position where all maps in which it might possibly be the case that the conjecture was false could be described, but there were very many of these and of great complexity. Then a computer was able to finish the proof by verifying it in each of these cases. It is hard to imagine any sense of beauty which could apply to such a proof and it evidently does not increase understanding at all, but the four-colour theorem, as it has become, is no longer a focus of interest. The proof is correct, even if not beautiful.

My second reason for disregarding the mathematician's concept of beauty in trying to pin down creativity is that it rests very much on notions of what has *gone into* the proof of a result. But I want to argue that creativity is encapsulated by how much *comes out* of a result in the future, and this is analogous to the use of the word in the other creative arts.

The second remark about proof is more apposite to my subject. It has become a commonplace since the Greeks that a correct argument can produce nothing new that was not already present (in a concealed form) in the assumptions. So the propositions of mathematicians, immensely varied though they seem, reflect no more about the world than the very small number of statements from which they are derived. And what is the logical status of these statements? In the eighteenth century, Kant questioned the view, which had begun to make some headway by that time, that the assumptions were a distillation of experience, and took them instead as the prime example of his synthetic *a priori*, that is, known independently of experience although the properties they predicate of objects do not inevitably belong to those objects but might have been otherwise. This ultimately untenable view of mathematics is an important step on the way to different twentieth-century views of the assumptions as freely chosen. Thus L. E. J. Brouwer holds both that 'Mathematics is synonymous with the exact part of our thinking' and that 'Mathematics is a free creation of the human mind.' He finds no paradox in holding both views, though their reconciliation requires an elaborate philosophy of mathematics and of logic which he elaborated but which is still largely rejected by mathematicians.

Most working mathematicians, on the other hand, are some variety of Platonists; they believe that they are describing the properties of actual objects that exist in some realm of Ideals. They create these objects by means of definitions which endow them with their properties. Here again the two halves of the doctrine sound paradoxical but in this case the adherents do not articulate these beliefs explicitly, and so can ignore the paradox. The intellectually more respectable version of the working mathematician's Platonism was provided by Hilbert, with the idea of a formal system of axioms and rules of inference, which allows the deduction of theorems from the axioms. Such a formal system may, in principle, be freely chosen, subject only to the requirement that it should be consistent: that is, that it should never allow the deduction of both a statement and its contradiction. So here is the same free creation as Hilbert's arch-enemy Brouwer claims. But the actual Hilbert enterprise is

not the frivolous multiplication of formal systems but rather the choice of
those which best represent the practice of mathematicians engaged in one
particular branch of the subject. There is not a unique system for each
branch and the creative choice of the system which best serves to provide
for the branch, but at the same time to provide for the utmost in extension
and generalization, is the most subtle of the occupations of the working
mathematicians.

This discussion of proof has brought me to the other essential aspect of
mathematics, that of abstraction. It is no surprise to anyone who has
understood what learning arithmetic involves, to be told that mathematics
deals with abstractions. For evidently $1 + 1 = 2$ is an abstraction from
endless examples of a pair of apples arising from taking an apple twice,
and so on. But this is only the beginning; the process of doing
mathematics is continually to abstract from the abstractions to further
abstractions. I will illustrate this by a simple example. Imagine that you
take a triangle, with its three sides all equal, cut out of a piece of
cardboard, resting on a table, and that you pencil round the outside of the
triangle so as to have the outline of it on the table. Now ask the question,
'How may the triangle be moved into new positions which still exactly
occupy the triangular shape on the table?' One way will be to rotate it
through one-third of a turn (120°), so each vertex moves round to the
position formerly occupied by the next one round. This can be done again,
making a rotation through two-thirds of a turn. A different kind of motion
is to pick up the triangle and put it face downwards, and this can be
combined with the one-third and two-third turns.

These five operations are the only ones. (The mathematicians would
alter the question slightly by deleting the word 'new' and so would include
also the sixth 'operation' of leaving the triangle untouched, but this is
merely a technical complication.) So far this mathematics is trivial, the
content of intelligence test questions. Now comes the abstraction. If two of
the six operations are carried out in succession, then the compounded
result on the triangle is to move it into a new position still occupying the
same shape drawn on the table and so, by what has been said, this result
on the triangle is the same as one of the other operations of the six. The
first step in abstraction is to forget the triangle and to consider any finite
set of operations with the property that any two can be compounded to
give a third. The second step is to dispense with the requirement to
identify with operations; any finite set of elements with the same property
(and some other simple properties which will suffice to make the collection
like enough to that of operations for the former results still to hold) is
called a finite group. A third step is to dispense with the condition that the
set should be finite, so that an infinite group is defined, and so on. At each
stage the next abstraction will preserve some of the properties but fail to

preserve others. The art of choosing the abstraction lies in which properties to preserve. So here again, as with the construction of a formal system (a process with which it has strong connections) the measure of creativity is, as with the other arts, what comes out as a result.

That will suffice for the present to answer the question 'What is mathematics' and I turn now to the main question of creativity and genius. During the long history of mathematics a number of outstanding mathematicians have arisen, all exhibiting a major degree of creativity in the ways I have described. If one were to make a list of a dozen or a score of the most creative, there would probably be fairly general agreement about whom to include, give or take one or two. Amongst these the title of genius might be more sparingly given to those whose insight and creativity were so great as to be inexplicable. I will select two cases as examples of this, not as the most outstanding, but as examples where the later consequences are easy to explain without too much technical detail.

My first example refers to an investigation carried out by Euler, the Swiss mathematician, in 1735 when he was 28.[1] His attention was drawn to an amusing diversion of the inhabitants of Königsberg, where the river Pregel flows from two branches on the east of the town, unites and then divides again to flow round an island (Kneiphof), before coming together

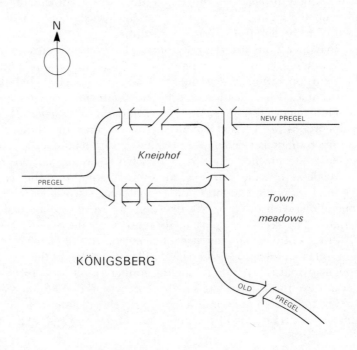

again on the west side of the island and flowing away to the west. The island was linked to the north bank by two bridges and to the south bank by two more. It was also joined to the Town Meadows, the eastern area between the two branches, by a single bridge. Finally, the Town Meadows were joined to the north bank by a bridge and to the south bank by another. The diversion of the inhabitants was to try to take a walk through the town which would return to its starting point having crossed every bridge exactly once. No one had succeeded in doing this, and some held it to be impossible but there was no clear consensus. (Königsberg is now Kaliningrad in the Soviet Union, and the destruction of its bridges in the Second World War has been repaired in a different pattern.)

Euler proves that the suggested walk is impossible, but the important feature for my argument is how he does it and what he says about it. It would have been very easy for him to have given some such argument as the following: any walk must pass at some time through the Town Meadows. There are three bridges joining them to elsewhere. In which direction are these bridges traversed? Either two must be chosen as exits and one as an entrance to the Meadows or vice versa. But it is clearly impossible to enter an area once and yet leave it twice or to enter it twice and leave it only once, on a circular stroll. But that solution is another example of an intelligence test argument and, though it is much shorter than Euler's, depends on an incidental feature of Königsberg. Euler sees at once that this particular problem is only one instance of a whole family of problems with any number of islands, bridges and branches. His method suffices for all such problems. He argues in this way: using N, S, E, I for north bank, south bank, eastern Meadows and Island, he observes that any bridge crossing can be denoted by a pair of letters, giving the part left and the part reached. In the crossing from the island to the north bank, for example, one would write IN. The next crossing in the chain must then start with N; if it goes over from the north bank to the Town Meadows on the east, one lengthens the chain to INE. Each successive bridge brings in one more letter and so, in order to satisfy the conditions of the problem (of crossing every bridge once only and starting and finishing at the same point) we have to find a string of letters, eight letters in length, starting and finishing with the same letter. There are five bridges joining the island to other parts and it is easy to see that if all these are to be crossed the letter I must come three times into the chain. In the same way, the north, east and south regions each have three bridges and it is easy to see that it will be necessary to have N, E and S twice each. Such a situation is impossible, since $3 + 2 + 2 + 2$ is 9, not 8.

So Euler exhibits some creativity in the generality of his solution and this is important, for the solution has led in the present century to a large-scale development in mathematics, known as graph theory. This development, in turn, has proved useful in many applications. But it would be fanciful to see genius in such a simple puzzle-solution, even a generalized one. What does show it is the introduction to the paper, where Euler refers to this problem as an example of a more general method and of a new kind of geometry, one in which measurement is no longer of importance (for it is clear that nothing depends on the size of the island or the lengths of the bridges, and yet the problem *is* a geometrical one). And this hint was taken up one and a half centuries later and has flowered in the present century in a major branch of mathematics called algebraic topology. This discusses a variety of problems of 'position', not only two-dimensional ones, by reducing them to algebraic form, just as Euler did for the Königsberg bridges. Topology proceeds, in fact, by relating the configurations in question to certain finite or infinite groups.

My second example arises in the investigations of the great German mathematician and physicist Gauss, perhaps the one mathematician who would be classed as a genius in any list, however selective. But this would be because of his immense range of activity. It has been said that everything discovered in mathematics for a century had been found but not published by Gauss. Such an exaggeration contains a grain of truth.

Gauss was in Göttingen and aged 41 when the great survey of the Kingdom of Hanover was begun in 1818.[2] The survey lasted nearly twenty years and Gauss was appointed as director. It was intended that his supervision should be very close in the initial stages. The process of a survey, just like the Ordnance Survey in Britain, consists of triangulation, that is, of measuring the angles between the lines of sight from a selected point to others visible from it, repeating the process from those points and so on. It proved more difficult than expected to make accurate measurements in Hanover, so these 'initial stages' took up ten years of Gauss's life.

At the end of that time Gauss published a paper which was a side effect of the survey. It arose like this: the points used in the triangulation are more or less on the spherical surface of the Earth, and the curvature of the Earth has to be taken into account in the survey. But the points are chosen on hill and mountain tops, for mutual visibility, so they are not on the exact surface of the Earth. Moreover, that surface is not exactly a sphere, for the Earth's rotation causes a flattening at the poles. So Gauss, generalizing as mathematicians will, asked how it would be possible to describe and calculate the curvature for any geometrical surface. He did this (and in this he was not entirely original) by asking how to measure the curvature of curves drawn on the curved surface. Of course these may curve more or less, according to how they are drawn, but because the surface is itself curved there is a limit to how straight they may be drawn. But now comes Gauss's touch of genius. If one draws a geometrical figure on a sheet of paper, and then bends the paper to form a cone or a cylinder, the cone or cylinder is a curved surface. Yet this surface is one on which the situation in the geometrical figure is unchanged. If two straight lines met at a certain angle before the paper was bent round, the corresponding curves will meet at the same angle after bending. So some aspects of curvature do not affect the geometry of figures drawn on the surface at all. On the other hand, the geometry on the surface of a sphere is different from that of a flat sheet of paper, because one cannot roll up a sheet of paper to make a sphere. As a result, the sum of the angles of a triangle drawn on the surface of a sphere exceeds the two right angles which make up the sum for a flat triangle. So there is also an aspect of curvature that affects the geometry on the surface, as well as affecting the relation between the points of the surface and the external space.

Gauss was able, by a detailed and rather technical argument, to sort out completely the description of those aspects of curvature which were intrinsic and those which were not. One can think of the intrinsic as being those properties which could be found by measurements carried out by two-dimensionsal creatures living on the surface. Those which were not intrinsic depended partly on the relation with the surrounding space. Gauss himself was pleased with his principal result; not a boastful person, he called it *theorema egregium* ('out of the common herd'), but even he could not have anticipated its generalizations within fifty years, mainly by the Italian geometers who worked out the corresponding theory for spaces of more than two dimensions.

To summarize the argument up to here: I have tried to show that the idea of genius is appropriate where one is left wondering at the totally inexplicable creative insight which results in such further developments of mathematics. The isolated character of mathematics means that most examples of this are complex and inaccessible but I have used two as examples in which it is possible to give a simple explanation. I now turn to the other, 'language of science', aspect of mathematics.

In some ways this is much easier to deal with, for the isolation of mathematics is overcome by discussion within the context of a known concrete problem to which it is applied. But the mystery is actually much deeper, for it seems utterly inexplicable that any applications at all of such an abstract subject should be possible. To put it slightly differently, mathematics speaks with absolute exactness, though it does no more than prove what was already in the mathematical assumptions. How can this be reconciled with telling us something new about the real world with all its inaccuracies? Nor is this mystery dispelled by taking the Platonist view that the application of the piece of mathematics is not to the physical world but to an idealization ('a model') of it. For this idealization is a mathematical model and so the mystery is simply transferred to the relationship between the model and the real world. I can offer no solution to this mystery, the existence of which is ignored by mathematicians, who thus perpetuate their own isolation. Fortunately this does not affect my discussion of genius. The inexplicability of genius does not reside in the existence of the results but in their discovery and I want to describe three instances in which such genius was clearly recognized by the larger community.

The first is Newton's celestial mechanics. It is just over 300 years since Newton's *Principia* showed that observed motions of the planets round the Sun could be explained by postulating that each planet was attracted to the Sun by a force proportional to its mass and inversely proportonal to the square of its distance from the Sun. Generalizing, by supposing that this inverse square force operated between any two bodies, later allowed the small deviations from the cruder seventeenth-century observed positions to be calculated. The assumption here was that these deviations were caused by the much smaller influences of the planets on each other. This celestial mechanics proved hugely successful. The details of Newton's book are geometrical, and not very simple. This did not prevent his recognition. For Pope,

> Nature and nature's laws lay hid in night.
> God said, 'Let Newton be!' and all was light.[3]

A grateful country found room for a grand tomb in Westminster Abbey and Newton's theory was a topic of conversation in the salons across the Channel. What was the secret that produced such popular acclaim? Partly, perhaps, the extreme accuracy of the predictions but, more importantly, the frisson of excitement at the postulation of the invisible but universal force, gravity. The result was the acknowledgement that the Renaissance had culminated in the Age of Reason, which saw what it wanted to see: reason successful in correlating a bewildering complex of observations into a few simple laws. It said less about what it would not have liked so much – the invisible unexplained force, as mysterious and irrational as the alchemy which took up so much of Newton's time and which was so much less successful. But the general community was right in attributing genius here, for the consequences of Newton's formulation of mechanics are immense and the process of discovery of the inverse square law (though the finished proof is set out in the book and, like all mathematics publications, conceals far more than it reveals) shows an inexplicable creativity.

Much as the salons discussed Newton's theory, the whole populace argued about Einstein's in the early twentieth century. And unlike the Newtonian case there is no mystery about why this should be so. Einstein made two outstanding contributions, one in 1905, the other ten years later. The general fame, however, came after the Great War and so tended to look at the two together. In 1905 Einstein addressed the problem of the speed of light. It had been known since the late seventeenth century that light travelled from one place to another with a certain high speed, but by 1900 it had become clear that something was strange about the speeds of objects when these were comparable to that of light, and indeed about the nature of the speed of light itself. There had been attempts to clarify this situation by seeing it as a feature of electromagnetism (which was, as it happened, where the experimental data accumulated). Einstein's solution was radically different. He pointed out that our descriptions of events as happening at a certain point in space and at a certain time contained an unsuspected metaphysical assumption, *viz.* that a (distant) event had a unique time of happening. All that an observer can really find by measurement – a measurement which necessarily involves sending and receiving signals between observer and event – is a time relative to himself. The metaphysical assumption, easily seen to be false, for it leads to an inconsistency, is that this relative time does not in fact depend on the observer. By dropping this false assumption, time ceases to be a numerical property of an event. Instead, the numerical measure has to be attached to the relation between the event and the observer. Amongst the more bizarre consequences of this is the well-known situation of the space-traveller who returns after a long voyage to find that less time has elapsed with him than those who stayed at home. This is only a puzzle so long as one retains the old concept of a unique time attached to a distant event.

Certainly the space-traveller drew attention to the theory but it is not the main reason for the adulation of Einstein. That reason, and it is much to the credit of those who thought about these matters in the twenties even when they could not understand the technical details, was that Einstein had taken the boldly original step of questioning the concept of time and proposing a radical reform of it. The general public did not find the reform much to their taste; it went too much against their intuition. But they did realize as a result that they actually held a definite belief about the concept of time, and that this belief was being questioned. It is reasonable enough to apply the term genius to such a radically creative action.

But the term fits much better, in my view, as applied to Einstein's 1915 contribution, the object of which is to reconcile Newton's gravitational theory with the 1905 results on time. It fits much better because the 1915 paper does three quite astonishing things. In the first place, it questions the mysterious, invisible gravitational force that the Age of Reason had perforce to tolerate. It goes back before Newton to Galileo, to the observation that two heavy bodies of different weights fall at equal speeds when they are released in a gravitational field. This, said Einstein, opens the possibility of analysing phenomena from a new point of view. Instead of looking from a point fixed to the Earth's surface, look instead from a freely falling point of view. Whatever things you may measure around you, gravitation will not be one of them, for in free fall everything is affected equally. We can see television film now of astronauts in just such a freely falling situation, so that 'weightlessness' has become common-place. In the nineteenth century, such an imagination as Jules Verne had quite the wrong idea and even in 1910 it cost Einstein a greater effort of imagination than we would now need. So his first astonishing step was to abolish Newton's gravitational field by a change of point of view.

But how can this be? For the planets must still encircle the Sun, not move in straight lines as they would under no forces. This comes about simply because the change in point of view is only a local one. As one gets farther and farther away the remains of the old gravitational field begin to come back because the point of view ceases to be the right one to abolish it, being applicable only over there where we started. Einstein's second astonishing step (owing something to 'my friend, the mathematician, Marcel Grossmann') was to find how to formulate the problem of relating the changing field to the presence of the Sun. But this leads on to the third astonishment. For the technique for doing this, though derived by Einstein and Grossmann from the work of the nineteenth-century Italian differential geometers, is really just a generalization of Gauss's theory of curvature of surfaces. Only it is no longer a two-dimensional surface which is under discussion here but a four-dimensional curved manifold. The four dimensions are needed because of incorporating both the position and the time of an event (since the event no longer has a unique time but one that depends on its position relative to an observer). The curvature of the manifold, which is what now produces the planetary orbits, is itself caused by the presence of the Sun. Instead of being mysteriously forced towards the Sun, the planets are envisaged as moving in the straightest possible paths in a space curved by the Sun. This curved manifold can be thought of, if desired, as lying in some higher-dimensional space just as Gauss's curved surface lay in a three-dimensional space. But there is no need for the mental tortures involved in such a visualization, for Einstein, taking the cue of Gauss's *theorema egregium*, uses only quantities which can be measured and discussed by the inhabitants of the manifold, no longer mythical two-dimensionals, but us. So in 1915 Einstein capped his radical reconstruction of time of 1905 by an equally radical one of space. Something of all three of these creative advances, but particularly of the first and the third, was understood by the general public and their judgement that it was a work of genius was the correct one. But this was so not only for the reasons they saw as obvious but also for the way in which disparate parts of mathematics were united by the creative step.

My last example of genius in the application of mathematics has had less popular acclaim but its creativity and insight are in no way less than Newton's or Einstein's. The application here was originally conceived to be to the activity of mathematics itself but it is much wider, and applies more or less to all complex reasoning. The mathematician involved was the Austrian, Gödel, in 1931. The context of his original discovery can best be seen as Hilbert's schema, which I mentioned above, seeking to describe the nature of mathematics as an interlocking family of formal systems, each with its axioms and its rules of inference for deducing theorems from the axioms. I say 'can best be seen' since Gödel actually directed his fire at a different target, Russell and Whitehead's *Principia Mathematica*,[4] a noble but failed attempt to find a secure basis for mathematics in a (suitably augmented) logic. The idea of one of Hilbert's formal systems, on the other hand, was that it would apply to some branch of mathematics, for example, geometry, and the axioms and rules of inference would then be chosen in the most convenient way to provide proofs of *all* geometrical results ('completeness'). And about such a system, as I said before, one would like to be assured of its consistency.

By 1929 Hilbert and his co-workers had managed to prove that many of their formal systems would be consistent if and only if the one for arithmetic was consistent. What Gödel then showed was that any such formal system, subject only to the condition that it was complex enough to include arithmetic (counting), suffered from one of two defects: either it was inconsistent or incomplete. Such a result strikes at our whole idea of codifying mathematics by means of a fixed set of assumptions, but it does much more. For this apparently successful way of proceeding in mathematics has served extensively as a model for discourse in many different fields, so that Gödel is really pointing to grave limitations in the way we argue about anything.

In the particular case of mathematics, he turns the screw still further. For in the Hilbertian construction of formal systems one might, perhaps, swallow the incompleteness as an indication that any system served only till the subject developed far enough to need another. But in that case, when there was, as it were, no absolutely correct or best system, one would need all the more, some kind of assurance of its consistency. But Gödel's proof proceeds by exhibiting a result which is 'evidently true' if the system is consistent, and yet is unprovable. Amongst various such results is one whose evident interpretation is simply that the system *is* consistent. So a consequence of Gödel's proof is that we can never have the desired assurance of the consistency of the system.

It is a work of genius indeed to discover the limitations involved in our processes of argument. But our surprise at this is compounded by even a slight acquaintance with the structure of the proof. Firstly, what role is played by the mention of arithmetic? The answer is that, if the system is sufficiently complex to express arithmetic, then it is also adequate to talk about its own expressions, syntax and so on, just as a natural language is. (The reason is simply that the system is expressed by means of a finite alphabet, so that the expressions in the system can be numbered off and described numerically.) But secondly, as soon as such a measure of self-regard is present, natural languages exhibit paradoxes. Thus, if I write

[The sentence in square brackets on this page is false.]

and ask about the truth or falsehood of this sentence, I am led from the assumption that it is true to the conclusion that it is false, and vice versa.[5] However, the element of paradox is a consequence of the use of the concept of truth. In a Hilbertian formal system the corresponding basic concept is not truth but provability from the axioms. The truth of what is provable is a derived property depending on the truth of the axioms and the consistency of the system. So Gödel replaces 'false' by 'unprovable'. And if the formal system is complex enough to include arithmetic, then it can discuss its own sentences and the use of square brackets can be replaced by a numbering of sentences. The Gödel sentence becomes:

Sentence number so-and-so is unprovable.

Now (and here is the further subtlety of Gödel's already very subtle proof) 'so-and-so' can be substituted by such a number that, when it is inserted, the result is a sentence whose number is exactly the number inserted. With this special number inserted, the sentence asserts its own unprovability. Now ask about the truth or otherwise of this sentence. If it is true, then it is a sentence which cannot be proved from the axioms, though it is a true one. In this case the system is incomplete. If it is false, then the sentence must be provable, so that the axioms provide a proof of a false sentence and the system is inconsistent.

So my final exhibition of genius has turned my argument full circle. I began by insisting on proof as the essential mathematical process and I finish by pointing to Gödel's surprising demonstration of the underlying weakness of such a view of mathematics, genius questioning its own foundations in a truly twentieth-century manner.

Notes

1 A translation of Euler's paper is in J. R. Newman, *The World of Mathematics* (4 vols, London, 1960) vol. i, pp. 570–80.
2 See W. K. Bühler, *Gauss, A Biographical Study* (Berlin, 1980), ch. 9.
3 Pope's couplet was 'Intended for Sir I. Newton'.
4 A. N. Whitehead and B. Russell, *Principia mathematica* (3 vols, Cambridge, 1913). A second edition differing considerably, 1927. A paperback of the first 56 chapters of the second edition, 1962.
5 This paradox, the pseudomenos, is described by Aristotle. It is better known in the less extreme form of the Epimenides, when St Paul, *Epistle to Titus* I.12–13 warns Titus about the Cretans: 'One of themselves, even a prophet of their own, said, The Cretians are always liars, evil beasts, slow bellies. This witness is true. Wherefore rebuke them sharply; that they may be sound in the faith.'

11
Genius and Mental Disorder: A History of Ideas Concerning Their Conjunction

Neil Kessel

Les choses les plus belles sont celles que souffle la folie et qu'écrit la raison.

(The most beautiful things are those that madness inspires and reason writes)

André Gide[1]

When the ancients expressed the notion, as they variously did, that *'nullum magnum ingenium sine mixtura dementiae fuit'*[2] ('there has never been any great *ingenium* without some touch of *dementia*') they did not ascribe to *ingenium* or to *dementia* meanings that translate persuasively into genius and madness. The long association between the two, that lingers on even today, begins in the sixteenth century. Shakespeare's audiences would have been unsurprised by his conceit that

> The lunatic, the lover and the poet
> Are of imagination all compact.
>
> (A Midsummer Night's Dream)

The lunatic being hallucinated, the lover frantic and the poet exhibiting frenzy. They were soon to hear from him, moreover, that

Love is merely a madness; and I tell you, deserves as well a dark house and a whip as madmen do.

(As You Like It)

Yet his reference to imagination was novel. The seventeenth and eighteenth centuries were to dethrone 'noble and most sovereign reason' from its eminence as the chief attribute of great men and replace it with originality and imagination. The artist came to replace the sage as the most exalted being, and with this change the modern idea of the genius was born. All subsequent writings about genius have carried the notion that supremely high intelligence is not the essential requirement. Contemporaneously, enlightened appreciation of madness began. In the seventeenth century, methodical description led to the beginnings of scientific understanding. During the latter half of the eighteenth century, a proper appreciation of mental disorder permitted a relationship with genius to be explored.

Nevertheless it was the poets, essayists and philosophers of the seventeenth and eighteenth centuries who most emphasized the conjunction with the notion of the melancholy genius. 'All poets are mad' proclaimed Robert Burton in 1621,[3] and added artists and philosophers for good measure. The couplet by Dryden:

> Great wits are sure to madness near allied
> And thin partitions do their bounds divide[4]

is better known than the same notion expressed by Pascal: 'Great wit is charged with madness just as is great defect.'[5] A century and a half later Lamartine, influenced, as we shall see, by theories then current, was even more absolute, referring to 'This illness that we call genius'. He explained: 'Genius carries in itself a principle of destruction, of death, of madness, as the fruit carries in itself the worm.'[6] Such writers freely expressed what were no more than beliefs. None examined the relationship with a view either to verification or explanation. In the nineteenth century other, milder, more determined, more reasoned, voices come to express doubts. Esquirol, the greatest psychiatrist of his time, wrote in *Des Maladies Mentales*:

Dryden has said that men of genius and madmen are very close to one another. If that means that men who have a very active or a very disordered imagination, who have very exalted or very mercurial ideas, present analogies with madmen, then it is correct; but if it is meant that great intelligence predisposes to madness, then it is wrong. The greatest geniuses, in both the sciences and the arts, the grandest poets, the most gifted painters, have retained their sanity into extreme old age. When one has seen painters, poets, musicians or artists become mentally ill what has occurred is that on top of a very active imagination these men have, in their lives gone from extreme to extreme. More than other men, their personalities have led them to this. It is not at all because they exercise their intelligence that they lose their reason; it is not at all at the door of science or art or letters that the blame should be laid: men who are gifted with great powers of thought or imagination have a great need for stimulation of feeling. Most painters, poets and musicians, urged on by the need to feel, yield themselves up to numerous excesses in their style of living, and it is these excesses, more than excessive study, which are for them, the real cause of the madness.[7]

Esquirol had observed countless mentally ill people from all walks of life and knew what he was writing about. He was thus able both to refute Dryden for his generalization and to proffer an explanation for the instances when geniuses did become insane. Charles Lamb too, had seen mental illness close at hand. He recognized the impossibility of madmen producing great works. In his essay 'On the Sanity of True Genius' he wrote: 'So far from the position holding true, that great wit (or genius in our modern way of speaking) has a necessary alliance with insanity, the greatest wits, on the contrary, will ever be found to be the sanest writers. It is impossible for the mind to conceive of a mad Shakespeare.'[8]

Whenever the relationship between genius and mental disorder comes under close scrutiny it seems to diminish. Indeed at first blush genius, the supreme flower of human endeavour, stands so opposed to the lowering condition of mental illness that we can scarcely contemplate their association. Nevertheless it has been thought of, off and on, for nearly 400 years and we need to examine the reasons. To do so we must pluck certain historical strands from the developing concept of genius.

The first of these is the idea of passion. We turn to Diderot: 'I have always been an apologist for strong passions. They alone move me. The arts of genius are born with them and die with them.'[9] We recognize at once that excess of passion – frenzy – bears close relationship to madness. Had it not been pointed out earlier by Young and by Shaftesbury? The genius seized by enthusiasm could be inspired, and, once he began working, 'This poet [. . .] in an instant he no longer knows what he does. He is mad. This orator [. . .] he is no longer in control of himself; he is mad.'[10]

As he grew older Diderot, as Goethe was also to do, came to resile from according passion the central role in genius, although he never completely discarded it. Observation and reason played the larger part. It is a fault and a blessing of ageing that this change takes place. Diderot also believed that genius, which he regarded as irreducible and not capable of being dissected into component parts, involved a one-sided development in a man, an abnormality which made of him a monster.

Diderot debated a further matter which is also important when discussing the relationship between genius and madness. He reflected indeterminately whether genius should be considered as something separate from a man, a faculty which could be thought about in the abstract, so that we might speak of a man 'having genius', or whether on the other hand his genius ought not to be considered as an isolated factor but so transformed the man that he became totally imbued with it, 'being a genius' or 'the man of genius'. This debate almost exactly mirrors a long-standing controversy about how we should think of illness. Goethe certainly took the first view, that genius consisted of a peculiar energy or organization of energy. The idea of genius as something that can be argued about exclusive of the man who, as it were, possesses it, makes it a more malleable concept. It also accounts for the man of genius being, except in his particular field of high achievement, except, that is, at special times and in special circumstances, quite an ordinary person to talk to and to be with. 'That's what I particularly like about men of genius' says Rameau's Nephew, Diderot's anti-hero scamp. 'They are only good for one thing. Outside that, nothing.'[11]

Diderot believed that genius was acquired from nature. This idea soon passed to Germany and dwindled into the *Naturphilosophie* and the romantic ideas of *Sturm und Drang*. 'It is with Romanticism, of course,' writes Porter 'that the indissoluble link between madness and artistic genius comes into its own as an autobiographical experience.'[12] Becker adds that 'a sizable proportion of, in particular, Romantic geniuses acted as the initiators of their "victimization" and more or less deliberately conveyed an impression that contributed to the "imposition" by others of the "madness" label [. . .] The aura of "mania" endowed the genius with a mystical and inexplicable quality that served to differentiate him from the typical man, the bourgeois, the philistine, and, quite importantly, the "mere" man of talent.'[13] Romantic artists and writers may still hanker after that notion.

Later, throughout the latter part of the nineteenth century, occurred a most curious, sad, and perverse linking together of genius and mental disorder. A series of errors and an awkward pun brought degeneration theories of disease to the fore. Ideas concerning evolution were then exciting all Europe. It was widely accepted that some sort of transmission from generation to generation occurred. Darwin proposed natural selection but in mid-century the mechanism by which evolution occurred was still improperly appreciated.

Degeneration theories postulated a double process causing the inherit-able state. It might spring from physical disease and it might be caused by defective moral behaviour. One of its tenets was of disease being caused by sin. Victims of degeneration thus came to be called degenerate, or, more kindly if just as pointedly, decadent.

In Germany, Griesinger opined: 'Whenever I hear of an instance of genius in a family I straight away ask whether there is not an idiot also to be found.'[14] The theory, however, was most developed in France, championed by the very influential physician Magnan. Alcoholism, syphilis, any of a host of conditions now mostly recognized as acquired were held to damage not only the individual but his children and all subsequent generations, till the line ended in extinction. First-generation offspring might well have nervous dispositions; the next would suffer from psychoses or idiocy. Genius was considered to be one of the possible outcomes. Epilepsy was particularly linked with genius. Moreau de Tours constructed an evolutionary tree called '*Etat nerveux héréditaire, idiosyncrasique*'. Its branches included afflictions of the sense organs, delusional illnesses, mood disorders, nerve pains, neuroses, infectious diseases of the brain and spinal cord, idiocy, alcoholism, prostitution and, near the top, exceptional intelligence in science, music and the arts. He began his book with this argument: 'Those dispositions of mind which act so that a man becomes distinguished from others by the originality of his thought, by his conceits, by his eccentricity, by the energy of affective state or by his transcendent intelligence, stem from the same organic causes as various moral [we might now say mental] troubles, of which madness and idiocy are the fullest expression.'[15] The theory also took root in Italy, particularly in the work of Lombroso. In *Genio e Follia* he wrote that: 'Genius is a true degenerative psychosis' and remarked 'the frequency of genius among lunatics and of madness among men of genius'. He had, he noted, 'been enabled to discover in genius various factors of degeneration which are the foundations and the sign of nearly all forms of congenital ['inherited' is meant] mental abnormality' . . . 'The giants of thought expiate their intellectual forces in degeneration and psychoses.'[16] In English similar notions were proclaimed by J. F. Nisbet. His study, *The Insanity of Genius*, published in 1891, purported to document significant mental abnormality in the person or family of practically every famous Briton who had ever lived.

Henry Maudsley's *Pathology of Mind* appeared in the heyday of degeneration theory. He preserved a relative coolness to such ideas but invoked a concept of altered neuro-physiology both in geniuses and in the insane.

It is undoubtedly true that where hereditary trait exists in a family, one member may sometimes exhibit considerable genius while another is insane or epileptic: but the fact plainly proves no more than that in both there has been a great natural sensibility of nervous constitution, which, under different outward circumstances or internal conditions, has issued differently in the two cases.

Sensibly he would not find the two cases in the same individual, since anyone insane lacked:

the power of calm, steady and complete mental assimilation and must fall short of the highest intellectual development [. . .] the truly creative imagination [. . .] he is not sound and comprehensive.[17]

Galton's *Hereditary Genius* appeared in 1869. Genius to Galton was not a special quality; he used the term freely as an equivalent for natural ability and

By natural ability, I mean those qualities of intellect and disposition, which urge and qualify a man to perform acts that lead to reputation [. . .] an adequate power of doing a great deal of very laborious work [. . .] a nature which, when left to itself, will, urged by an inherent stimulus, climb the path that leads to eminence, and has strength to reach the summit [. . .] Few have won high reputations without possessing these peculiar gifts.[18]

This book is devoted to the proposition, for which he provided detailed evidence, that genius runs in families. In the second edition of 1892, he addressed the problem of the relationship of genius to insanity. He derided Lombroso and others

whose views of the closeness of the connection between the two are so pronounced that it would hardly be surprising if one of their more enthusiastic followers were to remark that so-and-so cannot be a genius because he has not been mad nor is there a single lunatic in his family.[19]

Nonetheless he observed that:

there is a large residuum of evidence which points to a close relation between the two [. . .] I have been surprised at finding how often insanity or idiocy has appeared among the near relatives of exceptionally able men. Those who are over eager and extremely active in mind must often possess brains that are excitable and peculiar [. . .] They are likely to become crazy at times, and perhaps to break down altogether.

Since we know exactly what Galton meant by genius we know that he was not allying himself with the supposition with which he continued:

If genius means a sense of inspiration, or of rushes of ideas from apparently supernatural sources, or of an inordinate and burning desire to accomplish any particular end, it is perilously near to the voices heard by the insane, to their delirious tendencies or to their monomanias. It cannot in such cases be a healthy faculty nor can it be desirable to perpetuate it by inheritance.[20]

Yet this view of genius as inspiration or rushes of ideas was rife among those who steeped themselves in degeneration theory. That theory's course was nearly run, but its popularity coincided with the Europe-wide growth of asylums. As Porter rather opaquely puts it: 'And the coming of institutional psychiatry had invented peculiarly destructive nurseries of genius.'[21]

In this century, among psychiatrists, only Kretschmer has assiduously pursued degeneration ideas. He invoked evolutionary and degenerative concepts, although inviting his readers to consider genius less exclusively in relation to psychoses (as up to then had been done) and more in relation to neuroses and personality disorder.

Genius is from a purely biological standpoint an extreme variant of the human species. Such [. . .] show [. . .] a heightened tendency to degeneration [. . .] Mental disease, and more especially, those ill-defined conditions in the boundary of mental disease, are decidedly more frequent among men of genius. [. . .] [Such men have] a very considerable liability to psychoses, neuroses and psychopathic complaints [. . .] For some types of genius this inner dissolution of the mental structure is an indispensable prelude.[22]

He stressed

the psychopathic component [. . .] an intrinsic and necessary part, an indispensable catalyst perhaps, for every form of genius.[23]

We are almost back to the ancients. The mental disturbance is 'necessary', an 'indispensable' element of the genius. However, Kretschmer's views commanded little respect. Degeneration theories of disease had faded from scientific acceptance by the turn of the century, once the principles of inheritance had been properly understood. They could no longer be sustained by medical scientists and linger only among lay people in such phrases as 'he comes from poor stock.'

It is time to take up another historical strand and consider the genius in relation to society. Geniuses change our way of understanding things. Berenson's synoptic remark that 'we define genius as the capacity for productive reaction against one's training'[24] echoed Proust's earlier cognate thought:

The artist's genius acts in the manner of those very high temperatures which have the power of dissociating combinations of atoms and of grouping them in an absolutely different order corresponding to another type.[25]

Samuel Butler quintessentially expressed this aspect:

Genius points to change, and change is a hankering after another world, so the old world suspects it. It disturbs order, it unsettles mores and hence it is immoral. [. . .] The uncommon sense of genius and the common sense of the rest of the world are thus as husband and wife to one another; they are always quarrelling.[26]

And later on he all but coaxes us to agree that

genius is a nuisance, and it is the duty of schools and colleges to abate it by setting genius-traps in its way.[27]

If geniuses disturb society, if they misfit, then this is another characteristic they share with the mentally ill. Yet it is a dangerous conjunction to make because the reasons lying behind the two types of disturbance are so different. Unfortunately today we have good cause to know that there are places where to proclaim heterodox and heretical ideas risks being shut away as mad. The closeness of passion to frenzy and madness was a seventeenth- and eighteenth-century thought. Considering disturbers and misfits to be deranged has been a sad nineteenth- and twentieth-century preoccupation.

Another very readily understood characteristic – envy – can add to our eagerness to regard geniuses as mentally ill. By calling geniuses mad, by, so to speak, salting their exalted position with stigma, we somehow reduce them so that petty people like us can more comfortably accept their existence. Swift tells us that 'when a true genius appears in the world, you may know him by this sign, that the dunces are all in confederacy against him.'[28] Diderot has Rameau's nephew express it thus:

I am envious. When I can learn of some characteristic in their private lives which degrades them I listen to it with pleasure. It brings us closer to one another; because of it I can more easily put up with my own mediocrity.[29]

'Whom the gods would destroy, they first make mad' is a very human projection.

Lange-Eichbaum's compendious work, *Genie, Irsinn und Ruhm*, appeared first in 1927. Like Galton, he regarded fame as essential to genius. He related the factors of ability and mental state in geniuses by drawing up, as it were, a simple two by two table: high or ordinary ability set against mental illness or health.[30] He produced no quantitative data but his biographical considerations led him to believe that most geniuses had high ability and some mental abnormality. A lesser number had enormous ability but were mentally normal. A few had ordinary ability and were mentally unwell, and a very few had ordinary ability and were well; these had gained the soubriquet by the fortunate chance of having their name attached to a pyramid of work by others to which they had contributed only the final small but apical step.

Lombroso, Galton, Nisbet, Kretschmer and Lange-Eichbaum each produced catalogues of great men and women who had shown mental abnormalities, accompanied by brief supporting biographies. The cumulative effect of these long lists, certainly upon the authors themselves,

convinced them of the rightness of their theses. What none of them did
was to look at the evidence statistically. (Galton did so for the inheritance
of genius but not for its relation to mental illness.) They did not consider
rates. Their attention was captured by the size of the numerator but not
by that of the denominator, for they completely ignored the large numbers
of sane great individuals.

Whether there is a relationship between genius and mental illness has
to stand or fall by the facts. These require to be statistical and perhaps
also genealogical. Havelock Ellis in 1904 reported his biographical study
of 1,030 British men and women of genius culled from the entries of
eminent people in the Dictionary of National Biography. He sought as full
biographical details from other sources as he could. Only 4.2 per cent had
mental disorder (including senile dementia) and he concluded: 'It is rare
to find any true insanity in a man of genius when engaged on his best
work.'[31]

Catherine Cox studied biographical data of 300 'most eminent people'
from 1450 AD onwards, judging eminence by the space accorded to them
in biographical dictionaries and encyclopaedias. Most seemed to have had
high intelligence and great force of character, but in emotional balance
and control, up to the age of 27 (she did not follow them later) they were
not different from the normal run.[32]

The most important study is that by Adele Juda. She studied 294
acknowledged geniuses, from German-speaking countries since 1650.
Her proposition consisted of 113 artists (*Kunstler*) and 181 scientists
and statesmen, (*Wissenschaftler*) agreed by leading individuals in each of
their fields. She garnered extensive biographical and autobiographical
data and consulted medical records where available about the probands
and their relatives. It is a large and meticulous piece of work. 4.8 per cent
of the artists and 4.0 per cent of the scientists and statesmen suffered from
functional psychoses. These were all schizophrenic or indeterminate in the
case of the artists, all manic depressive in the cases of the scientists. Such
figures are higher than the expectancy rate in the general population, but
not very much so, particularly when one considers how extensively such
lives have been submitted to scrutiny and especially autobiographical
scrutiny, including diaries and letters in which the writer may readily
disclose abnormal mental states. The overwhelming proportion in each
group, over 95 per cent were sane. Psychopathy (which term includes, in
the continental usage, neurotic conditions), notoriously difficult of
mensuration, was found in 27 per cent of the artists and 19 per cent of the
scientists and statesmen, against an expected general rate of 10–12 per
cent. However, these rates for the geniuses were not higher than in an
intermediate comparison group of mainly professional people. Her
conclusions are important:

There is no definite relationship between highest mental capacity and mental health or illness, and no evidence to support the assumption that the genesis of high intellectual ability depends on psychological abnormalities. [. . .] Psychoses, especially schizophrenia, proved to be detrimental to creative ability.[33]

Juda reported no marked excess of either psychoses or neuroses in the families of her propositi. However, Karlsson found the likelihood of being listed in the Icelandic *Who's Who* (taken as a measure of 'giftedness') was almost twice as high for close relatives of psychotic patients as for the population at large.[34] This particularly applied when the psychosis was manic depressive in form, but in another study Karlsson, tracing a family history for 300 years, discovered an excess of 'giftedness' in the lines of the family that bore schizophrenic members.[35] Heston has used these data (and similar, though unsystematically gathered, information of his own) to argue that it might account for the persistence of the gene or genes for schizophrenia.[36] None of this genetic work, however, bears upon the conjunction of genius and mental disorder in the same individuals. In respect of that, Juda's conclusions represent the best statement of our present knowledge of the facts. Genius and insanity are not correlated.

Have we then done? Is the subject dismissed? If genius and mental disorder are not quantitatively found together in excess then perhaps there is nothing of substance to pursue further.

Interest in this century has come to centre on a cognate problem, that of a possible relation between creativity and mental instability. For one thing, there are those whose fascination with the subject would not let the matter drop. For another, neither genius nor madness was readily susceptible of exact definition. Mental illness, however, can now be defined operationally and operational criteria for creativity are, just, creatable.

Andreasen recently reported a neat, though small study in which, using standardized diagnostic questionnaire procedures, she compared the mental illness position of 30 members of a creative writers' workshop at the University of Iowa with those of control subjects matched for sex, age and educational status. 'The writers had a substantially higher rate of mental illness, predominantly affective type [i.e. manic-depressive] [. . .] There was also a higher prevalence of affective disorder and creativity in the writer's first degree relatives.'[37] It is a far cry, of course, from membership of a creative-writing programme to genius, or even to high levels of creativity, and it may be that what correlated with the manic-depressive features here was no more than drive and enthusiasm. Creativity itself would require these to be allied with judgement. However this study illustrates one facet of modern attacks upon the problem. As Hare points out: 'The association [of creativity] with affective disorder (especially in literature) suggests that the cyclothymic constitution may be a socially valuable trait.'[38] Storr, in chapter 12 of the present volume, offers another explantion for the conjunction, namely that writers, by virtue of the nature of their work, are not good at warding off depression.

Such notions lead us now to consider what ideas or speculations have been advanced to explain those individual instances where the conjunction does occur. Some of these have already been touched upon. In this century, and particularly in respect of artists, psychoanalytic views used to hold most sway. Art fascinated Freud, who again and again addressed himself to the subject.

Essentially, where Galton had seen genius as something biological stemming from sources external to the personality and its experiences, Freud's view of creativity was that the major motive force lay within the individual. He believed that the most essential part of the creations of geniuses come to them in the form of inspiration, as a result of unconscious thinking. Artists had the ability to tap lost images and feelings of their childhood, because they were less bound than most people by the repressive aspects of culture. They had more 'flexibility of repression'. His classical position is stated in the *General Theory of the Neuroses*:

An artist is once more in rudiments an introvert, not far removed from neurosis. He is oppressed by excessively powerful instinctual needs. He desires to win honour, power, wealth, fame and the love of women; but he lacks the means for achieving these satisfactions.[39]

The artist has 'a strong capacity for sublimation and a certain degree of laxity in the repressions' of his emotional conflicts, particularly excessively strong sexual excitations, so as to find an outlet and use in other fields.

Freud's theories, however, and those of his followers, reflect almost exclusively a wish to explain the content of art works and their implied symbolism. Psychoanalytic theories have therefore fallen foul of both art critics and literary critics, even when they have most wished to be sympathetic. Roger Fry, in his essay *The Artist and Psychoanalysis*, chided Freud and his followers because the theories explained content in terms of neurosis but ignored form and the techniques used to achieve form:

quâ artist the creator has other aims than that of wish fulfilment and [. . .] the pleasure which he feels is not thus directly connected with the libido

instead it was

a pleasure derived from the contemplation of the relations and correspondences of form.[40]

These are the aspects of artistic creation upon which the accolade of greatness most depends. Freud's monograph on Leonardo,[41] for instance, tells us something of why that artist may have chosen his subject matter but does not account at all for the impression of greatness that we receive. Trilling, in 'Art and Neurosis', found it

surprising that in his early work he [Freud] should have made the error of treating the artist as a neurotic who escapes from reality by means of substitute gratifications.

He even cavilled at Freud's 'assumption that, because the artist was neurotic, the content of his work was also neurotic.' His conclusions, in line with those of Fry, were that

granting that the poet is uniquely neurotic, what is surely not neurotic, what indeed suggests nothing but health, is his power of using his neuroticism [. . .] It is wrong, I believe, to find the root of the artist's power and the source of his genius in neurosis.[42]

The psychoanalytic view of the forces acting to produce creativity recently found support in an unexpected medical quarter. George Pickering, bedfast for a year because of illness, and having to forego the practice of medicine, cast a pathographic eye over six famous invalids, Darwin, Florence Nightingale, Proust, Freud, Mary Baker Eddy and Elizabeth Barrett Browning. In *Creative Malady* he wrote:

Passion is the chief characteristic that I can find which relates the psychoneuroses of the characters here described and the creative work which brought them fame. Psychoneurosis arises when there is a conflict between a wish and its fulfilment. The more passionate the desire the more likely is its frustration to lead to psychoneurosis. This in turn may make possible the fulfilment of the wish, or act as a spur to the mental catharsis which produces a great creative work. This seems to be the basis of the relationship between psychoneurosis and creativity. In brief, a psychoneurosis represents passion thwarted, a great creative work, passion fulfilled.[43]

This latterday orthodox Freudian statement is a lucid presentation of sublimation and catharsis theory. To Pickering, however, passion means no more than intensity of urge, with strong tones of sexual urge. To the earlier writers such as Shaftesbury, Young and Diderot it meant much more. Passion involved energy and enthusiasm, which could be truly allied to greatness, but even then, only with an admixture of judgement which ruled out their relationship with insanity.

Pickering puts forward another and novel advantage that may accrue to the creative individual by being neurotic. The nervous state, certainly in the cases of Darwin and Florence Nightingale, was deliberately used to shield them from society and its commitments and so protect their ability to work without interruption. Thus it permitted them to concentrate their energies, as Pickering himself was able to do, upon creative work.

Perhaps the best summing-up of the position regarding creativity and mental disorder is the authoritative statement by Slater:

Creative work is done out of the vigorous and healthy elements of the personality. Psychopathic features may give a slant to the work; neurotic fixations may lead to the selection of material of a particular kind for elaboration; griefs and sorrows may compel the artists to find some creative way of catharsis. But the creative work itself proceeds from strength and not weakness.[44]

Psychodynamic theory, by the interpretations it engenders of the content and symbolism of a work of art, may increase its appeal, but the theory signally fails to account for the greatness of the achievement. Its protagonists might do better to concentrate upon the search for psychological explanations for the outflow of productive energy that lies at the heart of creativity and of genius. We could do with knowing why some people approach whatever they tackle in life with much more energy than others. The answer, however, may as well depend upon metabolic as upon psychological factors. If we were looking to increase the number of geniuses we should try to increase the numbers of prodigiously energetic people.

So far the general direction of proffered explanations has been with how mental disturbance might produce creative response. It could be argued, however, that the arrow of cause of any association might lie in the reverse direction. Esquirol, as we have seen, believed that geniuses adopted styles of life that led to material self-neglect and consequently to mental illness. Recently, such an idea has been extended. Tentative suggestions have been made that the creation of certain types of writing brings mental illness in its inevitable train. Thus Alvarez, perhaps taking his cue from Goethe who said of his poems that 'they made me, not I them', has suggested: 'For Sylvia Plath suicide was an attempt to get herself out of a desperate corner her own poetry had boxed her into,'[45] and Anne Sexton's poem *Sylvia's Death* has the lines:

> what is your death
> but an old belonging,
> a mole that fell out
> of one of your poems?

I have elsewhere argued that this view is romantic rather than right.[46] In the case of Sylvia Plath there is good medical evidence to tell us where the cart stood and where the horse. Her first attempt to end her life was very serious yet made without there being any antecedent 'risk poetry'. Though life events and psychological experiences may condition art, there is no trustworthy evidence to convince us that the converse can hold.

Other explanations can be put forward to explain why someone who senses mental illness to be impending might turn towards artistic expression, why he might choose art rather than some other form of activity, and, if he has high abilities, great art might result.

First he will derive from art some of the six qualities that Lange-Eichbaum described as apparent when we come face to face with a work of genius. In particular, the alluring quality (*das Lockende*), the strange, otherworldly and eerie quality (*das Unheimliche*) and the wonderful and marvellous quality, transcending human experience (*das Besondere*) may exert a particular hold upon him for they will perhaps mirror what he dimly apprehends in himself.[47] Thus he may persuade himself that he cannot be as alien as he was beginning to fear. Out of a sense of imitation and attachment he may turn to a similar form of expression.

Second, there is about art an imprecision which may well appeal to the individual who, because of mental illness, is beset with difficulty in exact expression. Since a work of art does not give the same message to any two people it does not reveal that its creator is having difficulty with communication. This may be comforting.

Third, the enjoyment of art is private; the satisfactions of artistic creation do not require others; therefore they are particularly appropriate to the individual dislocated by mental illness. Elizabeth Hardwick, in her essay on Zelda Fitzgerald, neatly catches this point:

In Zelda's fight against insanity and dependence she turned, as many disturbed people turn – the educated ones at least – to the hope of release through the practice of art. This hope rests upon the canny observation, clear even to the deranged and sequestered, that artists do not require the confidence of society to the same degree as other workers.[48]

Talented people may turn to art because of madness therefore, or because of impending madness. But they achieve their greatness despite it, not because of it. The mentally ill are vouchsafed no extra powers that normal people do not possess; they have no true prophetic visions; they are not, although they may think they are, more inspired; they achieve no apocalyptic synthesis of ideas. They evince no consummate creative force, enthusiasm or passion. They are, on the contrary, reduced people. And creative work proceeds from strength and not from weakness.

Consideration of the relationship between genius and mental disorder is not complete without our addressing of the question whether it is possible to detect, say in a painting, that the artist was insane. Three general descriptive propositions have been made about pictures by the mentally ill. First, overcrowding of the canvas with detail, as can readily be seen in Dadd's 'The Fairy Feller's Master Stroke' or Ensor's 'The Entry of Christ into Brussels'. Both artists were schizophrenic. Second, figure–ground confusion, marvellously illustrated by the series of cat pictures painted by Louis Wain during the waxing of his mental illness. The cat becomes progressively more lost in the pattern until in the last picture the pattern is so dominant that it is hard to recognize even the vestige of the cat. Third is barrenness of composition, when contrasted with the artist's former fertility. There may be something to this suggestion, which is commonly made about Van Gogh's paintings of 1889 and 1890. But it is difficult to sustain when we compare, for instance, his painting of 'Mademoiselle Gachet at the Piano' with Lautrec's very similar but much duller painting of a similar subject done at exactly the same time. A study of Van Gogh's life, indeed, brings out an important generalization about mad artists. During their disturbed periods they produce very little work.

Does the art reveal the man? 'In the ideal I have of Art' wrote Flaubert in 1875, 'the man is nothing, the work is everything.'[49] The polarities of view about this have been expressed by two of the major formative literary influences of this century, both, I venture, geniuses. Virginia Woolf wrote: 'Every secret of a writer's soul every experience of his life, every quality of his mind is written large in his works.'[50] And T. S. Eliot wrote: 'The more perfect the artist the more completely separate in him will be the man who suffers and the mind which creates.'[51] We know the lady was from time to time psychotic, but we could not deduce it from her work. The noes, the separatists, have it.

Notes

1 The quotation continues: '*Il faut demeurer entre les deux, tout près de la folie quand on rêve, tout près de la raison quand on écrit.*' ('We should stay between the two, close to madness when we dream, close to reason when we write'.) A. Gide, *Journal for September 1894* in *Oeuvres Complètes d'André Gide*, ed. L. Martin-Chauffier (Paris, 1932), vol. I, p. 518.

2 Seneca, *De tranquillitate animi*, 17. 10.

3 R. Burton, *The Anatomy of Melancholy* (London, 1621) vol. I, pp. 128–9.

4 J. Dryden, *Absalom and Achitophel*, lines 163–4.

5 Pascal, *Pensées sur la Vérité de la Religion Chrétienne*, ed. Jacques Chevalier (Paris, 1925), vol. I, p. 170.

6 Lamartine, quoted in W. Lange-Eichbaum, *Genie, Irsinn und Ruhm*, 6th edn (Munich, 1967), p. 220.

7 J. D. E. Esquirol, *Des Maladies Mentales* (Paris, 1838), vol. I, p. 41.

8 C. Lamb, 'On the Sanity of True Genius' in *Last Essays of Elia* (London, 1823).

9 D. Diderot, *Oeuvres Complètes de Diderot*, eds. J. Assezat and M. Tourneux (Paris, 1875–9) vol. XIX, p. 87.

10 Ibid., vol. XI, p. 125. For a full discussion of 'Diderot's Conception of Genius' see the article of that name by Herbert Dieckmann, *Journal of the History of Ideas*, 2 (1941), 152–82, to which the author is indebted.

11 D. Diderot, *Le Neveu de Rameau* (Paris, 1891), p. 37. Text translated by me.

12 R. Porter, *A Social History of Madness* (London, 1987), p. 63.

13 G. Becker, *The Mad Genius Controversy* (Beverly Hills, 1978), p. 127. This is a useful source book of ideas.

14 W. Griesinger, quoted by R. Arndt, *Psychiatrie* (Vienna, 1883). It is not completely clear whether the word *Blödsinniger* here should be translated as idiot or madman. It matters little in this context.

15 J. Moreau (de Tours), 'Argument' to *La Psychologie Morbide ou de l'Influence des Névropathies sur le dynamisme intellectuel* (Paris, 1859).

16 C. Lombroso, *Genio e follia*, anonymous English translation, *The Man of Genius* (London, 1891), made from 5th edn (retitled *L'uomo di genio in rapporta alla psichiatria, alla storia ed all'estetica* (Turin, 1888), pp. 333, 361 and Preface v, vi.

17 H. Maudsley, *The Pathology of Mind* (London, 1867), p. 297.

18 F. Galton, *Hereditary Genius*, 2nd edn (London, 1892), p. 33.

19 Ibid., p. ix.

20 Ibid., p. x.

21 Porter, *Social History of Madness*, p. 81.

22 E. Kretschmer, *Geniale Menschen*, translated by R. B. Cattell as *The Psychology of Men of Genius* (London, 1931), pp. 13, 17.

23 Ibid., p. 20.

24 B. Berenson, *The Decline of Art*, cited in the *Penguin Dictionary of Modern Quotations* (Harmondsworth, 1971), but with only this bare reference. I cannot trace this essay but the aphorism is too good to lose. Berenson expresses the same thought though less concisely in *Aesthetics and History* (London, 1950), p. 175: 'for genius as distinct from talent means creative reaction against spiritual as well as material environments and its unavoidable by-product is neurosis.'

25 M. Proust, *A l'Ombre des Jeune Filles en Fleurs* (Paris, 1918), vol. III, p. 133, = vol. II, p. 223 of C. K. Scott Moncrieff's translation *Within a Budding Grove*, (London, 1924).

26 S. Butler, from *The Notebooks of Samuel Butler*, ed. H. F. Jones (London, 1918), p. 178.

27 S. Butler, *Samuel Butler's Notebooks: Selections*, eds. G. Keynes and B. Hill (London, 1951), p. 298.

28 J. Swift, *Thoughts on various subjects* in *The Works of Jonathan Swift*, ed. Thomas Roscoe, (London, 1841), vol. II, p. 304.

29 D. Diderot, *Le Neveu de Rameau*, p. 46.

30 Lange-Eichbaum, *Genie, Irsinn und Ruhm*. This is a very large source book.

31 H. Ellis, *A Study of British Genius* (London, 1904), p. 195.

32 C. M. Cox, *The Early Mental Traits of 300 Geniuses* in L. M. Terman (ed.), *Genetic Studies on Genius* (California, 1926). The quoted details are taken from Aubrey

Lewis's 1961 article, 'Agents of Cultural Advance'. This article contains much of value on the subject and may be found more easily reprinted in A. Lewis, *The State of Psychiatry* (London, 1967), p. 246.

33 A. Juda, *Höchstbegabung. Ihre Erbverhaltnisse sowie ihre Beziehungen zu Psychischen Anomalien* (Munich, 1953). A short version in English appeared in the *American Journal of Psychiatry*, 106, (1949), 296–309, from which comes the quotation.

34 J. L. Karlsson, 'Genetic Association of Giftedness and Creativity with Schizophrenia', *Hereditas*, 66 (1970), 177–82.

35 J. L. Karlsson, 'Inheritance of Schizophrenia', *Acta Psychiatrica Scandinavica*, Supplement 247 (1974), 81.

36 L. L. Heston, 'The Genetics of Schizophrenic and Schizoid Disease', *Science*, 167 (1970), 249–56.

37 N. C. Andreasen, 'Creativity and Mental Illness', *American Journal of Psychiatry*, 144 (1987), 1288–92.

38 E. Hare, 'Creativity and Mental Illness', *British Medical Journal*, 295 (1987), 1587–9.

39 S. Freud, *Introductory Lectures on Psychoanalysis*, English version in *Standard Edition of the Complete Psychological Works of Sigmund Freud*, ed. James Strachey (London, 1963), vol. XVI, 376.

40 R. Fry, *The Artist and Psychoanalysis* (London, 1924), pp. 13 and 12.

41 S. Freud, *Leonardo da Vinci and a Memory of his Childhood* in *Standard Edition*, vol. XI, pp. 63–81.

42 L. Trilling, 'Art and Neurosis' in *The Liberal Imagination* (New York, 1950), pp. 161, 165, 174, 169.

43 G. Pickering, *Creative Malady* (London, 1974), p. 309.

44 E. Slater, 'The Problems of Pathography', *Acta Psychiatrica Scandinavica*, Supplement 219 (1970), 209–15.

45 A. Alvarez, *The Savage God* (London, 1971), p. xiii.

46 N. Kessel, *Two Essays on Sylvia Plath*. Lectures to Whitworth Arts Society (Manchester, 1978).

47 Lange-Eichbaum, *Genie, Irsinn und Ruhm*, pp. 117–24.

48 E. Hardwick, *Seduction and Betrayal. Women and Literature* (London, 1974), p. 94.

49 G. Flaubert, Letter to George Sand 1875, in *Oeuvres Complètes: Correspondence 1873–1876* (Paris, 1930), vol. VII, p. 280, my translation.

50 V. Woolf, *Orlando* (London, 1928), p. 189.

51 T. S. Eliot, 'Tradition and the Individual Talent' in *Selected Essays, 1917–32* (London, 1932), p. 18.

12

Genius and Psychoanalysis: Freud, Jung and the Concept of Personality

Anthony Storr

What has psychoanalysis to offer to the study of genius? I must first make it clear that I am using the word 'psychoanalysis' in the wide sense of psychodynamic theory of every variety, not in the narrow sense of Freud's particular contribution. Psychoanalysis has nothing to say about the cognitive study of genius. That is, psychoanalysis is not concerned with studying or explaining what many people consider the most significant feature of genius: the possession of special gifts and abilities, like a gift for mathematics, or a capacity for musical composition. What psychoanalysis primarily studies is motivation: that is, the factors which drive men and women of genius to achieve what they do. Not every highly gifted person makes full use of his or her native endowments. Genius may not only be, as Carlyle put it, 'a transcendent capacity of taking trouble'; but it is certainly the case that great achievements require dedication and concentration over long periods of time, and that many people, however gifted, are not prepared to devote themselves whole-heartedly to objectives which offer few immediate rewards.

This obviously raises the question of whether men and women of genius are abnormal in some other sense than that of being abnormally gifted? Are they driven to achieve what they do by internal forces which are not operative in most of us? Are the achievements of genius dependent upon psychopathology? I do not think that there is a simple answer to this question; but the rest of this paper will be chiefly concerned with examining the problem.

Since the title of this paper makes reference to both Freud and Jung, I shall briefly summarize their views on genius and indicate why I find both unsatisfactory. Although Freud was widely read and himself a gifted writer who was awarded the Goethe prize for literature, he considered that art was primarily an escapist activity based on unrealistic phantasy. Freud wrote:

An artist is once more in rudiments an introvert, not far removed from neurosis. He is oppressed by excessively powerful instinctual needs. He desires to win honour, power, wealth, fame and the love of women; but he lacks the means for achieving these satisfactions. Consequently, like any other unsatisfied man, he turns away from reality and transfers all his interest and his libido too, to the wishful constructions of his life of phantasy, whence the path might lead to neurosis.[1]

Freud considered that phantasy was derived from play. He believed that, as children gradually gave up playing with real objects they substituted phantasies and daydreams. The creative writer, according to Freud, does the same as the child at play. He creates a world of phantasy which he takes very seriously. Freud had a low opinion of phantasy:

We may lay it down that a happy person never phantasies, only an unsatisfied one. The motive forces of phantasies are unsatisfied wishes, and every single phantasy is the fulfilment of a wish, a correction of an unsatisfying reality.[2]

Freud considered that phantasy, along with dreaming and with halluci-nation, was an unrealistic and infantile way of relating to the world based on the pleasure principle rather than upon the reality principle. He thought that the human infant at first hallucinated whatever it wanted, and only gradually relinquished wish-fulfilling phantasy in favour of directed, rational thinking. He wrote:

It was only the non-occurrence of the expected satisfaction, the disappointment experienced, that led to the abandonment of this attempt at satisfaction by means of hallucination. Instead of it, the psychical apparatus had to decide to form a conception of the real circumstances in the external world and to endeavour to make a real alteration in them. A new principle of mental functioning was thus introduced; what was presented to the mind was no longer what was agreeable but what was real, even if it happened to be disagreeable. This setting-up of the *reality principle* proved to be a momentous step.[3]

So life becomes real and life becomes earnest. Only by putting away childish things like phantasy and directing one's efforts towards reality, however disappointing, can one gain satisfaction for one's needs. It sounds like a Victorian re-creation of the story of the Fall of Man. The immediate satisfactions of the Garden of Eden must be abandoned. The phantasy that all will be provided without effort must be discarded in favour of the Puritan work ethic. 'In the sweat of thy face shalt thou eat bread, till thou return unto the ground.' There is no such thing as a free lunch.

It is true that Freud did not totally dismiss all art as escapist, in that he postulated that the artist found a way back to reality by making use of his gifts 'to mould his phantasies into truths of a new kind, which are valued by men as precious reflections of reality.'[4] But Freud's view of the imagination is essentially a negative one, and on that account I find it profoundly unsatisfactory. There is no such thing as a purely rational view of the world in which imagination plays no part. Even scientific discovery depends upon the use of phantasy. If Einstein had not been able to imagine how the universe might appear to an observer travelling at near the speed of light, he would not have formulated the theory of relativity.

Freud never seems to have entertained the notion that phantasy might be biologically adaptive. Although there are such things as idle daydreams, all daydreams are not idle. They may be ways of playing with ideas, making new combinations of concepts, experimenting with novel ways of looking at the world. Play, like phantasy, was dismissed by Freud as childish. But play is an essential aspect of creativity, as the Dutch historian, Johan Huizinga, claimed in his book *Homo Ludens*. Freud seems to have considered 'thinking' as a highly conscious activity, strictly directed toward a particular goal, as one might plan a journey from A to B. But most thinking, even scientific thinking, is not like this. Einstein once defined thinking as 'a free play with concepts'. He confessed that, in his own thinking, images predominated over words, and considered that thinking went on unconsciously to a considerable degree. Of course there are escapist phantasies: masturbatory daydreams, daydreams of winning the football pools, nonsense like thrillers and romantic novels. But not all phantasy is of this lowly variety. Without phantasy, neither the achievements of science nor the artistic masterpieces of civilization could have been produced.

Jung took a more positive view of the creative artist, although his vision is also flawed. He distinguished two varieties of artistic creation; the *psychological* and the *visionary*. To the first variety belong 'all the novels dealing with love, the family milieu, crime and society, together with didactic poetry, the greater number of lyrics, and drama both tragic and comic. Whatever artistic form they may take, their contents always derive from the sphere of conscious human experience – from the psychic foreground of life, we might say.'[5] Jung is not primarily interested in this kind of creative activity, nor in the psychology of the artists who produce this type of work, in spite of the fact that they constitute the majority.

The artists who interest Jung are those whose imagery belongs to the variety which he names 'visionary'. He includes Dante, Nietzsche, Wagner, Blake, and Goethe, in the second part of Faust, amongst such visionaries. Jung writes of Goethe:

The gulf that separates the first from the second part of *Faust* marks the difference between the psychological and the visionary modes of artistic creation. Here everything is reversed. The experience that furnishes the material for artistic expression is no longer familiar. It is something strange that derives its existence from the hinterland of man's mind, as if it had emerged from the abyss of prehuman ages, or from a superhuman world of contrasting light and darkness.[6]

Jung believed that this kind of visionary imagery could not be derived from the artist's personal biography. Whereas Freud would have interpreted such material as originating from early infancy, Jung postulated a level of mind which he named the 'collective unconscious'. Jung had an extensive knowledge of myth and of comparative religion. He also had considerable clinical experience with schizophrenic patients, which was not shared by Freud. Jung believed that the collective consciousness produced primordial images, or archetypes, which manifested themselves in different forms in different cultures, but which attested the existence of a basic, myth-producing level of mind which was common to all men. This concept has been vulgarly misinterpreted in terms of 'racial memory' and the like. This is not what Jung meant. I think his idea was originally derived from his studies of comparative anatomy when he was a medical student. He pictured the mind as being like the body: as having a structure which had a long history, and which produced the same kinds of basic images, just as the body produced the same kinds of basic organs.

Nevertheless, it was difficult for the average person, caught up in the toils of mundane, conscious existence to tap this level of mind except, perhaps, during sleep, when he might occasionally have dreams of a particularly impressive, visionary kind. Those who were mentally ill, or on the point of breakdown, might also be assailed with visions of a disturbing kind which could not be derived from personal experience. Jung himself experienced such visions when he went through a period of intense mental disturbance after his break with Freud.

In Jung's view, the visionary artist was gripped by this material, rather than inventing it. He writes:

Whenever the creative force predominates, life is ruled and shaped by the unconscious rather than by the conscious will, and the ego is swept along on an underground current, becoming nothing more than a helpless observer of events. The progress of the work becomes the poet's fate and determines his psychology. It is not Goethe that creates *Faust*, but *Faust* that creates Goethe. And what is *Faust*? *Faust* is essentially a symbol. By this I do not mean that it is an allegory pointing to something all too familiar, but the expression of something profoundly alive in the soul of every German, which Goethe helped to bring to birth.[7]

Jung conceived the individual psyche as a self-regulating system. This, again, is an idea which was probably derived from his medical studies. In terms of physiology, the body is a self-regulating system of checks and balances based upon 'feedback'. That is, it is so arranged that if, for example, the blood becomes more alkaline, mechanisms are automatically called into action to increase its acidity. These physiological mechanisms ensure homeostasis: a constant oscillation about a balanced mean.

Jung thought of the individual mind as functioning in the same way. Neurosis occurred when the individual became 'one-sided': that is, when he behaved in so extraverted a fashion that he lost touch with his inner life; or became so introverted that he lost touch with external reality. Neurotic symptoms were indicators of lack of balance: valuable pointers to what was wrong, not merely unpleasant manifestations to be abolished.

Jung also considered that whole cultures behaved like individuals, and might also become unbalanced in rather the same fashion. Thus, modern Western culture might be considered one-sided, in that the pursuit of material prosperity has taken precedence over the pursuit of spiritual health. Jung thought of artists of the visionary kind as prescient: as being in touch with unconscious factors which were as yet unappreciated by the ordinary person, but which are heralding changes in collective attitudes. He referred to artists of this kind as being ahead of their times. One might take as an example the revolution in how we perceive the world which was begun by the early Impressionist painters, who were at first reviled for their disturbing innovations. In Jung's view, to be an artist of this prophetic kind was often a harsh fate.

Art is a kind of innate drive that seizes a human being and makes him its instrument. The artist is not a person endowed with free will who seeks his own ends, but one who allows art to realize its purposes through him. As a human being he may have moods and a will and personal aims, but as an artist he is 'man' in a higher sense – he is 'collective man,' a vehicle and moulder of the unconscious psychic life of mankind. That is his office, and it is sometimes so heavy a burden that he is fated to sacrifice happiness and everything that makes life worth living for the ordinary human being.[8]

This conception of the artist fits, if it does not explain, some of those artists who do indeed sacrifice everyone around them and every other pleasure to their creative endeavours. Wagner and Strindberg are both examples of such ruthlessness. But not everyone will go along with Jung's conception of the collective unconscious as not only being the basic substratum of mind which gives rise to myth, but as a realm outside space and time which somehow exists 'out there' and which, as it were, exerts an influence on culture by operating upon, or entering into, the individual psyche of the artist.

It is worth remembering that Jung was considerably influenced by Schopenhauer. Jung's 'collective unconscious' bears a strong resemblance to Schopenhauer's 'Will'. Schopenhauer considered that individuals were the embodiment of an underlying Will which was outside space and time. Following Kant, Schopenhauer thought that space and time were human, subjective categories imposed upon reality which compel us to perceive the world as consisting of individual objects. Fortunately one does not have to accept the whole range of Jung's conceptual system in order to appreciate his considerable contributions.

In the area of creativity, one notable difference between Freud and Jung is to be found in their views of phantasy. As we have seen, Freud tended to put phantasy on a level with dreaming, hallucination and play as an immature form of mental functioning, which was primarily unrealistic and escapist. Jung, on the other hand, took phantasy seriously, and encouraged his patients to make use of it in their quest for mental health and stability. Jung encouraged his more advanced patients to enter a state of reverie, which he called 'active imagination'. They were encouraged to note what phantasies occurred to them, and to let such phantasies develop and take their own paths without consciously interfering with them. Then they were enjoined to write down, draw or paint whatever had occurred.

This technique developed as supplementary to the analysis of dreams, which was the main method employed in Jungian analysis. The object of this exercise was to achieve a new balance between conscious and unconscious. Jung specialized in the treatment of middle-aged people, many of whom were well established and successful, but who were suffering from a sense of futility or loss of meaning in life. In Jung's view, this was because the highly developed consciousness of such individuals had diverged too far from the unconscious. In other words, the individual had strayed from his own true path of inner development, and needed to look inward if he was to regain equilibrium and progress once more. The analysis of such patients became a quest for the true self; a spiritual journey, of which the end-point, never completely attained, was the achievement of inner peace, acceptance, and wholeness. By paying careful attention to the unconscious, as manifested in dream and phantasy, the individual comes to change his attitude from one in which ego and will are paramount to one in which he acknowledges that he is guided by an integrating factor which is not of his own making. Jung's name for this spiritual journey was 'the process of individuation'; a term which also derives from Schopenhauer.

This brief exposition of Jung's ideas may seem remote from the topic which I am supposed to be addressing, but I hope to persuade you of its relevance, though Jung himself might not have agreed with me. Jung's description of the process of individuation is closely paralleled by what we know of the process of creation in the arts and sciences.

First, the state of reverie which Jung advised his patients to cultivate is precisely the condition of mind in which most new ideas occur to creative persons. There are a few instances in which actual dreams have provided inspiration; for example, the idea of *Dr. Jekyll and Mr. Hyde* came to Robert Louis Stevenson in a dream, and the composer Tartini affirmed that the theme of his 'Devil's Trill' Sonata came from a dream in which he saw and heard the devil playing the violin. But such examples are rare. By far the majority of new ideas come to people when they are in a state intermediate between sleep and waking. Wagner's description of the state of mind in which the overture to the *Rheingold* came to him is typical.

Wagner had been suffering from dysentery, and was staying in a hotel in Spezia. He wrote:

After a night spent in fever and sleeplessness, I forced myself to take a long tramp the next day through the hilly country, which was covered with pine woods. It all looked dreary and desolate, and I could not think what I should do there. Returning in the afternoon, I stretched myself, dead tired, on a hard couch, awaiting the long-desired hour of sleep. It did not come; but I fell into a kind of somnolent state, in which I suddenly felt as though I were sinking in swiftly flowing water. The rushing sound formed itself in my brain into a musical sound, the chord of E flat major, which continually re-echoed in broken forms; these broken chords seemed to be melodic passages of increasing motion, yet the pure triad of E flat major never changed, but seemed by its continuance to impart infinite significance to the element in which I was sinking. I awoke in sudden terror from my doze, feeling as though the waves were rushing high above my head. I at once recognised that the orchestral overture to the *Rheingold*, which must long have lain latent within me, though it had been unable to find definite form, had at last been revealed to me. I then quickly realised my own nature; the stream of life was not to flow to me from without, but from within.[9]

Jung's concept of individuation was of a goal which is never reached. No one succeeds in realizing all his potential; no one achieves total integration or wholeness. Jung defined personality as 'the supreme realization of the innate idiosyncrasy of a living being'.[10] The achievement of optimum development is a lifetime's task which is never completed, a journey upon which one sets out hopefully toward a destination at which one never arrives. This is exactly how creative individuals describe their work. No genius is ever satisfied with what he has achieved. He is always striving after something better, always attempting to plumb new depths, or to find some new form which will convey his insights more effectively.

In my book *The Dynamics of Creation*, I quoted the composer Aaron Copland's remarks about composing music, which are so apposite that I will repeat them. They come from Copland's Charles Eliot Norton lectures of 1951–2:

The serious composer who thinks about his art will sooner or later have occasion to ask himself: why is it so important to my own psyche that I compose music?

What makes it seem so absolutely necessary, so that every other daily activity, by comparison, is of lesser significance? And why is the creative impulse never satisfied; why must one always begin anew? To the first question – the need to create – the answer is always the same – self-expression; the basic need to make evident one's deepest feelings about life. But why is the job never done? Why must one always begin again? The reason for the compulsion to renewed creativity, it seems to me, is that each added work brings with it an element of self-discovery. I must create in order to know myself, and since self-knowledge is a never-ending search, each new work is only a part-answer to the question 'Who am I?' and brings with it the need to go on to other and different part-answers.[11]

The parallel with Jung's description of the individuation process is very close. Is it reasonable to suggest that the forces which motivate people to embark on the journey of self-exploration which Jung describes and the forces which motivate people to undertake the journey of self-exploration described by Aaron Copland are also similar?

If it is agreed that this is so, some might argue that all I am saying is that creative people are neurotic. Perhaps those who are not creatively gifted embark upon Jungian analysis, whilst those who are conduct a self-analysis by means of their creative work. There is a sense in which this may be true; but one must bear in mind that the patients whom Jung describes were not suffering from any conventional form of neurosis like hysteria or obsessional neurosis, but from a sense of futility and lack of personal fulfillment. Jung wrote of these patients:

About a third of my cases are not suffering from any clinically definable neurosis, but from the senselessness and aimlessness of their lives. I should not object if this were called the general neurosis of our age. Fully two thirds of my patients are in the second half of life. This peculiar material sets up a special resistance to rational methods of treatment, probably because most of my patients are socially well-adapted individuals, often of outstanding ability, to whom normalization means nothing.[12]

These patients are very different from those whom the psychiatrist habitually sees in an outpatient clinic. They are not suffering from neurotic symptoms like phobias, compulsive thoughts and rituals, or even obvious difficulties in interpersonal relationships. What they seem to be suffering from is alienation from the unconscious, that 'impersonal force within which is both the core of oneself and yet not oneself', as Rycroft has called it.[13]

This impersonal force within might equally be called 'genius'. According to R. B. Onians, the original meaning of the word is 'the life-spirit active in procreation, dissociated from and external to the conscious self that is centred in the chest'. Genius was located in the head and was also that part of the person which was supposed to survive death. Onians writes:

The idea of the genius seems to have served in great part as does the 20th-century concept of an 'unconscious mind,' influencing a man's life and actions apart from or even despite his conscious mind. It is now possible to trace the origin of our idiom that a man 'has or has not genius,' meaning that he possesses a native source of inspiration beyond ordinary intelligence.[14]

So, what Jung's individuation process and the creative process have in common is first, that both involve making contact with the impersonal force within, whether this be called the unconscious or the genius: second, that both processes are concerned with integration or healing, especially in the sense of making new wholes out of previously disparate entities: third, that both processes are concerned with self-discovery in the way described by Aaron Copland: fourth, that both processes involve a journey which may bring many rewards *en route*, but which, by its very nature, is never completed.

Jung's patients were driven to seek his help by dissatisfaction with their lives, rather than by neurotic disorders of a clinically definable kind. Can we reasonably affirm that creative persons are also driven by dissatisfactions to embark on their journeys of exploration? I think that we can; although, as we shall see, the dissatisfactions may not simply be the sense of aimlessness and futility which Jung says was characteristic of his patients.

I think that dissatisfaction with what is is characteristic of man as a species. In my book *The Dynamics of Creation*, I called this 'divine discontent'. This dissatisfaction is biologically adaptive, in that it makes man use his imagination to explore new possibilities and make discoveries. Every human being uses imagination to some extent. No one is content merely with satisfying physical needs, as one might suppose that a well-adapted animal might be. Even so-called primitives, who appear to be well adapted in that they may have lived much the same kind of existence for millennia, entertain notions of a heaven in which they will be free of toil and relieved from pain and suffering. Dr Johnson referred to 'that hunger of imagination which preys incessantly upon life, and must always be appeased by some employment'.[15] Men use their imaginations in two ways. One way, as Freud rightly supposed, is to escape from the rigours of actual existence into wish-fulfilling daydreams. The other way, neglected by Freud, is by using imagination better to understand the world and ourselves, or to create works which, by combining opposites, symbolize new syntheses within the personality.

We are all divided selves in varying degrees, and we are all motivated to seek a unity which we never achieve. The first and most obvious way in which we do this is through love. Plato, in the *Symposium*, assigns to Aristophanes the speech in which it is supposed that human beings were originally wholes of three sexes: male, female and hermaphrodite. Because of their hubris, they were bisected by Zeus. All human beings are therefore compelled to seek for their lost halves, in order to regain their pristine unity. Love is therefore 'the desire and pursuit of the whole'.

The desire and pursuit of the whole can be sought in other ways than in physical unity with a beloved person. Jung's idea of individuation is really a search for unity within the psyche of the individual: a reconciliation between the opposites of conscious and unconscious. The process of creation in both the arts and the sciences is often characterized by finding a new synthesis between ideas which had previously appeared to be distinct or widely separated. The sciences and the arts share the aim of seeking order in complexity and unity in diversity. And when a painter or a musician solves an aesthetic problem, he shares the same pleasure, described as the 'Eureka' experience, which is enjoyed by scientists who have made a new discovery.

The human mind seems to be so constructed that the discovery of order in complexity in the external world is mirrored, transferred, and experienced as if it were a discovery of a new order and balance in the inner world of the psyche. This probably seems a fantastic statement. Let me support it by quoting from an early novel by C. P. Snow. The young scientist has just received confirmation that some difficult work he had been doing on the atomic structure of crystals has turned out to be correct.

Then I was carried beyond pleasure. I have tried to show something of the high moments that science gave to me; the night my father talked about the stars, Luard's lesson, Austin's opening lecture, the end of my first research. But this was different from any of them, different altogether, different in kind. It was further from myself. My own triumph and delight and success were there, but they seemed insignificant beside this tranquil ecstasy. It was as though I had looked for a truth outside myself, and finding it had become for a moment part of the truth I sought; as though all the world, the atoms and the stars, were wonderfully clear and close to me, and I to them, so that we were part of a lucidity more tremendous than any mystery.

I had never known that such a moment could exist. Some of its quality, perhaps, I had captured in the delight which came when I brought joy to Audrey, being myself content; or in the times among friends, when for some rare moment, maybe twice in my life, I had lost myself in a common purpose; but these moments had, as it were, the tone of the experience without the experience itself.

Since then I have never quite regained it. But one effect will stay with me as long as I live; once, when I was young, I used to sneer at the mystics who have described the experience of being at One with God and part of the Unity of things. After that afternoon, I did not want to laugh again; for though I should interpret it differently, I think I know what they meant.[16]

Given this intimate connection between inner and outer worlds, it seems to be reasonable to guess that those who are particularly strongly motivated to seek for unity and order, whether in the arts or in the sciences, are likely themselves to be particularly divided. This notion may conceivably go some way toward resolving the argument about the relation between genius and mental illness. I would suggest that men and women of genius are frequently driven by conflicts within their own personalities: conflicts which often make them unhappy, dissatisfied and restless, but which also make them imaginative, questing, and eager to find and experience the delights of unity and synthesis. So long as they are able to pursue their search by means of their work, they will often protect themselves against any form of mental breakdown, but, if their power to work fails them, or if it is rejected and they are particularly sensitive to rejection, melancholia or some other form of mental illness may ensue.

Throughout history, there have been two opposing schools of thought about the nature of genius. The one portrays the genius as exceptionally well balanced; the other asserts a close connection of genius with mental instability.

In *Born under Saturn*, the art historians Rudolf and Margaret Wittkower quote from Jonathan Richardson's *An Essay on the Theory of Painting* of 1715.

The way to be an Excellent Painter, is to be an Excellent Man.
A Painter's Own Mind should have Grace, and Greatness; That should be Beautifully and Nobly form'd.
A Painter ought to have a Sweet and Happy Turn of Mind, that Great, and Lovely Ideas may have a Reception there.[17]

Galton, writing in the second half of the nineteenth century, thought that genius was largely inherited, and that great achievements depended upon three gifts which he named as 'ability', 'zeal', and a 'capacity for hard work'. He wrote: 'If a man is gifted with vast intellectual ability, eagerness to work, and power of working, I cannot comprehend how such a man should be repressed.' Galton, who apparently took no notice of autobiographical accounts of the creative process furnished by writers, musicians, and mathematicians, entirely repudiated the idea that anything involuntary or inspirational could play any part in the activities of genius.

If genius means a sense of inspiration, or of rushes of ideas from apparently supernatural sources, or of an inordinate and burning desire to accomplish any particular end, it is perilously near to the voices heard by the insane, to their delirious tendences or to their monomanias. It cannot in such cases be a healthy faculty nor can it be desirable to perpetuate it by inheritance.[18]

Yet many creative people, not all of whom were notably unstable, have recorded the appearance of inspiration as something far removed from conscious effort, zeal, or hard work. Gauss, who had been trying unsuccessfully to prove a mathematical theorem for two years, wrote:

Finally, two days ago, I succeeded, not on account of my painful efforts, but by the grace of God. Like a sudden flash of lightning, the riddle happened to be solved. I myself cannot say what was the conducting thread which connected what I previously knew with what made my success possible.[19]

Thackeray wrote:

I have been surprised at the observations made by some of my characters. It seems as if an occult Power was moving the pen. The personage does or says something, and I ask, how the dickens did he come to think of that?[20]

One reason for the assumption that genius and insanity are connected dates from antiquity and is based on a confusion of insanity with inspiration which is still being expressed, eighteen centuries later, by Galton. Seneca's remark in his dialogue *De tranquillitate animi*, '*Nullum magnum ingenium sine mixtura dementiae fuit*' (There has never been any great *ingenium* without some touch of *dementia*) was echoed in Dryden's lines:

> Great wits are sure to madness near allied,
> And thin partitions do their bounds divide.[21]

But some scholars think that Seneca was using the word '*dementia*' in the sense of divine inspiration, the holy madness described by Plato, which was clearly distinguished from insanity. Today, with the recognition that there is an unconscious part of the mind which is constantly comparing, sorting, rearranging and, I believe, imposing pattern and order upon our experiences and thoughts, we should no more be astonished by solutions to problems appearing as inspiration than we are by dreams.

One form in which a tendency to mental illness commonly shows itself in men and women of genius is proneness to depression. Depression is a condition of mind from which none of us escape. We cannot avoid the hazards of loss, of bereavement, failure, rejection, disappointment in all its manifold forms. The reaction to such loss is depression. We invest whatever or whoever we want with hopes; our hopes are disappointed; the withdrawal of the investment we have made takes time. We cannot easily transfer what we have felt for one person or one object to another person or another object. Meanwhile, the world takes on a sombre tinge. It becomes weary, stale, flat and unprofitable. Locked in misery, we withdraw into ourselves. Life seems pointless, without object. Perhaps we long for it to end, or even contemplate bringing an end to it ourselves.

Depression is the lot of all mankind, but some are more susceptible to it than others. Their suffering is deeper, their loss of hope more profound. In most of us, loss of hope is not absolute. The loss of the person whom we love most leaves a void which can never be entirely filled. But, for the majority, there are others who can at least partially replace the loved one. If you and I fail to pass an examination, or are not appointed to a position we are seeking, we may experience severe disappointment and temporary depression, but hope is not totally extinguished.

This is not the case with those who are peculiarly susceptible to depression: the people whom I designate 'depressive personalities'. For them, what might in ordinary people be a temporary loss or setback appears to be the end of the world. They are plunged into a state of melancholia from which there appears to be no possibility of recovery. Their loss of hope is absolute, and the risk of suicide is never far away.

The reasons for this increased susceptibility to depression in the face of loss are multiple. Genetic inheritance is certainly a factor in many cases. Early loss of a parent seems rather often to increase the severity of the reaction to further loss. Social factors are also important. Severe depression in response to disappointment or loss is commoner amongst women who are poorly housed, and who have no one at home in whom they can confide. There are certainly other factors which space precludes me from pursuing here.

It suffices to say that, for one reason or another, depressive personalities seem to be lacking in any built-in sense of self-esteem. When things go wrong in our lives, most of us have some sense of inner resources on which we can fall back for reassurance. We have an inner conviction of our own worth, dating from childhood, which sustains us even if failure, rejection, or loss assail us. Depressive personalities have no such conviction. They are vulnerable because their sense of their own worth is entirely derived from external sources. This is why so much of the world's work is accomplished by depressives. Just as a drug addict requires recurrent 'fixes', so the depressive requires recurrent boosts to his self-esteem. This makes him work hard to achieve the successes which he cannot do without.

Recurrent depression is particularly often found amongst writers, more especially amongst poets. William Cowper, John Donne, William Collins, John Clare, S. T. Coleridge, Edgar Allan Poe, Gerard Manley Hopkins, Anne Sexton, Hart Crane, Theodore Roethke, Delmore Schwartz, Randall Jarrell, Robert Lowell, John Berryman, Dylan Thomas, Louis MacNeice and Sylvia Plath all suffered well-attested periods of depression. Five of these poets committed suicide. A recent study of 47 British writers and artists, selected for eminence by their having won major prizes, demonstrated that 38 per cent had been treated for manic-depressive illness or recurrent depression without mania. Of the poets in the sample, half had received treatment with drugs as outpatients, or had been admitted to hospital for other forms of psychiatric treatment.[22]

In the light of this information, one might conclude that there was certainly some link between liability to depression and creative writing, but one might also deduce that creative writing was not particularly effective in warding off depression, as I have suggested that it might be. I think that poets may be less successful than prose writers in using their talents for this purpose because of the intermittent nature of their work and their greater dependence upon inspiration. A prose writer may be able to make himself work regularly, even if what he produces is pedestrian. Poets, constantly in search of the *mot juste*, and usually concerned with an extremely concentrated form of expression, have little opportunity to engage in the regular, routine kind of writing which must play some part in the work of even the most inspired novelist. There are certainly a number of writers who recognize that what they do is connected with the preservation of their mental health. Graham Greene, for example, writes in his autobiography:

Writing is a form of therapy; sometimes I wonder how all those who do not write, compose or paint can manage to escape the madness, the melancholia, the panic fear which is inherent in the human situation.[23]

Depression is largely to do with difficulties in interpersonal relationships; with ambivalence toward other people; with an inability to handle aggression; with needing constant reassurance and boosts to self-esteem. The creative pursuits of writers who are prone to depression tend to be primarily concerned with the vagaries of human relationships. Amongst novelists, for example, Balzac is an obvious example of a man of genius whose enormous output was achieved because he worked compulsively. Balzac displayed the hunger for fame, for recurrent successes, which is characteristic of the manic-depressive temperament.

But depression is not the only condition against which creative work can provide a refuge and a defence. Deeper anxieties, especially those connected with disintegration, lead to an especial concern with the search for order and coherence. The great abstract thinkers, for example, seem often to be people who do not form close interpersonal ties. For them, concern with finding some order and sense in the world takes precedence over human relationships. There is a connection between fear of close relationships, anxiety about disintegration, and a feeling that the world is an unpredictable, unsafe place over which some form of control must be exercised if any security is to be attained. Those who suffer from such anxieties are often avoidant of others, as if they feared that close relationships might be destructive. It is certainly striking that the majority of the greatest philosophers of the Western world since the Greeks have not lived normal family lives or formed close personal ties. This is true of Descartes, Newton, Locke, Pascal, Spinoza, Kant, Leibniz, Schopenhauer, Nietzsche, Kierkegaard, and Wittgenstein. Some of these men of genius had transient affairs with men or women, but none of them married, and most lived alone for the greater part of their lives. The majority of human beings are to some extent preoccupied with making sense and order out of their lives as well as with interpersonal relationships, but I suggest that the higher reaches of abstract thought are usually only achieved by men or women who have time and opportunity to spend long periods alone, and who are less concerned with interpersonal relationships than most of us. Most of the greatest thinkers have been somewhat isolated.

What are the factors responsible for producing human beings with this kind of personality, which, when clearly pathological, psychiatrists call schizoid, but which, in lesser degree, is not uncommon amongst intellectuals? We can never determine accurately how much a particular type of personality owes to environment, how much to genetic endowment. There are a certain number of cases in which we know enough about the person's infancy to state with confidence that traumatic events played a part in creating anxiety of the kind described above. Newton, for example, was a premature child whose father had died before he was born. For his first three years, he enjoyed the undivided attention of his mother without suffering competition from any rival. Indeed, he required even more attention than most infants, because of his prematurity. Then, when he was just past his third birthday, his mother not only remarried, but moved house, leaving Newton in the care of others. We know, from his own diaries, that he passionately resented what he felt to be a betrayal. Amongst the catalogue of 58 sins which, in his self-punitive way, he accused himself of and recorded when he was 22, was his threat to burn his mother and stepfather and the house over them.

Newton's adult personality was pathologically eccentric. As a young Fellow of Trinity College, Cambridge, he conformed to the stereotype of the absent-minded scholar. He had very little contact with other people, took no exercise, often forgot to eat, and devoted his whole attention to his studies, seldom going to bed before two or three in the morning. He made no close relationships with either sex, and, in old age, told a visitor that he had never violated chastity. Although he was robust enough to have surmounted the hazards of prematurity and to survive into his eighty-fifth year, he was notably hypochondriacal, and constantly preoccupied with death, a trait he shared with Immanuel Kant.

He was also extremely suspicious, quarrelsome, touchy about priority in his work, and reluctant to acknowledge any indebtedness to other scientists and mathematicians. In 1693, when he was just over 50, Newton had a breakdown in which he expressed various paranoid delusions, including the belief that the philosopher Locke was trying to 'embroile' him with women.

I think it reasonable to assume that his early 'betrayal' by his mother made him feel, as a 3-year old, that human beings could not be trusted, and that the world was an unsafe place. His avoidance of other human beings contributed to his achievement, since he devoted himself to his work to the virtual exclusion of human relationships. His insecurity may have fuelled his desire to find order and predictability in a world which, when he was a child, had seemed arbitrarily governed by factors which he could not comprehend. One biographer writes of him:

To force everything in the heavens and on the earth into one rigid, tight frame from which the most miniscule detail would not be allowed to escape free and random was an underlying need of this anxiety-ridden man.[24]

A genius working in an entirely different field of creative endeavour who shared a number of the same traits of personality was Franz Kafka. Kafka was neither as suspicious as Newton, nor quite so isolated. But, as his writings demonstrate, he also regarded the world as an unsafe place, dominated by powers who could neither be reached nor understood. Both *The Castle* and *The Trial* depict nightmare worlds in which arbitrary power is exercised in inexplicable ways by nobles or judges who cannot be called to account. Kafka also shared with Newton a fear of letting others close to him. Kafka had a number of relationships with women, and was involved with Felice Bauer, to whom he became engaged, for five years. Yet, during all this time, the couple met on no more than nine or ten occasions, often for no more than an hour or two. Their relationship was almost entirely epistolary. When Felice writes that she would like to be near him when he is writing, Kafka responds by telling her that if she was there he could not write at all. Kafka had an unsatisfactory childhood and a bully for a father, but other factors must have contributed to his extreme insecurity. I have little doubt that his writing saved him from breakdown, serving as an integrating factor in a personality not far removed from insanity.

The examples I have given of creative individuals who were motivated by their psychopathology are, perhaps, too extreme. But, as in other psychological matters, the extremes teach us something. I began this paper by asserting that, in the study of creativity, psychoanalysis was chiefly concerned with motivation: with discerning and explaining why it is that men and women of genius invest their creative pursuits with so much energy, often at the expense of their human relationships and much else beside. There is no doubt that the difficulties encountered by those who are prone to severe depression encourage the use of the imagination for the reasons already given. Although severe depression requiring treatment can be regarded as an illness, every one of us experiences some degree of depression in response to loss, disappointment, or failure. By studying the way in which the gifted use their creative powers as a way of dealing with, or avoiding depression, we can learn something about ourselves.

It could be argued that we are less likely to learn much about ourselves from trying to understand such characters as Newton. However, Newton and some of the philosophers who turned away from interaction with their fellows to pursue abstractions to the limit, illustrate something about human nature which is today unfashionable and apt to be ignored. Psychoanalysts and their followers have preached the gospel that happiness and personal fulfillment are only to be found in interpersonal relationships. But reproduction and family life are not the only ends of man. If man was not a creature who is also passionately concerned with trying to make sense and order out of the universe, his greatest intellectual achievements could not have taken place. Man is not made for love alone. We owe an enormous debt to those men and women of genius whose need to make sense out of a world which to them appeared incoherent took precedence over their need to make human relationships.[25]

Notes

1 Sigmund Freud, *Standard Edition of the Complete Psychological Works of Sigmund Freud*, ed. James Strachey (London, 1963), vol. XVI, p. 376.
2 Freud, *Standard Edition*, vol. IX, p. 146.
3 Freud, *Standard Edition*, vol. XII, p. 219.
4 Freud, *Standard Edition*, vol. XII, p. 224.
5 C. G. Jung, *Psychology and Literature, Collected Works*, vol. 15 (London, 1966), pp. 89–90.
6 Ibid., p. 90.
7 Ibid., p. 103.
8 Ibid., p. 101.
9 Richard Wagner, *My Life* (London, 1911), vol. II, p. 603.
10 C. G. Jung, *Collected Works*, vol. 17, p. 171.
11 Aaron Copland, *Music and Imagination* (Oxford, 1952), pp. 40–1.
12 C. G. Jung, *Collected Works*, vol. 16 (London, 1954), p. 41.
13 Charles Rycroft, *Psychoanalysis Observed* (London, 1966), p. 22.
14 Richard B. Onians, *The Origins of European Thought*, 2nd edn (Cambridge 1954), p. 129, pp. 161–2.
15 Samuel Johnson, *The History of Rasselas, Prince of Abyssinia*, in *Samuel Johnson*, ed. Donald Greene (Oxford, 1984), p. 387.

16 C. P. Snow, *The Search* (London, 1934), pp. 126–7.

17 Rudolf and Margot Wittkower, *Born under Saturn* (London, 1963), p. 94.

18 Francis Galton, *Hereditary Genius*, 2nd edn (London, 1892), p. x.

19 Quoted in Jacques Hadamard, *The Psychology of Invention in the Mathematical Field* (Princeton, 1945), p. 15.

20 Quoted in Rosamond E. M. Harding, *An Anatomy of Inspiration* (Cambridge, 1940), p. 15.

21 John Dryden, *Absalom and Achitophel*, 163–4.

22 Kay R. Jamison, 'Mood Disorders and Seasonal Patterns in top British Writers and Artists', unpublished data.

23 Graham Greene, *Ways of Escape* (Harmondsworth, 1981), p. 9.

24 Frank A. Manuel, *A Portrait of Isaac Newton* (Cambridge, Mass., 1968), p. 86.

25 See further, A. Storr, *The School of Genius* (London, 1988).

Select Bibliography

Below is a list of some of the most important general contributions to the history of the idea of genius. More detailed bibliography will be found in the notes at the end of each chapter.

Abrams, M. H. *The Mirror and the Lamp: Romantic Theory and the Critical Tradition* (New York, 1953).

Currie, R. *Genius, an Ideology in Literature* (London, 1974).

Dieckmann, H. 'Diderot's Conception of Genius', *Journal of the History of Ideas*, 2 (1941), 151–82.

Fabian, B. Introduction to the critical edition of Alexander Gerard, *An Essay on Genius, 1774* (Munich, 1966).

Fabian, B. 'Der Naturwissenschaftler als Originalgenie', in *Europäische Aufklärung. Herbert Dieckmann zum 60. Geburstag*, eds H. Friedrich and F. Schalk (Munich, 1967), pp. 47–68.

Grappin, P. *La Théorie du Génie dans le Préclassicisme Allemand* (Paris, 1952).

Jones, H. M. 'The Doctrine of Romantic Genius', in *Revolution and Romanticism* (Cambridge, Mass., 1974), pp. 261–95.

Kaufman, P. 'Heralds of Original Genius', in *Essays in Memory of Barrett Wendell* (Cambridge, Mass., 1926), pp. 191–217.

Klibansky, R., Panofsky, E. and Saxl, F. *Saturn and Melancholy* (London, 1964).

Lowinsky, E. E. 'Musical Genius', in *Dictionary of the History of Ideas*, ed. P. P. Wiener (New York, 1973) vol. 2, pp. 312–26.

Nahm, M. C. *The Artist as Creator* (Baltimore, 1956).

Poirier, R. 'The Question of Genius', *Raritan*, 5, 4 (Spring 1986), 77–104.

Porter, R. 'Madness and Genius', in *A Social History of Madness* (London, 1987), pp. 60–81.

Schmidt, J. *Die Geschichte des Genie-Gedankens in der deutschen Literatur, Philosophie und Politik 1750–1945* (2 vols, Darmstadt, 1985).

Simonsuuri, K. *Homer's Original Genius: Eighteenth-century Notions of the Early Greek Epic (1688–1798)* (Cambridge, 1979).

Smith, L. P. 'Four Romantic Words', in *Words and Idioms* (London, 1925), pp. 66–134.

Tonnelli, G. 'Genius: from the Renaissance to 1770', *Dictionary of the History of Ideas*, ed. P. P. Wiener (New York, 1973), vol. 2 pp. 293–7.

Wittkower, R. 'Genius: Individualism in Art and Artists', ibid., pp. 297–312.

Wittkower, R. and M. *Born under Saturn, the Character and Conduct of Artists: a Documented History from Antiquity to the French Revolution* (London, 1963).

Zilsel, E. *Die Entstehung des Geniebegriffes. Ein Beitrag zur Ideengeschichte der Antike und des Frühkapitalismus* (Tübingen, 1926).

Index